plays from the boom box galaxy

theater from the hip-hop generation

edited by kim euell
wth robert alexander

theatre communications group new york 2009

Plays from the Boom Box Galaxy: Theater from the Hip-Hop Generation is copyright © 2009 by Theatre Communications Group

Introduction copyright © 2009 by Kim Euell

Plays from the Boom Box Galaxy: Theater from the Hip-Hop Generation is published by Theatre Communications Group, Inc., 520 Eighth Avenue, 24th Floor, New York, NY 10018-4156

This publication is made possible in part with public funds from the New York State Council on the Arts, a State Agency.

TCG books are exclusively distributed to the book trade by Consortium Book Sales and Distribution.

Library of Congress Cataloging-in-Publication Data

Plays from the boom box galaxy : theater from the hip-hop generation / edited by Kim Euell with Robert Alexander.—1st ed.
p. cm.
Includes bibliographical references and index.
ISBN 978-1-55936-292-4 (alk. paper)
1. American drama—African American authors. 2. Experimental drama, American. I. Euell, Kim. II. Alexander, Robert.
PS628.N4P55   2009
812'.6080896073—dc22   2009005979

Cover art copyright © 2009 by Radcliffe Bailey, adapted by the artist from his "Door of No Return" series
Cover, book design and composition by Lisa Govan

First Edition, November 2009

For Malakai

contents

acknowledgments

this anthology was a labor of love that could not have been completed without the contributions and support of numerous organizations and individuals. First I wish to gratefully acknowledge everyone in the hip-hop theater community who sent Robert and me a script to consider or took the time to speak with us about this project. Your names are too numerous to list here, but please know that your efforts contributed meaningfully to this process and are deeply appreciated.

I am extremely grateful to each of the gifted artists who contributed plays to this volume. Thank you Zell, Cristal, Carl, Psalmayene 24, Tommy, Dan, Jake-ann, Bamuthi, Aya and Will for your vision, brilliance and patience. Many thanks to Radcliffe Bailey for his inspiring cover artwork and to Will Power for pointing me in his direction. Major gratitude goes to Kathy Sova and Terry Nemeth at TCG for their ongoing support and guidance throughout this process.

I am deeply grateful to Kamilah Forbes (Artistic Director) and Clyde Valentin (Executive Director) of the NYC Hip-Hop Theater Festival, who were gracious in assisting me from the very beginning. Six of the plays included in this volume were presented at the HHTF, so in many ways their vision and dedication helped make this anthology possible. Thanks also to founder Danny Hoch for his time, and to writer/performer Holly Bass. Special thanks to professor Daniel Banks of NYU for providing the transcript of the first HHTF symposium and for other support. Thank you to Laurie Carlos, artist extraordinaire, and curator of the late-night series at the Pillsbury House Theatre in Minneapolis for bringing the work of Zell Miller III to my attention. Thanks also to Amy Mueller, Artistic Director of the Playwrights Foundation/Bay Area Playwrights Festival for providing a crucial missing draft of *Death of a Ho*.

Major thanks goes out to Alan MacVey, Chair of the Theatre Arts Department at The University of Iowa, and professors Art Borreca and Dare Clubb. A special thank you to professors Sydné Mahone and Tisch Jones, also of the Theatre Arts Department, for reading several drafts of the introduction and asking the questions that spurred me on. Thank you to professor Richard Turner of UIOWA's African-American Studies program and to deans Sandra Barkan (emeritus) and Minetta Gardinier for their invaluable support. A very special thank you is extended to professor Harry J. Elam, Jr., of Stanford University, for providing detailed and insightful notes on the introduction. His time and expertise are greatly appreciated. Thanks also to Donnell Barnes, aka Khalij D'Gree, and spoken-word artist Louis Hale, for their feedback.

I thank professors Lou Bellamy and Allen Isaacman at the University of Minnesota for their support and encouragement at an early stage of this project.

I thank professor Rose Malague, Director of the Theatre Arts Program at the University of Pennsylvania, for the opportunity to be in residence. Much appreciation is extended to Kevin Chun at Penn's Theatre Arts Program and to Ancil George, Reference Librarian for Africana Studies at Penn, for their valued assistance. Thanks also to my students at Penn for their input: Joshua Bennett (an acclaimed spoken-word artist), Laird Edge, Chioma "Chichi" Erondu, Jodine Gordon, Morgan Rogers, Samaria Shipp and Kristina Ward.

A shout out to Jeff Chang whose presentation at The University of Iowa inspired further investigation into hip-hop's historical origins and whose book *Can't Stop Won't Stop* was such an invaluable resource. I also wish to acknowledge Murray Forman and Mark Anthony Neal for their outstanding collection of writings on the cultural roots and aesthetics of hip-hop: *That's the Joint! The Hip-Hop Studies Reader.*

Shout-outs also to artist/activist Rha Goddess, Eisa Davis, Melisa Riviere and Rachel Raimist, founders of B-Girl Be (the Minneapolis-based Celebration of Women in Hip-Hop); Baraka Sele at the New Jersey Performing Arts Center; Professor Rickerby Hinds at UC Riverside and to everyone at UMASS Amherst's New WORLD Theater.

Frances Wilkinson, Theresa Isaacs, John Kaufman, Karen Ransom, Susan Smuoluchowski, Andrea Sohn and Cathy Carr each provided invaluable support at key times as did my mother and sister, Grace Euell and Yuma Euell-Hazard. A special thank you to Michael for his unwavering support throughout. Thank you all for being there for me.

I want to acknowledge Robert Alexander, whose idea it was to create this anthology. Thanks Rob, for inviting me on this journey, for naming the book, and for keeping an open mind.

Peace.

shango's mixtape: a contextual frame

by Kim Euell

The first time I heard the term "hip-hop theater" was during a conversation with Will Power back in fall 1997. I was immediately intrigued when he called to pitch me a hip-hop musical he'd written and produced. As the director of play development at a regional theater that was only beginning to diversify its mainstage programming I regretted not being able to offer any immediate possibilities. "But keep me informed about what you're doing, I suggested, "I'm very interested on a personal level." And so he did

By the time Robert Alexander first approached me about working on this anthology in 2001, I was full of enthusiasm for this emerging genre. I loved its energy and inventive approaches to language, but most of all I loved its social relevance. It was the kind of work that had inspired me to commit to a life in the theater. Simultaneously I harbored some reservations about hip-hop itself. I had been a fan from the early eighties until 1991 when the first of several disturbing incidents involving gangsta rap music (beginning with NWA's *Efil4zaggin*) caused me to distance myself. You could say that for a period of time, I unwittingly allowed the industry of hip-hop to come between me and the culture of hip-hop. Some years later through many affirming experiences with hip-hop theater, I not only renewed but deepened my relationship with the culture.

My first conscious experience with this new genre occurred in 1999 at San Francisco's Theater Artaud, where Will Power shared the bill with Sarah Jones. *The Gathering* was Power's homage to the spaces where African American men congregate for their male bonding rituals. I was highly impressed by his virtuosity in portraying a five-man basketball squad in action as well as his rhythmically inflected text delivery, and the empowering values imbedded in his work. I was equally awed by Jones's solo turn in *Surface Transit*. The skillful writing and performance of both pieces left me wanting to know more about hip-hop theater.

Next I was captivated by Universes' performance of *Slanguage* during a special performance as part of Mark Taper Forum's New Work Festival in 2001. This led me to a hip-hop theater conference convened by Rickerby Hinds at UC Riverside, where I first met Kamilah Forbes, artistic director of both Hip-Hop Theatre Junction and the Hip-Hop

Theater Festival (HHTF). The work I saw there inspired me to attend the third annual NYC HHTF in 2002, where I was riveted by performances by Festival founder Danny Hoch, London's Jonzi D, Psalmayene 24 (his *Free Jujube Brown!* is included in this anthology) and Will Power and his powerful adaptation of Aeschylus' *The Seven Against Thebes*. The show that spoke to me most directly however was Aya de León's *Thieves in the Temple: The Reclaiming of Hip-Hop* (a slightly revised version is included here). Created in response to the violence and misogyny in gangsta rap lyrics, Aya boldly confronts these issues from the perspective of a female operating within the culture.

As I was exposed to more and more examples of this genre, I realized that this was not my initial exposure to this type of theater, this was just the first time that I'd heard it labeled "hip-hop theater": in 1991, I'd caught *Erotic Justice*, Robert Alexander's spoken-word performance piece at San Francisco's Lorraine Hansberry Theatre; in 1992, I'd been mesmerized by Carl Hancock Rux's *Geneva Cottrell* and *Waiting for the Dog to Die* in New York City; in 1995, I'd seen the first commercially successful hip-hop musical, *Bring in 'Da Noise, Bring in 'Da Funk* at The Public Theater (twice) before it transferred to Broadway; in 1997, I'd attended Danny Hoch's amazing solo work *Jails, Hospitals & Hip-Hop* (then titled *Evolution of a Homeboy*) at Berkeley Rep.

I also recognized that several of the plays that I'd worked on as a dramaturg, including Robert Alexander's *A Preface to the Alien Garden* and Jake-ann Jones's *Death of a Ho* (included in this anthology), belonged to this emerging canon. Roger Guenveur Smith's touring solo work *Frederick Douglass Now*, which I'd presented while serving on the staff of Oakland Ensemble Theatre in 1992, seemed to fit neatly into this category. I also thought of several other plays from the early nineties in this context, such as Ifa Bayeza's *Homer G. & the Rhapsodies in the Fall of Detroit (Part I)*, which attracted a Kennedy Center Fund for New Plays Award in 1994, and Michael Henry Brown's acclaimed *Generations of the Dead in the Abyss of Coney Island Madness*.

Going back even further, I recalled Ntozake Shange's groundbreaking choreopoem *for colored girls who have considered suicide/when the rainbow is enuf* and Charles Fuller's OBIE Award–winning *Zooman and the Sign*. These plays, which were first presented in New York City theaters by African American companies, were written between the mid- to late seventies. Could these be classified as early examples of this genre? Certainly the poetic text, nontraditional structure and underground origins of *for colored girls* (the show debuted in an East Bay women's bar) all make a very strong argument that this could have been the first hip-hop theater piece. (Shange acknowledges working with Gylan Kain of The Original Last Poets, on the development of the piece.)

Fuller's subsequent creation of the gang-banging character Zooman, who appears onstage dressed in hip-hop attire and accompanied by a boom box playing signature music, clearly represents a facet of the culture. The playwright's use of direct address monologues for each of his major characters combined with his goal of engaging the community in taking responsibility for gang violence also connect this play with those that emerged during the nineties and beyond. At the very least, these two classics form an evolutionary bridge between the Black Arts Movement of the sixties and seventies and the hip-hop theater movement that emerged during the nineties.

During the third annual NYC HHTF in 2002, Kamilah Forbes and NYU professor Daniel Banks organized the first hip-hop theater symposium (many more would follow) devoted to grappling with many issues, such as defining hip-hop theater. This session revealed that although this process of defining is still very much in process, hip-hop theater artists are deeply committed to the goal of self-definition and of critiquing the culture. Being in the room during these discussions, I knew I was home.

Before delving into the definitions of hip-hop theater and introducing the plays in this volume, I'd like to examine the origins of hip-hop culture, beginning with the conditions leading up to its birth in the Bronx during the first half of the seventies. Since cultures do not evolve in a vacuum, this perspective combined with that of locating hip-hop within the cultural continuum of the African Diaspora allow us an expanded contextual frame for appreciating the plays.

the birth of hip-hop

Hip-hop was born from an apocalyptic landscape. The year was 1974 and the Bronx was burning. Factories in the South Bronx closed one by one, contributing to a youth unemployment rate of sixty to eighty percent. Hip-hop historian Jeff Chang wrote in his meticulously researched epic *Can't Stop Won't Stop* (St. Martin's Press, New York, 2005): "If blues culture had developed under the conditions of oppressive, forced labor, hip-hop culture would arise from conditions of no work." When the factory jobs left, so did many of the borough's white population. Simultaneously a city-sponsored plan to move poor people out of Manhattan relocated thousands of African Americans, blacks and Latinos of Caribbean ancestry into the borough's public-housing projects and rent-controlled apartment buildings. Once the demographics of the tenants changed, landlords frequently allowed these buildings to fall into disrepair. As conditions deteriorated, many owners turned to "arson-for-hire" when the value of their insurance policies exceeded the income they were able to legally derive. Between 1973 and 1977, thirty thousand fires were set in the South Bronx. The area resembled a war zone with block after block of burned-out abandoned buildings.

When these new black and brown youth first moved into these neighborhoods during the late sixties, they were often targeted for beat-downs by the area's Irish and Italian youth. Initially gangs formed for self-protection, but then some evolved into social clubs, surrogate families and even activist organizations. These gangs proliferated and street violence escalated to epidemic proportions as young people battled for dominance over turf and colors. *The Warriors*, a cult film set in New York City during this time period, vividly captures the flavor of this era.

Out of this bleak scenario emerged a man with a vision. Cornell Benjamin, aka "Black Benji," was a member of an influential gang known as the Ghetto Brothers. The Puerto Rican Melendez Brothers formed the Ghetto Brothers initially as a musical group, but it evolved into a fairly constructive gang committed to community activism, among other things. Whereas most other gangs had warlords, Black Benji became the peacemaker for the Ghetto Brothers. But in December 1971, when he tried to diffuse an erupting confrontation between the Mongols, the Black Spades, the Seven Immortals and the Savage Skulls, they converged on him, viciously beating and stomping him to death. After the funeral, tensions ran high as everyone expected the Ghetto Brothers to declare war on the other gangs in order to avenge Black Benji's death. Instead, the Ghetto Brothers called for a meeting of all the gangs to talk peace. In this moment of transformation, when the decision was made to move toward light rather than darkness, the ground was laid for the birth of hip-hop.

Once peace prevailed, young people in the Bronx had the option of redirecting their considerable energies to more constructive outlets. What do people do when a war ends? They party. Hip-hop was born at the party scene that gradually filled the vacuum created by the decline of the gang era.

hip-hop's founding fathers

Appropriately for a movement that began as an extended party, the originators were all DJs. Clive Campbell, aka Kool DJ Herc, is widely acknowledged as the father of hip-hop. Born in Jamaica, he lived there until he was twelve before coming to the U.S. in 1967. In Jamaica (as in many black communities in the U.S.), there was an established tradition of DJs toasting and rapping over the music. Herc's primary innovation at the turntables was called the "merry-go-round": simultaneously working two turntables cued with copies of the same record to extend the song's climatic instrumental breaks, inspiring the crowd to new dancing heights. Soon Herc's parties attracted so many people that he had to take them outdoors. He created a portable sound system with enormous speakers (and volume), allowing him to roll up to parks and schoolyards facilitating massive summertime block parties. These events usually featured an MC, a young man or woman who rocked the mic, showcasing his/her verbal dexterity in the role of master or mistress of ceremonies. Initially Herc doubled as an MC, but as the art of DJing became increasingly demanding, MCing became a distinct role. Rapping and rhyming to the DJ's beats formed the essential core of hip-hop music, which in turn seeded an entire subculture.

If Kool Herc is the father of hip-hop culture, then Afrika Bambaataa is the godfather. Born Kevin Donovan in Manhattan to parents from Jamaica and Barbados, Bambaataa is a former Black Spades warlord who participated in the historic gang summit that led to the truce. After becoming a DJ, he was the first to define hip-hop as a culture containing four elements: DJing (or turntabling), MCing (or rapping), breaking also known as B-boying (and/or B-girling), and graffiti-writing (which evolved separately, but was invited to join the party). Bambaataa envisioned using these skills to battle for dominance as an alternative to the violent, physical battles that plagued the gang era. He founded the Universal Zulu Nation as an alternative to gang warfare. An organization that began essentially as male and female break-dance crews (Zulu Kings and Queens) during the seventies has since evolved into an internationally recognized cultural organization, the first dedicated to hip-hop culture. Their website states: "The Universal Zulu Nation stands for knowledge, wisdom, understanding, freedom, justice, equality, peace, unity, love, respect, work, fun, overcoming the negative to the positive, economics, mathematics, science, life, truth, facts, faith, and the Oneness of God." Bambaataa officially designated knowledge to be the fifth element of hip-hop.

Grandmaster Flash is the third member of the DJ triumvirate. Born Joseph Sadler to parents who immigrated here from Barbados, Flash developed his streak of technological genius partially as a result of learning to repair electronic equipment at a vocational high school in New York. He became known for refining the technique of DJing by making the transitions more seamless and precise. He popularized innovations such as scratching and punch-phasing, bringing a new level of showmanship to the art. Grandmaster Flash performed with the first crew of rhyming rappers, The Furious Five. Together they became known for their seminal monster hit *The Message*, which contains the best known rhymes in the history of hip-hop: "Don't push me 'cause I'm close to the edge / I'm tryin' not to lose my head / It's like a jungle sometimes, it makes me wonder / How I keep from goin' under." *The Message* marked the turning point when hip-hop music evolved into a vehicle for social commentary, giving voice to previously unheard inner-city youth.

Hip-hop began some time between 1973 and 1974 with the beats laid down by Kool Herc. Afrika Bambaataa articulated the vision that helped transform hip-hop into a global, multicultural youth movement. Grandmaster Flash and his crew's innovations helped raise the artistic level of DJing and MCing, while injecting commentary and protest into the music that served as the foundation for this new highly theatrical subculture. By the late seventies hip-hop was already influencing the aesthetic of black theater.

Many leading African American playwrights have identified black musical genres as major influences in their work. August Wilson cited the blues in this regard. When asked during an interview, published in the collection *Conversations with August Wilson* (Jackson R. Bryer and Mary C. Hartig, editors; University Press of Mississippi, Jackson, 2006), if rap music has anything in common with the blues, he responded:

> Oh sure, without question . . . It's part of the tradition. They're defining the world in which they live, they're working out their social manners, their social intercourse—all these things they're working out through the rap. And it's alive and vibrant. You have to listen, and a lot of us are unwilling to stop and listen.

hip-hop's african roots

In a lecture given on hip-hop culture in Oakland in 2007, sociologist Michael Eric Dyson said: "In the beginning, hip-hop represented an index of a Diasporic moment in the global expansion of black consciousness, articulated in a moment of postindustrial collapse." In Nelson George's interview with Afrika Bambaataa, first published in *The Source* in 1993 (later reprinted in *That's the Joint! The Hip-Hop Studies Reader*; Murray Forman and Mark Anthony Neal, editors; Routledge, New York, 2004), Afrika Bambaataa defined the term "black" in a Diasporic context: "Now one thing people must know, that when we say black we mean all our Puerto Rican or Dominican brothers. Wherever the hip-hop was and the Blacks was, the Latinos and the Puerto Ricans was, too."

For those readers who may be unaware, the African Diaspora consists of all the places in the Caribbean, Central America, South America and North America where enslaved Africans were forced to settle. This list includes but is not limited to: Jamaica, Barbados, Cuba, Puerto Rico, Haiti, the Dominican Republic, the American South and even New York City. Drawing upon their rich cultural traditions, the transplanted Africans sowed the seeds from which new subcultures emerged, combining elements of African, European and indigenous culture.

References and themes related to the African Diaspora are like threads connecting the plays in this anthology. In a recent conversation with Will Power (whose play *Flow* is included here), he referred to his ancestral roots in Haitian and Louisiana's Creole culture: "It's deep in us," he observed. "When we perform, we channel, and our African roots come through. A guy from Nigeria came up to me after a performance of *Flow* and said that my movements reminded him of a dance the people did back in his village."

the significance of "the beat"

One essential feature that African Diaspora cultures share is their emphasis on "the Beat" and on drumming as a core component of worship, communication and everyday life. According to Rene Thompson, my Cuban dance instructor who came to the U.S. as an adult: "Diaspora cultures are characterized by rhythms based on a four-beat measure, which is one reason why it is so easy for us to dance to each other's music." Even after drumming was outlawed in the American South in the wake of slave rebellions, slaves invented new ways of perpetuating "the Beat." They rhythmically pounded large sticks on the ground, clapped hands, stomped feet and slapped their chests and thighs as part of their worship and communal activities. The ancestors kept the Beat going because the Beat kept them going.

Most African cultures are also characterized by a call-and-response dynamic between the drummers, dancers and singers. According to *That's the Joint!*: "Traditional African music rarely existed apart from dance and vocalization." These African retentions are easily discernable in hip-hop. When Kool Herc laid down the beats that formed the basis for the culture, his turntables represented the latest technological incarnation of the African drum. B-boying or breaking was the highly competitive, physical response to the call issued by the Beat. MCing (or rapping) emerged as a verbal accompaniment, but it gradually took on its own role as a call, evoking its own spirited verbal and physical response from the crowd.

It is worth noting a few of the many creative ways in which the Beat manifests in this collection of plays. *The Evidence of Silence Broken* by Zell Miller III opens with "a layered breathing made from several voices, becoming more and more rhythmic, turning into its own drum/track." *The No Black Male Show* by Carl Hancock Rux is performed with an onstage percussionist who is part of the cast. The script also incorporates hand "claps in four/four." As indicated by the title of Tommy Shepherd and Dan Wolf's play *Beatbox*, the two central characters beatbox. In Jake-ann Jones's play *Death of a Ho*, the central character is hooked up to a heartbeat monitor, which at times dissolves into a beatbox rhythm. In *Word Becomes Flesh*, Marc Bamuthi Joseph's inspired tap-dancing provides one of several expressions of the Beat, along with his trap-drummer's rhythms. In each of the plays, the Beat is emphasized in the performance of the text, but, in Will Power's *Flow*, it *is* the text: "Baba-dee-da-dabeydoo-dee-da!"

the african roots of rap

In *Conversations with August Wilson*, the playwright reiterated his belief that African Americans are fundamentally African in their worldview. He elaborated:

> Because Africans are not Europeans they have different ways
> of looking at life . . . we value and prize linguistic ability. This
> is one of the values of our culture—the ability to rap.

Musician/Writer David Toop (in *The Rap Attack: African Jive to New York Hip-Hop*; Pluto Press, London, 1984) managed to trace the origins of rap in a single sentence:

> Rap's forebears stretch back through disco, street funk, radio
> DJs, Bo Didley, the be-bop singers, Cab Calloway, Pigmeat
> Markham, the tap-dancers and comics, The Last Poets, Gil
> Scott-Heron, Muhammad Ali, a cappella and doo-wop
> groups, ring games, skip-rope rhymes, prison and army
> songs, toasts, signifying and the dozens, all the way back to
> the griots of Nigeria and Gambia.

From childhood I can recall men who had shoeshine stalls and other low-status occupations but gained stature in the community for their rhyming and oratorical skills. Eventually I understood that the activity of manipulating one's language through rhythm and rhyme builds confidence in one's ability to extend that control to other areas of life, a major reason why this skill continues to be valued in disenfranchised communities. I was reminded of this recently by a scene from Charles Burnett's independent film classic *Killer of Sheep*. Set in California's Watts neighborhood in the mid-seventies, it is a story about poor working-class blacks, some representing the first generation up from the Deep South. Casting real people as opposed to professional actors, it is a rare document of authentic African American culture at this place and time. What struck me was a scene in which the central character's family is headed to the racetrack for a rare outing with friends. When one of the car's tires blows out, the outing is derailed for lack of a spare. One of the men vents his frustration by busting a rhyme in the middle of the road.

The ability to rap, rhyme and improvise are all central values of hip-hop culture. The rituals of battling and of the cipher, the posturing of rap, the wordplay of rhyming, the improvisational aspect of free-styling, the emphasis on creative self-expression—these aspects of the culture all contribute to hip-hop's inherent theatricality. Will Power, Tommy Shepherd and Dan Wolf, all included in this anthology, are also highly respected for their skills as MCs.

african spirituality in hip-hop

Several of the plays included in this anthology reference traditional African spiritual beliefs. Along with the Beat, the Yoruba religion is another definitive aspect of African culture that thrived in the New World. The two primary tenets of the Yoruba religion are reverence for ancestors and worship of the Orishas. The Yoruba believe in one God who has many intermediaries known as the Orishas. While they are associated with manifestations of nature, these Orishas have human personas. For example, Shango, the God of Thunder, is often depicted as a virile warrior riding a horse, while Oshun, the River Goddess, is shown as a beautiful woman wearing an armful of brass bracelets. These deities crossed the Atlantic Ocean in the consciousness of our African ancestors and continue manifesting as a presence in many African Diaspora cultures, particularly through dance. The Yoruba religion evolved into Santeria in Cuba, Obeah in Jamaica, Vodun in Haiti, Candomblé in Brazil, and it is practiced in various forms around the U.S.

I see aspects of Yoruba deities manifesting in hip-hop culture. I see Oshun, the River Goddess, who rules love, sensual movement and the arts in the bodacious dancing and provocative videos and fashion of hip-hop. I see Oshun, controller of money and yellow metals in the bling of hip-hop. I see and hear Shango, God of Thunder, owner of the drum and, by extension, the turntable, in the traditions of DJing, MCing and the spoken-word aspect of hip-hop. Shango is also the patron saint of preachers, politicians, pimps and con-artists (flashy characters who have a way with words). He is often depicted with lightning bolts shooting from his mouth, symbolizing his ability to illuminate through his verbosity.

To me, hip-hop is primarily an expression of creative energy. Both nebulous and potentially transformative, it can be tapped for constructive or destructive ends. Some argue that hip-hop is indefinable because once you attempt to define it, it transforms into something else. This shape-shifting, trickster aspect of hip-hop is one that some scholars attribute to the influence of Esu-Elegba. In her article entitled *Dance in Hip-Hop Culture* (also included in *That's the Joint!*), Katrina Hazzard-Donald compares Public Enemy's Flavor Flav's movements to those of the Yoruba deity Elegba. She writes: "Flavor Flav resembles the contemporary urban Esu-Elegba, or deity (principle) of uncertainty and unpredictability, also known as the trickster deity." She elaborates further in her notes, connecting Flav's highly theatrical persona to additional figures found throughout the Diaspora: "During performance, Flavor Flav bears a striking resemblance to other New World African performers—King Warrin of the John Canoe celebrations, Haiti's Baron Samedi and even the Uruguayan 'el Gramillero.'" All exhibit aspects of Esu-Elegba.

Similarly, Henry Louis Gates, Jr., links the trickster element inherent in black language to Esu-Elegba in his landmark work *The Signifying Monkey* (Oxford University Press, New York, 1988). "Signifying" is a well-established ritual deeply rooted in the African American ethos. In his book, Gates argues that African American literature is "double voiced," with texts talking to other texts, offering critique and revision. He labeled this process "signifyin'." It can be argued that signifyin' is another way of describing two core values of hip-hop culture: sampling involves taking a section of previously recorded music and looping it to create a new song. The practice of sampling reflects the African tradition of paying homage to what has gone before. In theater, one way we sample is by taking a classic play and "flipping it into new meaning," the way Will Power did when he adapted the Greek tragedy *The Seven Against Thebes* into the hip-hop musical *The Seven*. Keith Antar Mason engaged in a different form of signifyin' when he was inspired by Ntozake Shange's *for colored girls*, revising it into a black male version entitled for *black boys who have considered homicide when the streets were too much*. (After debuting in Los Angeles, this production toured nationally in 1993.) Several of the plays in this anthology signify on other well-known works in the canon of black dramatic literature.

the spoken-word poetry movement as incubator

During the early nineties, when the explosion of the rap music industry and the rise of gangsta rap were commanding the mainstream's attention, the underground spoken-word poetry scene mushroomed into a major outlet for the creative expression of authentic hip-hop culture. Whereas hip-hop originated in the inner-city among Diasporic youth, the spoken-word poetry movement attracted young people of all ethnicities and class backgrounds. Performance venues sprang up around college campuses, at cafés, community-based theaters and alternative performance spaces. By November 2002, Def Poetry Jam had landed on Broadway.

While the cipher tended to be a male-dominated forum, spoken-word poetry and its competitive forum, the poetry slam, were much more accessible to women. Everyone had an opportunity to step up to the mic and passionately speak their truth. Characterized by its distinctive use of rhythm, rhyme and repetition, spoken-word poetry is written expressly for performance. Not surprisingly, many of the theater artists who became associated with the hip-hop theater movement started out writing and performing spoken-word poetry. Several of the writers in this anthology, including Zell Miller III, Carl Hancock Rux, Marc Bamuthi Joseph and Aya de León are also acclaimed spoken-word artists.

While the spoken-word movement was gathering momentum, so was hip-hop theater. Throughout the nineties, as previously noted, hip-hop theater was performed at African American theaters, regional theaters, alternative spaces, on college campuses and on Broadway, where *Bring in 'Da Noise, Bring in 'Da Funk* won two Tony awards.

The first theater festival devoted to hip-hop theater was presented at the Kennedy Center in June 2000 by Jennifer Nelson and The African Continuum Theatre Company. Later in 2000, the NYC HHTF debuted. Since then, the HHTF has begun producing full productions of new plays, while expanding its presenting activities into Washington, D.C., San Francisco and Chicago. Celebrating cultural diversity and hybridity, the HHTF has established itself at the forefront of the hip-hop theater movement. Like spoken-word poetry, hip-hop theater is a decentralized activity and continues thriving in a variety of venues around the country. Hip-hop theater has successfully infiltrated every level of American theater. It is here to stay.

defining hip-hop theater

There are several definitions of hip-hop theater. The original definition is: theater that uses at least one of the four elements of hip-hop culture (MCing, DJing, etc.) to tell a story. Robert Alexander elaborates: "For something to be truly a hip-hop theater piece it has to contain certain elements of schizophrenia and rebellion, creativity and destruction." (Quoted by Holly Bass in *American Theater*, November 1999.)

The NYC HHTF embraces a far more inclusive definition, based on one originally coined by W. E. B. DuBois, when he advocated for the creation of a black theater movement. The HHTF proclaims (Danny Hoch, *American Theatre*, December 2004):

> Hip-hop theater must fit into the realm of theatrical performance, and it must be by, about and for the hip-hop generation, participants in hip-hop culture or both.

This definition has been expanded to include "participants in hip-hop culture," a significant inclusion because HHTF's original definition focused on the hip-hop generation, as does the definition espoused by writer/performer Holly Bass in her essay "Can You Rock It Like This? (*The Fire This Time: Young Activists and the New Feminism*; Vivien Labaton and Dawn Lundy Martin, editors; Anchor, New York, 2004). Bass, who has served as a curator for the HHTF writes:

> Any production that captures the energy and feeling and drive of this hip-hop generation, its issues and concerns, its larger cultural aesthetic, is hip-hop theater. And hip-hop theater is more than just what is on the stage; it's who's in the audience as well. A theater work can have all the beats and rhymes and slick moves it wants, but if the production excludes the hip-hop community from the audience, it loses a valuable synergy. The interaction between the performer and the audience is a crucial element of the work.

Another thoughtful definition harking back to the culture's origins, was put forth at the NYU symposium by an unidentified female audience member who said:

> I guess what I imagined hip-hop theater to be is a merging of what hip-hop culture is and what theater is. And hip-hop culture to me is a culture of a people who took something and made something out of nothing. Like the people who said: "I can't afford a canvas, so I'm gonna take me some spray cans and I'm gonna make me some wall art. I can't afford a big, expensive drum set, so I'm gonna make the music with my mouth." When I think of what hip-hop theater is, I think they're the same thing. And I feel like it's like what the music is: it's rebellious, it's political, it's vibrant. It should be explosive and daring . . . If it's going to merge with theater, of course there should be an aesthetic to it. There

should be a director behind it, somebody that knows something about theater but somebody who knows something about hip-hop, because if you're going to represent theater, you got to know what it is. And you got to be able to bring both of those things to the stage and let it shine. Hip-hop theater should be theater that created something out of nothing.

the plays of the boom box galaxy

Because the definitions of hip-hop theater were continually evolving during our selection process, we tended not to think of this as an anthology of hip-hop theater but rather as a collection of plays that are in some way informed by hip-hop culture. I did find it useful, however, to utilize the various definitions in describing the plays.

In curating this volume we sought work primarily by the generation of theater artists who grew up alongside the culture. These plays are the work of both emerging and mid-career writers. Interestingly, the geographical representation of the writers parallels that of the creative evolution of the rap music industry with representation by the East Coast, West Coast (Bay Area) and the South. Puerto Rico, Haiti and other Diasporic cultural hotspots are also represented, if only through ancestry.

The proliferation of solo work is consistent with the definition of hip-hop theater as theater that creates something out of nothing. But more importantly this level of activity reflects an artistic evolution that began with rapping and MCing, progressing to spoken-word poetry and culminating in solo performance. Solo shows are the theatrical equivalent of a masterful MC rocking the mic, demanding the same level of bravado, verbal dexterity and virtuosity.

The Evidence of Silence Broken, Free Jujube Brown! and *Flow* are all shows featuring a solo performer who is accompanied by a DJ. The other two solo plays bend this tradition: *Word Becomes Flesh* utilizes a jazz trio onstage while Aya de León's *Thieves in the Temple* is performed without a DJ. What distinguishes these solo works from other traditional solo plays is the incorporation of spoken-word poetry, verse poetry and/or syncopated beats into the text. This is mostly true of the ensemble plays collected here as well.

From the Harlem Renaissance era up through the mid-seventies, the domestic drama or family play was one of the most popular genres in the canon of African American theater. However, hip-hop debuted at a time of increased family dissolution that accompanied the postindustrial economic stagnation. This reality is reflected in the plays in this anthology. The families that we encounter are almost all fractured and under siege. In Cristal Chanelle Truscott's *Peaches*, the central character's fruitful marriage is shattered by the sudden and mysterious murder of her husband. In Carl Hancock Rux's *The No Black Male Show* we look in on a traumatized Southern family mourning the death of a son who barely attained manhood. The family unit in *Beatbox* consists of two stepbrothers struggling to survive in the wake of their parents' death. In *Word Becomes Flesh*, the central character takes up tap-dancing as a youth because his father isn't listening to him anymore. Years later he reluctantly accepts the role of fatherhood when it is thrust upon him as the result of an affair outside of his primary relationship. The play that is a possible exception is Zell Miller III's *The Evidence of Silence Broken* in which the Poet's parents are lovingly and memorably portrayed. Whereas the divorce of the Poet's parent's is poignantly chronicled, the Poet voices his determination to keep his own marriage intact.

In the remaining plays, parental figures are nonexistent. This absence is particularly noticeable in the case of *Free Jujube Brown!*, because we hear from every other significant character in his life. Where are Jujube's parents? Probably out somewhere working three jobs to make ends meet.

The plays of this anthology have been subdivided into three groupings to facilitate further investigation: "Ruminations on Identity," "Cautionary Tales" and "Transformationals."

ruminations on identity

Identity issues are integral to the process of maturation. But when one is the member of a marginalized population, the process of constructing identity becomes much more critical as the images projected by the media and entertainment industries are usually limiting and frequently damaging. NYU professor Tricia Rose highlights the significance of identity within the culture in her seminal work *Black Noise: Rap Music and Black Culture in Contemporary America* (Wesleyan University Press, Middletown, CT, 1994):

> Hip-hop culture emerged as a source for youth of alternative identity formation and social status in a community whose older local support institutions had been all but demolished along with large sectors of its built environment. Alternative local identities were forged in fashions and language, street names and, most important, in establishing neighborhood crews or posses.

It's not coincidental that several of the playwrights here have chosen to explore identity issues, but here the focus is either on the individual or an archetype. *Death of a Ho*, a cautionary tale examining identity dilemmas, both begins and ends with the sound of a mirror breaking. Similarly, the protagonist in *The No Black Male Show* is depicted as nameless and voiceless.

"Ruminations on Identity" begins with Zell Miller III's *The Evidence of Silence Broken: A Spoken-Word Performance Concert*. This solo work is an autobiographical self-portrait of a young poet discovering his own voice. He writes:

So it was begins or should I say began with this:

> bus rides
> > books
> > > oral stories
> > > > words
> > > > > broken hearts . . .

The piece begins appropriately with "the Beat." Initially we hear the sound of breathing—a rhythmic layered breathing—which evolves into a drumbeat, which evolves into a heartbeat. During his journey of self-interrogation, we hear the Poet's thoughts as he passes through myriad colorful experiences: running contraband on the city buses, misdirecting rage toward white Americans as a result of scrutinizing our history, equating manhood with violence, and seeing a meaningful connection to God. There are also lovely moments that are completely unexpected: the Poet witnessing his unflappable mother's sudden vulnerability when she divorces his father after more than twenty years of marriage, a moment of longing on a first date evoking a Yoruba worldview: ". . . I want you to wake up my ancestors with that kiss / make my unborn children know they are loved / with that kiss . . ."

Miller's play signifies on Keith Antar Mason's *for black boys who have considered homicide*, extending the conversation initiated by Ntozake Shange's work. A major difference that distinguishes Miller's show from Mason and Shange's is that it is a solo work. Both Mason and Shange end their plays with their characters finding God within themselves. In Miller's play, the Poet's onstage journey ends symbolically with him moving purposefully out of darkness into the light.

Peaches, by Cristal Chanelle Truscott, is a lyrical exploration of a black female's journey across the ages. Beginning with the stereotypical image of an angry black woman, the playwright has peeled away the layers revealing a deeper truth. Peaches, the archetypal "round-the-way girl," is first glimpsed as a young slave girl in love, reminding us that, despite their harsh condition, some slaves managed to experience some tender moments. We also encounter Peaches as a depressed blues singer and a twenty-four-year-old widowed mother of four. In a segment called "Love Chain Peaches," various characterizations of Peaches, representing the varying hues of African American skin, converge for a lively exchange about black male-female mating dilemmas. As with *The Evidence of Silence Broken*, *Peaches* signifies on Shange's *for colored girls*, while creating its own unique rhythms as it sweeps us along, surprising us with unexpected shifts and turns.

In *The No Black Male Show*, by Carl Hancock Rux, the playwright defines the central character: "the hypothetical black male figure" of sociological studies," as "victim." While the black male in *The Evidence of Silence Broken* engages in the process of self-interrogation, in Rux's play the black male figure is interrogated by society. A "DJ mix of questions" functions as a kind of Greek chorus:

> Tell me about your mother . . . please
> Tell me about your father . . . please
> Do you own a gun?
> Tell me about hip-hop.

Like hip-hop, *The No Black Male Show* is a pastiche—incorporating Rux's poetry, prose, song lyrics and dialogue, along with sampled preexisting texts and songs, intercut with striking visual imagery—all signifying on the black male experience in American society. The following stage direction demonstrates the way the playwright invokes imagery to make his points:

> The DJ mix of questions resumes. The Black Male stands with his back against the wall, unaffected. There is an outline of his body scrawled in chalk behind him. New DJ mix of gospel, basketball, hip-hop, TV sitcoms, cut and layered over each other, filling the air. The Woman in Slip and Shawl takes a seat before the Black Male. She plugs her ears with cotton and waits for him to initiate the conversation. The Woman in Gown takes her seat in front of him, plugs her ears with cotton and waits for the Black Male to do something she can applaud. They both cross their legs, fold their arms . . . Every now and then the Black Male adjusts his jacket, pinches the crease of his trousers, unaware of the chalk outline. He looks to them for approval. Nothing.

The characters in *The No Black Male Show* engage in a discussion of identity and the lack of. A brief excerpt:

> WOMAN IN SLIP AND SHAWL: Your failure to perform as a
> Black Male is our failure to detach ourselves from our
> inherited perception of you.
> BLACK MALE: Thus I may have been unable to perform simply because at that moment I was unable to perceive
> myself . . . in this room.

Rux also manages to comment on a litany of related Diasporic issues. In the following excerpt from one of the show's songs, he slyly indicts white culture's appropriation of African American culture without acknowledging the source. His lyrics connect this behavior, which is rooted in the slave experience (Rux uses minstrel masks to allude to this), to its effect of psychically damaging and undermining the self-esteem of black people:

> If I could black like Eminem
> Oh Lord maybe then . . .
> If I could black like Britney Spears
> Oh Lord no more tears . . .

Carl Hancock Rux is a contemporary Renaissance man and this play showcases the breadth of his vision and artistry. *The No Black Male Show* is a sophisticated play of ideas and imagery that demands return engagements.

cautionary tales

Cautionary tales enable us to survive in hostile territory by warning us of hidden perils. The sixties produced two exemplary plays of this genre: *Dutchman* by Amiri Baraka and *Funnyhouse of a Negro* by Adrienne Kennedy. The "Cautionary Tales" section opens with Psalmayene 24's *Free Jujube Brown!* This movement-infused work investigates the circumstances surrounding an incident in which a "promising" black youth is accused of shooting a Washington, D.C., police officer. Through a series of monologues, a disparate group of richly drawn characters offer their unique perspectives on the central character through their responses to the incident. This solo work serves as a testimonial to the fact that encounters with a hostile police force are often an inescapable reality for young, urban black men. In performance, the monologues are book-ended by two choreographed spoken-word segments, which showcase Psalma-yene's accomplished dance background while framing the story. A particularly satisfying sequence occurs when Hip-Hop himself makes a surprise appearance to express his outrage at the way his name is being exploited and disparaged. True to form he is not quite who we expect him to be.

Beatbox by Tommy Shepherd and Dan Wolf incorporates beatboxing and B-boying, as it chronicles the story of two orphaned stepbrothers struggling to survive. When their effort to extract a livelihood from their street-performance skills comes up short, the older brother turns to dealing drugs and the younger brother to robbery. The situation is exacerbated when the older brother's best friend returns from a successful touring engagement, and the younger brother finds himself in a losing battle for his sibling's attention. Written entirely in rhyme, *Beatbox* shows the inevitable downward spiral resulting when a troubled youth equates violence with manhood. While depicting the severe circumstances that some inner-city youth must contend with, its ending still offers a glimmer of hope. In performance, this multicultural ensemble work exudes boisterous, streetwise energy as it re-creates environments where hip-hop culture flourishes.

Death of a Ho, by Jake-ann Jones, exemplifies Alexander's definition of hip-hop theater: "to contain certain elements of schizophrenia and rebellion, creativity and destruction." In the play, a young black woman's fragile and fragmented sense of identity leaves her vulnerable to media-fed feelings of self-hatred. In the wake of a suicide attempt, she is granted three wishes, but even they go horribly awry. This play graphically depicts the dangers of "selling out" and losing one's sense of identity in the quest to "make it." The author uses a video score to depict a parallel zombie universe that entraps the unwary. Her indictment of the role of music videos in undermining the self-esteem of young women is central to the vision of this potent multidisciplinary theatrical experience. This intense play of ideas signifies on Kennedy's absurdist classic *Funnyhouse of a Negro*. In both plays the central character sees suicide as a means of staunching the pain of being black and female in America. In *Death of a Ho*, Jones replaces *Funnyhouse*'s Kafkaesque vision of American racism with an MTV nightmare inhabited by the central character and her various "selves" as she lies suspended in a state between life and death.

transformationals

As previously alluded to, hip-hop also has a spiritual dimension. It emerged from the space created by the desire for transformation; the repudiation of gang violence in favor of peace. Many of the plays infused with the spirit of hip-hop reflect this impulse to move toward the light. Each of the plays in this section utilizes spoken-word poetry to tell a story. Each story culminates in a transformation.

Word Becomes Flesh, by Marc Bamuthi Joseph, traces the writer/performer's journey from reluctant "Baby Daddy" to embracing full-fledged fatherhood. *Word* relies on Bamuthi's command of various dance forms to expand on the story told through letters to his unborn son during various stages of the son's in utero development. Grippingly candid, the author/performer confesses:

> Three months in the womb
> I am wishing you away
> Inside your mother
> You are an emblem of infinite possibilities
> Inside my mind you are a symbol of disappointment . . .

This performance piece's elegant spoken-word text reveals both the author's sophisticated worldview and unmistakable hip-hop sensibility. The jazz ensemble also elevates the level of artistry onstage. This work culminates in a breathtaking nod to the Yoruba faith when the writer/performer's dying grandfather encounters the unborn son in the passage of transition. This moment calls to mind a similar scenario described in the classic play *Death and the King's Horseman* by Yoruba writer/activist Wole Soyinka. By the end of this play's journey Bamuthi's son, M'kai, has been provided the space by his father's transformation to evolve into a source of unconditional love and inspiration.

Thieves in the Temple: The Reclaiming of Hip-Hop was inspired by Aya de León's feelings of betrayal related to the rise of gangsta rap. While *Thieves* functions effectively as a black feminist critique, Aya's profound understanding that nothing can be solved by condemnation is the source of this piece's power. Instead, she seeks transcendence through revelation and healing. Early on, Aya connects with her audience by using call-and-response while performing "Cellulite," a poem about self-acceptance. Subsequently, she presents characters, recalling all too familiar types from rap videos: the gangsta rapper and video vixen. Then she strips away the braggadocios' façade, revealing the pain and vulnerability lurking underneath. Watching her performance, I recalled the hostile response that Ntozake Shange received from many African American men back in the seventies when she called them out on misogyny in *for colored girls*. The response to Aya's performance was markedly different, as young men of various ethnicities leapt to their feet, alongside the women, and gave her a cheering ovation. Clearly she accomplished her goal at the 2002 NYC HHTF, with this heartfelt, issue-oriented performance piece.

Will Power's solo work *Flow* presents the often humorous but unsentimental story of an urban community, home to seven storytellers who represent diverse ethnic identities and storytelling styles. After meeting each of them and watching them ply their craft, we learn of the various circumstances surrounding their sudden deaths, prompting a call to action. Will Power's nuanced portrait of this community challenges the media's overly simplistic portrayal of the 'hood as a tense and dreary site of violence, revealing a highly complex intersection of lifestyles and values. Functioning in part as a cautionary tale, *Flow* embodies hip-hop as a way of life. Power, an MC and a pioneer of the hip-hop theater movement, invents a new language in this piece—the language of the drumbeat. His text not only rhymes, it scratches while speaking in beats and rhythms:

> Zuu ta kaa-beedee-beedee-beedee
> Zuu ta kaa, Beedee-ka-ka uh-huh
> Zuu ta kaa, Beedee-ka-ka OK . . .

This is a contemporary urban griot at work, looking to pass the baton to us, the audience, so it is highly appropriate to end this volume with *Flow*.

Together these artists form a diverse collection of voices speaking to a range of experiences and issues they felt most compelled to address. The expanse of their talent is dazzling. They are poets, novelists, rappers, actors, dancers, choreographers, musicians, as well as playwrights, and these various talents inform their work. It's thrilling to hear this generation of artists reinventing their relationship with language, a hallmark of the hip-hop generation.

Back in the seventies when hip-hop was invented by African American and Caribbean American youth in the Bronx, no one expected that it would grow to become the dominant global youth culture. Now that its influence and longevity are undisputed, we can only anticipate that it will continue to transform the American cultural landscape for years to come.

June 2009
Oakland and Los Angeles

ruminations on identity

the evidence of silence broken

a spoken-word performance concert

written by zell miller iii
music by dj brainchild and dj kitundu

author's statement

This was never intended to be a play. Like all my other work, this was to be an experiment. This piece was solely intended to help me, as a performance poet, get booked in theaters under the banner of a "one-man show." But for me it was essentially going to be the work of a performance poet unfolding over hype, hip-hop beats, while tricking the audience into thinking that there was a story behind it all. But as my friend Daniel Alexander Jones said, quoting his friend Robbie MacCauley, "The writer has no idea what he/she writes." Once the first draft of this piece was done, I realized that it was one of the most autobiographical pieces of writing I had ever created. I quickly came to understand that this work is about the creation—the birth, if you will—of a poet, and how that poet came to be who he is. The series of vignettes that make up this piece all represent a poet's experimentation and his growth, leading up to the final image of maturation. Important quotations appear throughout the work; those quotes are intended to be read aloud by the Poet. The quotes and the "breaths" are used as transitions between the moments. They should also be used as opportunities for the Poet to catch his breath and connect to the audience, such as when a musician wipes his/her face with a towel or takes a sip of water and uses that moment to catch a glimpse of the crowd. If the budget is big enough, the quotes can also be displayed in some cool way by film or video, but it is so crucial to the work that they be spoken by the Poet, because these quotes represent the influences that helped to create him/her.

The Poet addresses the audience in three ways: as an MC speaking over the music, as a poet storytelling about his childhood in monologue form or meditating on his/her life in direct reflection to the audience. The changes happen very quickly, sometimes even blending together.

But these transitions must be understood, because at no time does the Poet ever completely drop one voice for another. It is important to note that each personality lives and feeds off the others'. Again, budget permitting, there should be a DJ onstage with the Poet, much like the call-and-response of original hip-hop music. The Poet and DJ work together to create atmosphere and context for the text spoken by the Poet. The stage directions are such as they are, and must be followed; there is not one word, one direction, one moment that can be spared in the telling of this story.

production history

The Evidence of Silence Broken: A Spoken-Word Performance Concert received its world premiere on April 18, 2003 at the Pillsbury House Theatre in Minneapolis, MN. It was produced by Pillsbury House Theatre and Trú Rúts Endeavors. The director was Daniel Alexander Jones. The Poet was Zell Miller III and the DJ was Walter Kitundu. Set design was by Seitu Jones, graffiti art was by Roger Cummings and lighting design was by Mike Walgen.

It was subsequently produced by the Hyde Park Theater in Austin, TX. The director was Ken Webster. The Poet was Zell Miller III and the DJ was DJ Brainchild. Set and lighting design were by Don Day, sound design was by DJ Brainchild and Zell Miller III.

set

A Saturday morning hangout. Think the Cosby kids from *Fat Albert*—very animated. Brightly colored graffiti covers the walls, several lights hang from the ceiling. Several times during the play, the actor will turn the lights on and off. Read *The Invisible Man* by Ralph Ellison: that should give you a clear idea.

a note on the text layout

The three incarnations of the Poet are indicated in part by the way the text is designed on the page: the Poet as MC speaks over the music; his monologues are set like run-in poems, the line breaks indicated by slashes. The Poet as the storyteller of his childhood speaks in poetic rhythms; these stories are set like poems, with a varied use of spacing. The Poet speaks in direct reflection to the audience; these lines are set like traditional verse. The stage directions also work to make these transitions clear.

In total darkness, we hear the sound of prerecorded breathing. The breathing becomes its own character—a layered breathing made form several voices, becoming more and more rhythmic, turning into its own drum/track.

Green and blue lights fill the stage. We see a white backdrop and a black floor. Centerstage is an empty mic stand, a music stand and stool, all in black.

The breathing continues. The lights remain at less than half. We hear the voice of the Poet, over the breathing, from backstage, or from the audience, but he/she remains unseen.

The breathing decreases to the sound of a regular heartbeat.
The Poet laughs.

POET:

My heart b
      b my heart
b

          beating

(The Poet takes a deep breath.)

When I was
    I became
        then I touched
        and I saw
then there was
    the first
        the first time
          I heard my own
      voice
        I . . .

(The recorded breathing stops. There is a brief moment of silence.)

Let's get it going.

(A mid-tempo hip-hop beat screams out of the speakers. The lights come up to full. The Poet is onstage taking on the spirit of an MC, cordless mic in hand. He takes over the entire space.)

I am the amplified / amplification of an amplifier / resonating with resounding resolve / receiving / unsolicited pornographic emails / that keep my Hotmail account on lock / pop culture keeps me drunk / with rumor and innuendo / and in a hazy recollection / I see Arafat trapped in his compound / with an M16 / locked and loaded / he is ready to French-kiss the concept of martyrism / and the blind stares of a million pairs of eyes squared / can't see the significance / or maybe they do / but like me / they are drunk off pop culture / and would rather bounce and sway to the oh so gritty grimy street level / but oh so pop friendly vocals of a Ja Rule / now can't nobody see this bitch-ass nigga is stealing everything Pac did? / and the equivalent of Arafat shut down in his own compound / would be like militants crashing a tank through the White House / 'cause they felt that 9/11 was somehow the government's fault / . . . and it is but I don't think that Bush would have his hands around an M16 / this muthafucka can't spell M16 / and is all this shit some poorly written dream / I mean / aren't we the dreaming of unrequited love / aren't we after all the deferment of a dream / that is cracked and shrunken by the sun / in the quiet of night / if I listen close enough / I can break dance to the ultrasound of my blood flow / I'm told it's a new world / but is it one of order / Cornel West said that / "America has been niggerized" / meaning that the false security of those privileged individuals / and the ones who move with privilege / even though their bank accounts is in the amounts / of equal / or lesser than mine / but they still move with privilege / well their false security has been HIJACKED / and now they question why a group of people hate them so / and blacks try to take a collective breath . . . out / 'cause the powers that Be now got themselves a new nigga / right / but me / I'm not breathing / I'm putting my exhale on layaway / I'm setting up a payment plan / 'cause little Georgie under orders from his pops / is nowhere near through with the cleansing of evil / it seems to me that it coincides with skin tone / and no one wants to talk about Vice President Cheney's secret tape recordings in California / when he was talking about running an oil pipeline through the territory of the so-called evil Taliban / it seems to me that patriotism is misspelled nowdays, it should be g-r-e-e-d / I am the amplified amplification of an amplifier / I am / the moan and weeps of Strats / who cry for Mary 'cause Jimi never played them / and now it seems

Jimi's sounds are to rebound into this new neo-black revolutionist movement / you know them cats / they still dining on the shattered memories and theories of the Black Panthers / and wasn't it the Black Panthers / who told Jimi Hendrix he wasn't black enough / you know them cats / they talk all that revolutionary shit / but you never see them niggas with a gat / you know them cats / quote all that 5% shit but never studied the legit / see it was Clarence 13 X who was suspended by Malcolm / like Elijah suspended Malcolm / but Clarence in all his wis-dumb / only took 120 lessons / that's why them niggas always screaming they studying 120 / see them cats can't even complete a full 360 circle / you know them cats they quote Robert Nesta to the hills and valleys / but what about the white blood running through Marley's veins / do you only love half of what he says / and in the dirt with clean fingers / I wanna write a scripture only to be shared by the wind / I wanna know what the Christians did the Saturday before the resurrection / I mean what do you do when you wake up and you think God is dead / and I ponder that / while Arafat sits in his compound under attack by Israel / I picture him sitting there with his M16 locked / and loaded / and maybe to himself in the middle-night when it's quiet and right / and he has maybe vomited from the funk of a stopped-up toilet / and the heat, fear and sweat of the others locked up with him / maybe in the mirror / alone he says / I am the amplified / amplification of an amplifier / resonating with resounding resolve / resolve / resolve / resolve / resolve . . .

(The music fades out.

The following quote and others like it throughout the play are projected and read aloud by the Poet.)

      Quote: "If you afraid to tell the truth, then you don't even deserve freedom."

                                        —MALCOLM X, MINISTER

(We hear prerecorded breath.)

So it was begins or should I say began with this:
bus rides
    books
        oral stories
            words
                broken hearts

lies
truth
speaking to myself
belief and mis-truisms
so it was Change kept Rage like a favorite nickel from childhood.

> **Quote:** "You can't create in a vacuum of hate."
>
> —TONY DESHAY, FILMMAKER, BIG BROTHA

So it was
    bus rides
        long walks
            dead night
wisdom in the beholder of those
who have no place to lay their heads
right there Change in the biggest brown eyes I will ever see
looking like his mother
acting like me
like fallen stars
and in the quiet of the moment there is a prayer she prays:

(In a sacred-sounding whisper:)

Our father, our father in heaven
Sacred be thy name, forgive us our trespasses
As we forgive those who trespass against you . . .

That prayer she prays.

(The blue lights come up and we hear a mid-tempo hip-hop beat.)

There is a prayer she prays / on running days and often unsupported nights / there is a soundtrack to it the prayer / she is called out for loitering these days / but she still believes in the wait / cannon of echoes reside with her / her eyes embarrass those not secure with their walk / it comes from her mother's wail I think / that prayer she prays / there is a prayer she prays in unestablished establishments / there is a low gutter gut bucket to the sound / angels of the city only answer when called, she protests / so she don't call them that often / but they still seem to find her doorstep / often when they have been set free and now need a landing strip / hard liquor in the air / contends with the smoke and hopes / that escape through the sighs of crowds / filled with soulless travelers / like

Miguel Pinero / like Jean-Michel Basquiat / like Jim Morrison / maybe they have forgotten / or maybe they were never told that they walk in divinity / that they are worthy / that they matter / that prayer be on some nonlinear shit / it comes like unmentionable moans and stains the air with permanent markers never to be removed / she gestures that prayer / it's in that stumble some call a walk / it's in that skid to a place where she stands to extend what some call her misery / but it's not really misery / it's quite the opposite / hear that prayer / feel that prayer / taste that prayer / smell that prayer / see that prayer / man / she got a history and a conjure about it / fuck around too close to her edge and you will lose your way and never really be able to find it again / so I listen at a distance / and interrupt my own listening sessions so not to have the full weight of the words / I've been bitten by that prayer once before / but she saved me from myself / she let me walk on / she said I carried a message inside / and until the completed message was sent out / I would be here / meeting people like her / and learning how to breathe / like the people who own my lineage / see we people of the sun / learned how to breathe when there was no air / we learned how to live when there was nothing around us but death / she did however take my grandfather / she took him on September 17, 2001 / but he was ready / to dance home / free / home free / home free home free . . .

(The Poet makes a rhythm out of "home free." He claps his hands and moves in a circular motion, repeating the phrase several times. The music fades out to a count of five. The lights return to the original setting.)

Quote: "Everything will change. The only question is growing up, or decaying."

—Nikki Giovanni, poet

Lying becomes easy enough
Especially when you learn the world rewards those that do
So my pen became extinct
A Jurassic relic in my modern times of acceptance
I learned how to maneuver around the truth with precision, alone
Walking under a street light
Walking in with mist and hazy colors and sounds of the night
Dreams are not supposed to walk up and pinch you, right?

(The Poet's breathing becomes more ancient in its rhythm.)

Dreams are less, or more, than we can afford sometimes
Once on the back of a bus
                    close to midnight
        I got a glimpse of:

(He creates an image with his body, sort of like a snapshot.)

                    self-portrait left title-less
Against the canvas
                the painter would have used small brushes
to illustrate his/her vision
                    the painter would have chose maybe
        midnight yellows and
                    hot-weather blues
but
                the poet, in his attempt to infuriate the night
spoke to himself in hushed mumbles
                    and fatigued pauses
and when the argument with his self was done
                    the page lay
            open to
                    give
birth
and it said
                    in his handwriting:
the night
                    in its mystery, confused the sound
it misdirected itself for the sake of peace
                    the night spoke with caution
it said:
        "Let's engage the middle,
            give the beginning a chance to breathe
and
                let the ending have a chance to rest."
Sound responded:
                    "Can you identify them places in yourself
where conversation becomes a calling card unused and low
on minutes?"
            before them
                I thought:
"My thick tongue illuminates my growth place. I stand for you to sit,
but that's how my mama raised me."

my mama
     my mama
          my mama . . .

*(We hear a banging hip-hop music track. The Poet stands under the blue
lights and continues to perform, now over the music.)*

In a semi half circle
     blue bulbs provide electric light
incense on the ceiling
          Indian-style in my approach
     what's native to me
          is my tongue
familiar subject matters
          keeps me focused
     Lord knows through these current political times
I have been forced into ADD
     Attention
          Deficiency
             Dominates
scripture says
          nothing to me
             is that the problem
in trying to get closer to God
          I listen to beats by Brainchild
he's the son of a minister
             like I'm the Son of God
     but I'm not holy no longer

feeling kinda heretic-ish
          remembering like my beginnings
1142 Mercer, apartment 108
remembering kissing bony Nessa under a cardboard box
     remembering how I blacked out
and woke up with
          a scar on my forehead
my mother smoking Viceroys
          my pops smoking Kools and I had
asthma
          dig it see
             caught up in the contradictions
     I wanted to get closer to God

so I invited them to dinner, they agreed
                    but sent Kahlil Gibran instead
Kahlil was good company
                    he brought greens
they were sweet like ambrosia.

(The music stops. The Poet does mock karate moves across the stage and then transforms into the Mother. His hand gestures indicate he's holding a cigarette and a can of Pepsi soda.)

Umm, umm, umm ummmmm
standing in her doorway in a well-furnished apartment
cigarette smoke from her left hand and Pepsi can in her right
my mother has coffee skin
coffee like three creams and two sugars, that's how she takes it
I always thought she could have been a mob boss
not like some Tony Soprano boss
more like a Marlon Brando-type boss
she would give you plenty chances to come clean with the truth
always showing you respect
but when you didn't come through with the truth
well
she would raise her left eyebrow
and like a mob boss
she would
        bust your ass
or put a hit out to have your ass busted
I always wanted to be cool like that
like this one time she was in a grocery store
and this little baby
little white baby in the meat section
he looks at my mom and he says:
"Are you a nigger?"
now me
I would have lost it, I probably would have tried to knock the
     shit out the kid's parents
but my mom
well
she just smiled
raised that left eyebrow, gold crown showing, and she said:
"No sweetheart, but your mother is."
And the little baby was like:
"Mommy, are you a nigger?"

that type of shit
I have never seen her shaken
finding them dirty magazines under the bed
when my brotha told her she was going to be a grandmother
and he was still in high school
cuts
bruises
hospital visits
whatever
I just remember her calm and collected
but on this day
she was visible shaken
she felt it necessary to explain to me why after twenty-eight years of
marriage
she had finally decided to leave my dad
this was a joke in our home
'cause she said it so much:
"I'm going to be by myself soon."
we just never believed her
but at twenty-two when I walked in the house and boxes were
    packed
and she asked me: "Who do you want to live with?"
I just became numb
so not like my mom
so she spoke
and the more she spoke
the more she cried
the more she cried the more beautiful she became
not that I never thought that my mom wasn't human
I just never thought anything got to her
she would never raise her voice to get her point across
she would never disagree with you

> **Quote:** "If you argue, and you know you're right,
> then you're an asshole for arguing."
> —VERNELL MILLER, MY MOMMA

I know I got my use of language from her
strength, I thought, was the ability to be strong when the pres-
    sure on
but today, on this day, to see her standing here like this
now all that had changed
I had to change

see, I judge women by my mother's mold
I never realized that I never gave them or my mother a chance
to be
to be human
I had it all fucked-up
now all that had to change
I had to change
'cause my mother was not who I thought she was
and maybe just maybe I wasn't who she thought I was
maybe that's why she was able to stand here and show me a side
of her I never dreamed existed
so here we were
me and Mom
standing in her doorway
talking, laughing, crying
together
I made peace with my myths about her
but she is still cool
          cool like a muthafucka.

(A quick blackout. The lights come up.
   In total darkness, the Poet whispers very eerily:)

Heart beating
     breath breathing
          what happens if I don't
use breath
take breath
sound breath
body breath
     I will die
         right . . .

*(The Poet pulls on a light cord, the light turns on. In a very conservative,
clichéd white man's voice he says:)*

Quote: "Still working on my nerves man, like son you
got to get your soul clean. Before they blow them horns
like Coltrane."

              —BENNIE SEGAL, MC

(Blackout.)

heart beating
    breath breathing
        what happens if I don't
use breath
take breath
sound breath
body breath
    I will die
        right . . .

(We hear street noise and the sound of a bus coming to a stop. The lights create a glowing street scene. The street noise fades out and we hear gangsta-style music with a hip-hop beat.)

Down 11th Street / walking with skipped strokes / and tuition-free knowledge / gliding with intellect / bending corners in this urban-renewal-gone-bad / to just plain fucked-up / badges and bunches hunch together / can't tell the good from the bad / everybody is looking to get by / get that thing to get you high / induced at seven months there are children here / children here who look like me / I'm a product of these streets / armed with a fear of my parents so I never walked too far outside the line / but I've been a mule in tight times / and for several months on the back of steel worms, city transit / I, under the slant of hip-hop beats / holding until the theories cracked all around me / *The Isis Papers* by Francis Cress Welsing / Malcolm's face on my chest / nestled safely in my book bag / was a 9 or a 380 to be specific / and I had the heart and the shrunken-ball, big-dick syndrome, if backed against a wall I would click it / my 380 riding along with the package I was delivering / I'm Southern and not knowing / I'm country and still growing / down 11th Street I glide / making sense out of abuse / in unlaced kicks and saggy jeans / I'm the means to an end / who wants to die today / I'm looking to make you famous / put you front page of the *Austin American-Statesman* type shit / feet pressed against the back seat, it's an immovable object / FUCK THAT / I am the immovable odyssey / I'm Orpheus / half God and pissed 'cause my lover died by my own hand / I'm greeting the beginners with old handshakes / I'm stomping / leaving holes in cement / I got these niggas so shook / I can walk half a block and they would still feel the after-shock / cigarette in palm / will never be lit / just hold it to remind me to stay free / can't be like my brothas on these blocks I'm different / my eyes are the cross-section of a traffic accident / I watch everyone and wait for the energy to pop off / I'm caution and alone / always alone / the city-bus door moans open / and down 11th Street I glide / down 11th Street I glide / down 11th Street I glide . . .

(The music fades out very quickly.)

> **Quote:** "Why is it that when we talk to God we're praying, but when God talks to us, we are schizophrenic."
> —LILY TOMLIN, COMEDIAN

Once on the back of a bus
Sacrifice sat 2 seats in front of me
me on a crossroad balancing between responsible acts
and artistic freedom
the hum of the frequent stops made writing an adventure
at a glance I was distracted by Sacrifice
who snagged the nickname of Chris
he wore no shirt
    torn jeans
        and the big disease with the little name
he was silent and still
        'cept for the crumpled 10 in his right hand
and a freckled composition book in his left hand
his pen hung loose from his lips
with ink drying in the corners of his mouth
I rang the bell . . . *(Beat)* I didn't want to pass him
but the back door was stuck
there is a nerving in the uncomfortable
echo vibrated
see the example
    crossroad got straight
Chris leaned into me he found my rumbling tummy funny
the 10 now balanced in my palm but I thought
I never wanna be the one who has to choose who gets to eat
    crossroad
so I learned
    I learned to maneuver around the truth with precision
'cause the truth is company unwelcome
in this reality of the unspoken
and speaking it only makes it livable
and if you have to sacrifice for your art
then

I
  can
  not
   I
   will
    not
and my heart b
      my heart b
       beating
beating
                    b
pauses   blood

blood
      pauses . . .

(The Poet takes three breaths.

    His breathing becomes rhythmic, gets very loud, then fades very quickly and quietly. He carries a chair center stage and places it down. Then he brings in a beautiful flower in a glass vase. This represents his lady love.)

Imagine, if you will. There is a booth right there and shit.

(He sets up the booth with his hands. When he speaks of the two characters he places a hand over each of their heads to establish where they are sitting.)

And then, there is like, OK people there. And. She wears her upbringing in the way she holds a glass. And. He is under-protected and reaching. Imagine that for like a second; can you see it? Close your eyes if you have to. When you see it. Then you will understand.

They
            they sit
they sit at a
                they sit at a table
they sit at a table
      ordering
and
she
  be
she

be cool
      she be cool
like
she be cool like the
                       mahogany
she be cool like the mahogany of her
eyes
      eyes
he
    is
      he is unlaced
         he is unlaced and locked
she
      she smiles with
         she smiles with anticipation
or
is it
  control
      she is under
control
he
he is the opposite
         nervous and impatient
laughs out of place
they
are
                    funny
each
      each waiting
each waiting for the other
to
  just
say
      to just say
kiss
    me
they talk about everything but *that*
she says:
"I'm here
      I'm here not going anywhere."
he waits
      wonders
to

him
    self
he
says
to
him
    self:
"I bet
I bet she
I bet she taste like
I bet she taste like peppermint
I bet she taste like peppermint if you
I bet she taste just like peppermint if you kissed her right
right?"
but
neither
will
    neither will just
neither will just say
    neither will just say
kiss
neither will just say
      kiss me
Kiss me / kiss me like you think the world is going to explode / and
your last action on this planet / is kissing me deep / touching my
soul with your tongue / I want you to wake up my ancestors with
that kiss / make my unborn children know they are loved / with
that kiss . . .
But
  they
sit
    sit at a
      sit at a table
     sit at a table ordering
when they
when they should
when they should just
     KISS
get it
get it over
get it over
   with
     they

they sit
>they sit at a
>>table
>>>they sit at a table
ordering
>ordering.

(He takes a breath.)

Quote: "In the end, we will not remember the words of
our enemies, but the silence of our friends."
—MARTIN LUTHER KING, JR., MINISTER

(The Poet takes a big breath. The sound of a hip-hop beat begins.)

I'm 93,000,000 miles from the sun / no gray coat define / weathering heights / not the movie / take flight Assata Shakur / innocent like a Peltier / damn if I b corruptible like a Huey P. / never see me in a senate's seat like a Seale / no babies outside my marriage / like a Jack-Son / won't be no visits to the White House to counsel the weakness of the president who soled the knees of twenty-one-year-old interns with my pregnant mistress like a Jesse fucking Jackson / had to say it twice for clarity / I will just be a poet / yeah / like a Lorca / yeah / Lorca / never thought that urban streets could lead me to his door / or / that those same urban streets / could lead me to a transcendentalist's belief / or / the proletarian simplicity could unclothed me to the sweater of an Edgar Allen / patterns like crop-dusting spectacles / I make the sound 'scape / but keep it entertained with my voice / JUST MY VOICE / to the beat of my drum / focus quiet enough / I can sustain the rhythm of my blood flow / write to it in spaces of time / that are now declined / canceled by the energy of my son / who says: / "Let's be castaway, Daddy / but not like Tom Hanks." / escape on sunrays at dusk / make dawn prohibited . . .

(The Poet creates another snapshot-like image. This image should echo or be repeated several times. The music fades out. The Poet establishes a section of the stage where his father is working; the next moment unfolds in this place.)

Quote: "If you are not a reality, whose myth are you? If you are not a myth, whose reality are you?"
—SUN RA, MUSICIAN

Proud, he smiled. with eyes, never seen. until. *(Takes a breath)* my father has little boy eyes. mischievous and innocent. under the stifling sun his beautiful black skin shines like new money. we work in one of his customer's yards; in between, we laugh. my father is whole again. after the divorce, he was split and shattered. it was more about him not having a home for his children, but now he understands that he, the physical him, is all we need. he has also learned how to shut up, or at least quiet the voices of alcohol when it comes knocking. we finish the job, and I load the tools back onto the truck and try find time to get a little breather before the next job. my pops will be out here all day hustling. he told me one time that he just likes to make money, not that he likes money all that much, says he just likes to make it. he says: "I tell ya, you can get a hustler off the streets, but boy if you a hustler you gonna always find something to hustle." he laughs out loud and follows it with his signature: "Shiiiiitttt." we laugh together. we are done, ready to move on the next job, but my pops is standing there for several seconds. watching the yard and smiling. he has this intense look of joy on his face. I have caught him looking at me and my brothers and my sister like that. my curiosity gets the best of me and I ask him: "What you doing Pops?" he looks at me like I just woke him from a pleasurable dream. he smiles, says: "A man, or woman, hell, for that matter. a man or woman ain't shit if they don't complete their work, son. you look at this yard, remember how it looked before we got started? now look at it. shiiitt, it's pretty as hell now. see that boy, Shiiittt. we did a good job on this yard. and when it's all said and done, that's all you can really hope to do, son. a good job." I listen, almost on the edge of tears. 'cause I know that's how he looks at me. so I ask, just for my own sake: "So in other words, you're proud of the job, Daddy?" he smiles and says: "Yes I am. I sho proud of the job, baby." and with that nothing else needs to be said. I say to myself. my father is proud of me. my father has been proud of me long before I ever knew the definition of the word. imagine that. proud he smiled. with eyes, never seen. until . . .

(The Poet takes a big breath and executes movements to suggest an expectant father in a delivery room, helping his wife deliver their baby. He wipes her head, holds her hand, breathes, helps her push, etc.)

There *(Breath)*
    is *(Breath)*
       a prayer she prays *(Breath, breath)*

there *(Breath)*
is a prayer *(Breath)*
    she prays
she
is
a
prayer? *(Breath)*
are we
    the prayer
        she prays?

Quote: "Have you ever seen a crackhead? That's eternal
fire."

—TUPAC AMARU SHAKUR, MC/POET

*(Blood red lights flood the stage. The Poet stands on the chair. He makes
a noose with the mic cord and wraps it around his neck as he talks.)*

Connection
the meter waits for nothing
        source
breath of my breath . . . *(Beat)* literally
intake
      cord
connecting to an outside source making room for amplification
amplifying
    am I
      first teacher
unopened lessons left
      want to blame
caught me
      want to make like it's
left hook to the jaw
      her fault
Joe Frazier–style
      need for responsible acts
left me swollen
      separation
still trying to hold on to my *(Grabs his crotch)*
have to learn how to *(Breaths in and out)*
    like Ali
my ego will not allow me to keep silent
      have to learn

right at the brim
                teach me
right under my skin
                        separation forced
right at the source of codes
                        mine theirs ours his
baby bird pushed from nest
                danger
red hot
                explosion
looking for a connection through
                my obsession
fascination with *(Grabs his crotch)*
                did she
you could have
told me
why didn't you
(Whispers) tell me
is this punishment for my premature arrival?
'cause I can't wait
she says you have to be
but
patience is only for those who can't wait *(Deep breath)*
                cord
extends
I speak life into this mic that goes out through
                like birth
people are looking for me to
                        feed them
but
I'm
still
                hungry
myself
looking for answers between
she says
and I don't listen with intensity
separation
split and whole
connection
cut like
cord.

(He takes four quick breaths. He stares out into the audience and begins to remove the mic cord from his neck. He sits on the chair and takes four long breaths.)

Quote: "A coward is incapable of exhibiting love; it is the prerogative of the brave."
—MOHANDAS K. GANDHI, PEACEMAKER

(A hard-hitting hip-hop beat comes on.)

In the throes of a city blocker / I glide down Guadalupe / more of an excursion than a hobby / backpacking on the steel worms / I turns / and seize the chance to advance through space / but I'm caught by hate / head filled with facts and the exact measurements of my history / and Laurie Carlos says that I have a right / if I'm going by facts alone / that I have a right to take 45s / sit on top of buildings / and blast every white face I see / that's my right / if I'm going off facts / but do I wanna deal with God's truth / because facts and God's truth are polar opposites / and she says there are thems that sits with facts going mad over the skin game / and baby / you better learn to see it's all the same / she says / soft hands holding my face / she is telling me to look past the obvious / question my existence / take a trip to Europe / see where the lies sits / I listen / but financial concerns won't let me burn that hole over the ocean and land in foreign soil / so / I transfer / take the 15 Red River back North / in my voice is the choice / allow my pen to bleed me dry / removed the X hat from my head / asked God to enter my cipher / there is an echo saying: / "I've been here, I've been here since you could remember and even before that." / I'm right and exact / no longer packing / just wishing to be a fraction / of the truth that is God / on the steel worm I turns / and bends / extends my seat / headphones are a thin barrier / but it's enough / it's enough for now / it's enough for now / it's enough for now . . .

(The music slowly fades out.)

Quote: "They who dream by day are cognizant of many things which escape those who dream only by night."
—EDGAR ALLEN POE, POET

(The Poet sits surrounded by books. His movement in this next moment is all metaphor; it's how he lost himself in his books at this period of his life. So he should build a barrier or execute some type of movement series

with the books to relay that metaphor. The books should fly out of his hands very quickly as he scans and then adds them to the barrier.)

"Our father who. our father in heaven. our mother earth. sacred be your name. forgive us for our trespasses, as we forgive those who trespass against you."

> **Quote:** "I start with a picture and then finish it, I don't think about it when I'm working, I think about life."
> —JEAN-MICHEL BASQUIAT, ARTIST

There are times when you breathe. then there are times when you never imagined breathing . . . *(Beat)* again.

> **Quote:** "I paint self-portraits because I am so often alone, because I am the person I know best."
> —FRIDA KAHLO, ARTIST

The first time, I heard, I heard, my own . . . *(Beat)* voice.
　Prince says:

> **Quote:** "There is lonely, then there is lonely, then there is what I'm feeling right now."
> —PRINCE ROGERS NELSON, MUSICIAN

I remember the clash. It's that place that resides in all of us.

> **Quote:** "God has been replaced, as he has all over the West, with respectability and air conditioning."
> —AMIRI BARAKA, POET

Many may never reach it. pray you never do. there is a prayer that she. prays! "Our father, holy mother."

> **Quote:** "Excuse me while I kiss the sky,"
> —JIMI HENDRIX, MUSICIAN

There have been pistols on my temples more times than there should have been. trigger drawn back, but I thought. what if the bullet just stays lodged in my brain forever? and I live. or, what if my hand shakes at the moment of truth and the bullet travels out of my eyesight and into the body of somebody else's body. it's funny / that thing that has kept me from breathing all these years

/ kept breath in my lungs those many years ago / there comes a point when fear must remove itself from your footsteps / but who makes that choice / you or fear? / there are times when you breathe / and then there are times when you can't imagine breathing again / I know both / the trick is / waking and knowing which one to choose / daily . . .

    Quote: "Memories come down on me. Once again, I'm caught without an umbrella."

                          —MICHAEL FRANTI, POET/MC

        Hands
soft
           woke
said
            said:
b
     my
heart
       heart
b
my— *(Blackout)*

(The Poet pulls on a light cord and does his best Bill Cosby impression:)

My wife is a Scorpio female
and
I'm a Scorpio male
now that is a novel adapted into a three- or four-day miniseries
but my son
my son
is a
Virgo male
and if you know anything about the zodiac
you will understand me and my wife's pain.

(The Poet turns the light off. A spotlight comes up on him sitting stage right.)

Once on the back of a bus. a man, average man, suit-wearing man. suit-wearing man, wanted to sit down. sit down next to me. suit-wearing man in white skin and wet hair, and long day, looking for a sit-down. suit-wearing man said: "May I sit down." black man, me. black man in revolutionary mode. I. revolutionary mode. me. saw white man as reflection of all white men. in search of change, me: "By any means necessary," misquote. me. acted no better than them who I wanted to change / kill / teach. see learned oppression from an oppressor. but this man. this average man, suit-wearing man. only wanted to sit down. but I. me, revolutionary, said: "You stand your ass up, my people had to stand for four hundred years, so you stand your punk ass up." average man, becoming unaware. him in long day. misunderstands. noise of bus drowns out rage of me. so he tries to sit. average man, suit-wearing man, tries to sit down. didn't I? say I. naw, wait, to myself say. he ain't trying to. me. black man. tells white man in suit: "If you sit down, I will break your muthafucking jaw." silence! *(Looking out into the audience with a face of pure rage)* stand off. nothing moves but the motion of the bus. there is some contact. some contact through eyes. a man, average man, suit-wearing man. suit-wearing man in white skin, wet hair, and long day. turns away and stands. me. black man, feeling. a revolutionary victory. but. silence. pause. change. was that change? later, much later, I get an understanding. now me, wiser, older, father. looks, every once in a while. looks through crowds. looks through crowds for, a man. average man, suit-wearing man. suit-wearing man in long day looking for sit-down. so I can say. the. unspoken. *(Breath)*

(The spotlight fades and another spotlight comes up stage left. The Poet walks to the new spotlight. As soon as he is there, a slow hip-hop beat begins.)

                    there beyond my reach
sits safety
closed off by barbed wire
                    barking dogs
                         armed bushes who house
rifle men
I
have
to
rethink
my
tactics to get to her
the ability to seem
invisible escapes
                    me

like
ancient love songs
like an infant I need warmth
body to body
but
I'm to be denied
I take this denial with favor
seeking in myself resolution
empty caverns
treeless forest
reminds me that Mother Nature is tired
she cannot pretend like she cares anymore
so she does not put energy into rejuvenation
I try to mentally reach Safety, who smiles like a shameful demon
but my transmission is blocked
codes shatter off into space
then disappear
honey-colored reasoning taste bitter, in this infant trance I longed
to be rocked
              rocked gently soft and fall asleep in arms of Safety
but she can't hear me
                    I can't get to her
                         I could
                              climb the cold side of
her tower
but
                              that's not a guarantee
to her
I imagine her in a straightjacket mumbling off secrets of the
universe to a padded cell
feed twice a day
once in the morning
shock treatment for lunch
                                        dinner at six

she needs me like I need her
(I can feel it)
I'm trying to escape this labyrinth
trying to remember the cracks in cement as my markers but
I confuse footprints for reasoning
I find myself licking asphalt for direction
I hope she is not dead
Safety, who wore black combat boots and chewed on her
fingernails for

thought process
I tried to love her
but a lover is not what she seeks from me
I got lost in my own wanting ability and forget that a relation-
    ship requires two
her hands
are soft petals
she gathers cosmic energy in her hair
so I caress it then put in my pocket for later
I stand outside the gates busting verse free poetics
to the beat of barking dogs
knowing my limit I stand at a north-eastern direction
for bullets could fly from bushes
I don't think she can see me
                    maybe her eyes are covered
                                    ears plugged
                    treatment *they* say
she's been here fifty-four minutes
                    fourteen hours
                    two days
                    seven months
I just think that I want to taste her like the salt on my upper lip
but I know that I must lay in her arms
if she were here would she hold me
could she hold me
maybe my pain is prickle like a porcupine
then I get to blaming myself for her free admission to this asylum
I leave under the cloak of not knowing
trying to return to the sun but its warmth is dry and in this infant
    trance
I curl up and wait for nightmares to
                    shake

                        my

                            sanity

                                to

                                    sleep

there beyond my reach sits

                                    Safety.

*(The music fades out. The same lights come up from the prior booth scene.
The Poet sits the chair down again, and then places the flower on the
chair.)*

Back at the booth
     between ordering and waiting
they
     they sit
          sit at a table
              ordering
and he says
          under his breath
          he says
if   I
     if   I   could
I would write
     I would write you a
I would write you a psalm
and it would read
     it would read like this:

(A beautiful mid-tempo, hip-hop jazz song begins.)

You are divinity personified
squared in the circle
I'm the specialist in the language of living
I dreamed of this meeting while test-tasting the existence of sound
breath work and gesture communication keeps me abound
is there a once-supposed beginning
but there is no beginning
'cause my feet have crushed past broken glass in every city block
since cities were blocks and stocked with human cattle branded
    and sold
we be the same atom or Adam and Eve we exist in the same cosmos
I'm the you
you think you wanted to be
and you're the me I think I'm hiding from
there is a dawn
and it smiles like you
faded and beautiful with orange burst of optimum illumination
there is a creation in this work of definition
born of collaboration with syncopated and complex simplistic
    memory
that beams out in a reminiscent and strange nostalgia
there is no beginning just *now*
the intersection of time is present

what's your cross street? I ask as crossing your conduit on my cell
    phone
we meet under the influence of divinity
drunk and aware, balanced and off center
music heightens the senses
your introduction is epic and full of consequences
our eyes made new colloquy
our laughs make crescent indentions upon the surface of breath
before we take inhale
the night is upon us
twisting the identification and theater of the vernacular
your corner-smile writes the lament with rushed inertia
heading me steadfast beyond intricate sagas
we now shock ourselves into affidavits of conjure and soothsayer
    potential
we make sport of truth and divorce ourselves from the concepts
    of love
in this passageway of God's tears
enkindle in our strides we make mirror moments
and repeat with pictorial perfection that: "You are divinity per-
    sonified"
You are divinity personified, you are divinity personified
the personification of divinity is you.

(The Poet pulls on a light cord, turning on the light.)

My son has old man's eyes
mischievous and innocent
when he's angered
        he raises his left eyebrow, arches it like an arrow.

(Pause.)

How are you supposed to discipline
the mirror
when it reflects right back to you?

> **Quote:** "Don't compromise yourself, you're all you've
> got."
> —JANIS JOPLIN, MUSICIAN

*(The Poet takes a look over the space. He begins to turn on all the lights and
pushes the hanging bulbs so that they are swinging. The music comes in*

easy and smooth. He starts the poem just as smoothly. He increasingly builds in intensity, while the music stays the same.)

Make night hot with sync / I sent decibels / rider of the thunder make the earth quake like Hannibal / equalization in the balance of my mother's eyes / submit the wisdom give space for sun to rise / I skip amethyst rocks across the surface of the sun / I toil my oxygen crops on the light side of Mars / I watch Satanists close, they're sent to earth to be rock stars / I lace instrumented sounds with subliminal freedom / and I vacation on Pluto in solstice / anticipate parabolic curves in unison / I am the what was before / before / before / before Solomon translated my song / I usta whistle it to him / before he touched the earth's ground bound by rosary beads of Jupiter's sacred stones / we moan in unison to the rotation of the third sun / I keep my time ship idle / slip between matter because of my gray matter / shift shape to hollow drums / a piece of my soul stirs every time we come / looking to reshape these dead trees / give them new life with these inscriptions of new dimensions in numerology / we sanctify the blessings of deep breaths / I taught the wind how to race / running water in stationary position / I'm waiting on thieves in the temple to drink so they can be poisoned / overcoming death is easy when you understand what you are living for / I moon trace / amongst your face / retrieve my identity / in the soft spaces of your smiles I find divinity / passion comes in threes / I'm the pleasure principle to these quiet stares when your silence says a novel to me / I am on again / I am on again / I am witness to the night / cousin to the silence / sista to the drum / we be the penetration of the drum / conversation happens over fizzling coca beans / me in saggy jeans and questions / you in comfortable fabric and perfection / and stroking the inside of your hands I have no choice but to say morning.

(He lets out a big laugh, takes a moment, then speaks directly to the audience. The lights come up to full.)

I once by accident found my voice asleep. I wanted to hide from it. but it was too much like a sleeping child. so caught in its beauty. I waited until it was awake and it said:
image one
    alone with self is never alone
when I was
    I became
        then I touched

                        and I saw
then
        there was
        the first
                the first time
I heard my own voice
                        naw . . .

(He sees the mic cord on the floor and crosses to it.)

Shit
it was the bass line
                        that bass line helped me to sit up
finally hear what my voice was trying to say to me
                                        so now I dance to the bass
                line.

(He picks up the mic and its cord and begins to dance around with it.)

        I
         I
          I
           I
                IIIIIIIIIIII . . .

(He unplugs the mic from the cord and throws the cord to the other side of the stage. He sees a beam of light break through the space like the sun, and he is drawn to it. He crosses to the light beam and with his back to the audience says:)

                The evidence of silence broken.

(We hear the hard-hitting hip-hop beat. The Poet continues to laugh as he crosses into the light.)

THE END

Zell Miller III is a Southern-bred interdisciplinary artist who was voted Best Poet/Writer 2004 by the *Austin Chronicle*. In 1999, D. Denby Swanson of the *Chronicle* said: "Zell Miller III is an incendiary device ready to explode." His one man show *The Evidence of Silence Broken* was voted Most Outstanding Theatrical Event 2003 by the *Minneapolis Star Tribune*. He was a featured poet at the South by Southwest Music Festival in 1999, 2001, 2002 and 2004. His work has been featured in numerous anthologies, as well as the 2003 InRadio compilation, *Roller Coaster*. He has opened for legendary poets such as Nikki Giovanni and The Last Poets. His play *Arrhythmia* was presented by Penumbra Theatre Company's Cornerstone Reading Series in 2002. His one-man show *M.A.D.I.Z.M* was nominated for a B. Iden Payne award for Best Original Script of 1999. He was a contributing writer for Laurie Carlos's *Alaskan Heat: Blue Dot*. He is also a veteran stage actor.

peaches

a staged essay,
a dream sequence,
a theatrical hodgepodge,
inspired from a song
by nina simone, a slave narrative,
some black girls in america and
a six year old's dream time line

written by cristal chanelle truscott
music by maiesha mcqueen

author's statement

The dream from the start was simple: Take a stereotype. Just one. A popular one that would be easy to recognize and then, break . . . it . . . down. Have it appear in all of its grandeur of one-dimensionality and then infuse its stock caricatures with the boldness of multi-dimensionality. Don't be afraid to be mis-understood. Invest in the notion that sometimes misunderstanding leads to understanding. Don't try to appeal to everyone or parade the banner of uni-versality. Trust that in respecting the particularities of an experience that what is universal will ultimately become clear. Don't timidly approach anger when the audacity of anger is necessary. Insist on anger as being multifaceted, as having a place among and a connection to the other great emotions of love, joy and sorrow. Break down the stereotype—it's only an exercise. A reminder that every identity that is pummeled by judgment and dehumanized by one-dimensional assessments and images has the right to humanity. Take what has been simplified and make it intensely, unapologetically . . . complicated.

Mostly and always, *PEACHES* is about deepening the popular iden-tity of the Black girl or woman who may, at any time in her life, be called "angry." This play has in some way been brewing since I first heard Nina Simone's classic song "Four Women," when I was just really beginning to articulate how my Blackness and femaleness shaped my thoughts and dreams. Fascinated as I was (and still am) by archetypes and by the social effects of cultural stereotypes, I was enraptured as Simone introduced Aunt Sarah, Sefronia and Sweet Thing. But, it was at the end of "Four Women" when she yelled "PEACHES!" over a roaring piano, that I knew I would someday write something about who I understood "Peaches" to be.

Of course not all Black women identify with "Peaches." And that is partially and precisely the point. But, rare is the soul who hasn't experienced the frustration and injustice of being characterized as a type rather than an individual or being judged before you speak and robbed of the opportunity to represent yourself because another's perception of your cultural stereotype has already spoken for you. The point is to reject these fantasies of cultural, ethnic and spiritual identities as being singular in support of the reality of cultural plurality, hybridity and diversity that manifests in everyday life.

PEACHES is inspired by those women—both past and present—who would be called, labeled "Peaches," an "angry" Black woman. It is not an autobiographical piece, but it is influenced by stories—both imagined and real—heard in my life, as I listened intently to all of the Black girls I have ever known, and soaked up the wisdom imparted to me by the women I know who were once Black girls. It is a refusal of the mentality that treats African American female identity (and, by extension, any identity) with a lack of depth. The dream, intention and hope—from the start—has been that this small offering be of assistance, God willing, toward peace, understanding and progress.

acknowledgments

First, I must thank my artistic family and beloved friends whose willingness to take risks and contributions to *PEACHES* were essential in bringing this dream to life. Thanks beyond words go to music composer and actor Maiesha McQueen, my dear friend, sister and artistic partner, for her immeasurable support in all ways. Thanks, pal, for enriching *PEACHES* (and all my plays!) with your incredible music and for your unwavering passion, sincerity, creativity and dedication—from day one—to building Progress Theatre. An extraordinary thanks to my dear friend, actor Dana Bowles, who completed the ultimate ensemble cast for *PEACHES* and whose sincerity toward this work as an artist and human being helped to build Progress Theatre.

Thanks also to editor Kim Euell and TCG editor Cassandra Csencsitz for their kindness, assistance and patience; Kevin Kulke and Rosemary Quinn from NYU's Experimental Theatre Wing for their support of *PEACHES* as a student project and beyond; Aaron Goodson for his contributions to Progress Theatre; NYU's Daniel Banks for his feedback and ongoing support; Beth Turner of *Black Mask Magazine* for her unmatched support and mentorship since those early days at NYU; and historian Robin D. G. Kelly, for his brilliant scholarship, amazing professorship and for encouraging my work as an artist. Many thanks to Roberta Uno, founder of New WORLD Theater and to the National Performance Network for being the first to commission *PEACHES* post-NYU along with Performance Space 122's former artistic director Mark Russell. Particular thanks to producer Mark Russell for daring to see a student production of *PEACHES* and whose ongoing support over the years since has been invaluable.

Great thanks to my comrades and personal friends: Yasmina Jacobs, from the first production, for being hilarious, sincere and so giving; my friend, actress Elizabeth Cunningham from the original *PEACHES* ensemble, for being the first on board and for always being willing to jump back in during a crunch; Akintoye Moses, photographer extraordinaire, for sharing his talent and enthusiasm from the very first performance and still; Christine Saidi, scholar and friend, for giving great feedback, sewing great costumes and sharing a great house(!); Greta Galuszka, artist and dear friend, whose sincerity and ongoing support I truly treasure; musician Hanq Neal, whose amazing arrangements of the spirituals captured my heart as a child; and to the best drama teacher ever, Suzanne Jennings from HSPVA.

Special thanks to my entire family for their unconditional love and support: cousins Aza Tucker, Natalie Guillory, Natalia Jewel and Kenneth David Jones; Uncle Edgar Tucker, Aunt Charlotte Jones, godfather Claude Merritt, godbrother Keith Merritt and goddaughter Tyra Merritt. Elevated thanks to my wonderful godmother, Virginia Eason.

Exclusive thanks to my soulmates: my extraordinary brother, Cassel David Truscott II; my inspirational nephews, Cassel David III, Cole Davis and Carter Daniel; my phenomenal sister, Courtney Rochelle Truscott; and my amazing parents, Rosa and Cassel Truscott, for their unparalleled encouragement and support throughout my entire life.

And again, to my mom Rosa Elizabeth, my greatest teacher and best friend, who gracefully defies all stereotypes and exemplifies the beauty of complexity.

Heartfelt thanks and appreciation go to my husband, Saeed Muhammad Muslim—my closest friend, my soul's mate, my daydreams fulfilled and my prayers answered—for whom a few words of customary spousal gratitude could never suffice.

And, all praise and gratitude is ultimately for Allah, the Most Merciful.

production history

PEACHES: A Staged Essay . . . was first developed as Cristal Chanelle Truscott's independent student project at the Experimental Theatre Wing at New York University's Tisch School of the Arts. *PEACHES* premiered at NYU in December 2000 with the cast of Elizabeth Cunningham, Maiesha McQueen, Robert Stines, Cristal Chanelle Truscott and Wanita Woodgett. In 2001, *PEACHES* was co-commissioned as a National Performance Network (NPN) Creation Fund Project by New WORLD Theater in Amherst, MA, in partnership with Performance Space 122 in New York.

Performances of *PEACHES* as a Progress Theatre production include a co-production by New WORLD Theater with the Ko Festival of Performance at Amherst from July 27–29, 2001; a performance at the National Black Theatre Festival in Winston-Salem, NC, in August 2001; in P.S. 122's fall 2001 season; a feature performance at "Intersection: Future Aesthetics" at New WORLD Theater in April 2002; "A-NIGHT-IN-PROGRESS" at the Walker Stage in New York City in November 2002; at NPN's annual meeting at the Kennedy Center in Washington, D.C., in December 2002; 651 ARTS in March 2003; New Jersey Performing Arts Center Alternate ROUTES: Sacred Circle in February 2004; Yerba Buena Center for the Arts as part of Nexthetics: An Exploration of Theater, Hip-Hop, Spoken Word and Dance in May 2004 in San Francisco; Aaron Davis Hall International Series in New York City in March 2005; The Heinen Theatre in July 2005 in Houston; 14th Street Playhouse in Atlanta in July 2005; Theatre Project in Baltimore, MD, in October 2005; Tampa Bay Performing Arts Center in November 2005; 14th Street Playhouse in January 2006; Apollo Theater in April 2006 in New York City; Theatre Project in May 2006; The Heinen Theatre in October 2006; University of Georgia in Athens; Theatre Project in February 2007; Abrons Arts Center in February 2007 in New York and the World Music Theatre Festival in March 2008 in the Netherlands.

characters

PEACHES #1, aka Slave Peaches, Big Mike's Peaches: a woman.

PEACHES #2, aka Diva Peaches: a woman.

PEACHES #3, aka Blue Peaches: a woman.

PROGRESS MAN, aka Thad, Homie, Preacher Man, Pimp Man, Boyfriend: a man.

LOVE-CHAIN PEACHES: alternately played by all of the women.

PROGRESS PEACHES: alternately played by all of the women.

ensemble

The play is performed by an ensemble of four actors (three females and one male), all Black, who perform all of the charcters in the play. The female actresses should vary in complexion, representing the wide range of people of African descent.

musical numbers

All of the musical numbers are a cappella. The other sound cues are pre-recorded.

"Work on, Pray on" is a public domain, Negro spiritual, inspired by an arrangement by Hanq Neal, adapted by the author and Maiesha McQueen; "Lord, Above" is a public domain, Negro spiritual; "Care about Nothing" is written by Maiesha McQueen; "Blue" is co-written by Maiesha McQueen and Wanita Woodgett; "Say a Prayer for Me" is written by Maiesha McQueen; and the lyrics to "Mí Amor" are written by the author, with music by Maiesha McQueen.

design note

The costumes and set design should be very simple and minimal, allowing an open canvas for the work of the actors to transform the time and space, and to redefine and complicate Peaches' identities, representing the same archetype, voice and identity across the various time periods in the play. The design should support a fluid rhythm to the show: seamless scene transitions and costume changes that can be managed easily by the actors alone. For the set: uniform chairs and a few platforms, moved easily by the actors, will suffice, in addition to creative, visceral lighting used to give certain effects.

The female actors should wear identical "base" costumes throughout: a simple black or gray pants-and-top combination that is loose fitting for ease of movement with a matching head wrap. Costumes should be tailored to minimize any physical differences between the actors themselves, such as body type, complexion or hair—differences which might serve any preconceived notions about their authenticity or lack thereof as a "Peaches." The women's tops should be long-sleeved and able to double as dresses or suggest the look of a dress for certain scenes. The male's base costume should match the women's in color to establish the unity of the ensemble, but it should be decidedly masculine. The base costumes should be neutral enough in appearance so that they are easily transformed by shoes, a few accessories and props to accommodate the specifics of each scene. For example, in the slavery scene, the actors may only wear burlap sacks across their shoulders (for picking cotton); the Diva Peaches, a shoulder shawl and a rose, á la Billie Holiday; the Preacher Man, a suit jacket and Bible; Big Mike's Peaches, name-plated earrings and belt with a faux-fur jacket, etc. The details in these accessories should reaffirm the theme of complexity and serve as an emotional gift to the actors and audience, but not become a distraction.

There is no intermission.

scene 1: the dream

The theater is completely dark. Music plays as the lights rise to reveal the three Peaches standing onstage looking out into the distance. They are still and calm, yet brewing and thoughtful, as they prepare for the journey through stereotypes and time they are about to take. When the song ends, the women take a moment before speaking to the audience.

PEACHES 1, 2 AND 3:
> My name is Peaches.
> I've recently been wonderin'
> how I came to be
> like
> why I think
> and feel the way I do
> and why carelessness
> has never been an option
> for me.

(In the following, the three Peaches speak in overlapping phrases, finishing each others sentences in a very fluid, natural way.)

When I was six years old / I dreamed about the slaves / my ancestors. They were in the fields picking cotton / probably because all I knew about slavery then, was that slaves picked / cotton all day and that slaves were whipped nearly to death / by White folks / —even six year olds. Oh yes / and that slaves sang songs.

(The Peaches sing a concert version of "Swing Low" or "Ezekial.")

I remember I asked my mother if it was true that / I would have been a slave. She said yeah and / nothing she said after that could make me understand why. / Slavery weighed heavily on my mind as a child and sometimes I'd dream about it.

(In unison:)

From what I can remember
what I imagine
what I recall from my dreams
it would all start with the love story
of Peaches and Thad.

PEACHES #1: The third generation out of Africa.

scene 2: slave peaches

Spotlight on Peaches #1. As she speaks to the audience, she becomes the Slave Peaches, an enslaved girl of fifteen. Although she is well aquainted with the harshness of slavery, when it comes to love she is as shy, naive and romantic as any teenager on the verge of their first love. This is the innocent "dream" romance of a six year old. The character types are very heightened but should read sincere, not negating the reality of the slavery environment. The other Peaches reprise the concert version of "Swing Low" or "Ezekial" as they become the "pigs" of the scene.

SLAVE PEACHES *(To audience)*:
> I wuh sittin' wid de pigs
> so'tin' dey food from ahs
> try'n a pick de bes'
> o' de slop fuh us slabes
> when . . .
> Thad come 'long.

> *(Progress Man enters. He plays Thad, a big country-looking, cotton-picking, enslaved teenager. He is serious and proud, and therefore prone to receive whippings. But he is also—all at once—young, kind, frustrated, shy, angry and beautiful.)*

> I wuh sangin' . . .

> *(Slave Peaches leads the others in a call-and-response chant:)*

> A y'all eat dis

ALL:
> 'N' we eat dis.

SLAVE PEACHES:
> A y'all eat dis

ALL:

> 'N' we eat dis.

(Slave Peaches sits on the floor and mimes throwing scraps of food, first on "A y'all eat dis" to the pigs, and then, to her other side, for those enslaved. The pigs lay lazily at her feet and observe the scraps she throws them nonchalantly. In this scene the Peaches act as a sort of chorus. They do not mimic pigs and are only known as such from Slave Peaches' reference to them.)

SLAVE PEACHES:

> A y'all eat dis

ALL:

> 'N' we eat dis.

(She pauses to scold the pigs.)

SLAVE PEACHES:

> If'n y'all ain't de lazies'
> bunch a pigs.
> Ain'tchu gon' eat?

(Thad has been watching from a distance. He slowly, hesitantly approaches with an empty wooden crate in hand, embodying the description the Peaches/Pigs give him. Slave Peaches and Thad make brief eye contact and smile. The following is said to the audience.)

PEACHES #2: Here he come.

PEACHES #3: Mild as a sheep.

PEACHES #2: Dumb as a calf.

SLAVE PEACHES: Thad got to lookin' at me soon as I wuh grown.

ALL *(Including Thad)*: Dat is fifteen on de plantation!

SLAVE PEACHES: I had to ask dat nigga right out wut his 'tentions wuh fo'
I get him a bleat out dat he lub me.

PEACHES #3: Now, here he come.

PEACHES #2: Mild as a sheep.

PEACHES #3: Dumb as a calf.

(Thad, having mustered the nerve, places his crate facedown. He grunts, mumbling in a "manly" way, motioning for Slave Peaches to move from her post onto his crate. She moves and sits marveling at him.)

SLAVE PEACHES *(To Thad)*: Well, goodday a you, too, Mr. Guntharpe.

PEACHES #2 *(To audience)*: Him name Thad Guntharpe.

THAD: Uh . . . all right and uh . . . goodday.

(He takes her position on the floor and begins sorting the slop. He is serious about his job and mumbles her little chant, "A y'all eat dis," to keep focused.)

SLAVE PEACHES: Mr. Guntharpe—

THAD: Huh? Unh-huh?

SLAVE PEACHES: You folla me nigh' and mornin' a dis pigpen—

THAD: Unh-huh.

SLAVE PEACHES: You happen a be in lub wid one ub dese pigs?

THAD: Aw, come on nah, gul!

SLAVE PEACHES:

> If so, I lak ta know
> which one 'tis
> so I kin come down heah
> by ma-sef
> 'n' tell dat pig
> 'bout yo' 'fections.

(He slides over to her on his knees, laughing a quiet laugh. She always seems to get him to laugh in spite of himself. Then he speaks seriously.)

THAD: I-I-I cain't sleep.

SLAVE PEACHES: Well, I don' reckon none ub us sleep much. 'Tween de missus steady callin' me 'n' de massa steady wakin' me. De Lawd know I don' get much sleep.

THAD: Now-Now-Now . . . he *wake* you?

SLAVE PEACHES *(Changing the subject)*: Now, how yo' back, Mr. Guntharpe?

THAD: Raw. Always raw.

PEACHES #2 AND #3: Always raw.

THAD: Ain't come talk 'bout ma back.

PEACHES #2 AND #3: Always raw.

SLAVE PEACHES: Well, ya sho ain't come down heah ta help feed no pigs. I do mighty fine sloppin' de hogs by ma-self.

THAD: Now-Now-Now—

(She takes pity on him and speaks to him "mighty plainly.")

SLAVE PEACHES:

>Now, Mr. Guntharpe
>you mus' limber up yo' tongue
>and say what you mean
>wantin' to visit dese pigs so often.

THAD: Uh . . . awright and . . . uh—

SLAVE PEACHES: Mr. Guntharpe, I say, limber up yo' tongue!

(She abruptly turns from him, impatient, yet hopeful. He rises too quickly, forgetting his back, raw from whippings. She turns back, noticing him wince in pain.)

PEACHES #2 AND #3 *(Softly, to audience)*: Always raw.

THAD *(Standing, with newfound determination)*: Awright den, Peaches. So, let's get married!

SLAVE PEACHES: Oh Lawd!

PEACHES #2 AND #3 *(Jumping up, fearfully remembering where they are)*: Oh Lawd!

(The stage becomes frantic with movement. The "pigs" become slaves and begin forming lines for picking cotton. They approach Slave Peaches.)

SLAVE #1: Girl, is you try'n' get killed?

SLAVE #2: How long it take you to mess up slop?

SLAVE PEACHES: I wuh try'n' a fin' de good ones fuh us.

SLAVE #1: Chile, slop is slop!

>Now, come on heah!

(They join the other slaves picking cotton and sing wrenching, wailing versions of "Swing Low" and "Wade in the Water," in stark contrast to the concert version of "Ezekial" sung earlier. All make heavy breathing sounds. We may hear the sound of whips cracking. As the lights and the slaves' movements begin to indicate the passing of time, Slave Peaches begins to faint. As she hits the ground, Thad rushes to her side, speaking softly to her as he continues to work.)

THAD: Got to work on, now, my Peaches.

SLAVE PEACHES: I cain't.

THAD: Aw, come on nah, Peaches.

(The others begin a call-and-response with Slave Peaches that eventually turns into the Negro spiritual "Work On, Pray On." The song is one of

those spirituals with a double meaning about running away. They sing
while continuing to pick cotton.)

ALL:

Work on, work on . . .

SLAVE PEACHES:

Lord, I cain't . . .

ALL:

Work on . . .

SLAVE PEACHES:

How can I? . . .

ALL:

Work on . . .

(Slave Peaches gets the "message" and resumes her work.)

SLAVE PEACHES:

I don't wanna . . .

ALL:

Work on . . .

SLAVE PEACHES:

But I gotta . . .

ALL:

Work on
Pray on
Work on . . .

SLAVE PEACHES:

Lord, please help me . . .

ALL:

Work on
Pray on
Da time ain't long chi'rren
Work on . . .

SLAVE PEACHES:
>   We gonna make it . . .

ALL:

>   Work on . . .

SLAVE PEACHES:
>   We gotta make it . . .

ALL:

>   Work on . . .

SLAVE PEACHES:
>   I know we'll make it . . .

ALL:

>   Work on . . .

SLAVE PEACHES:
>   We gonna make it . . .

ALL:

>   Work on
>   Pray on
>   Da time ain't long chi'rren
>   Work on
>   Pray on
>   Da time ain't long
>
>   Walk togethuh chi'rren
>   Don'tchu get weary
>   Dere's a great camp meet'n
>   in de Promised Land
>
>   We gonna walk
>   An' nevuh tie-yuh
>   We gonna walk
>   Walk Walk
>   Walk and never tie-yuh
>
>   Work on
>   Pray on
>   Da time ain't long chi'rren

Work on
Pray on
Da time ain't long
Ain't long
Ain't long.

(The lights fade for a transition. The song ends and they are all exhausted, yet determined to survive. During the transition light, the spiritual becomes a short, jazzy skat using the words "Ain't Long.")

scene 3: diva peaches

The lights come up on the three Peaches seated in café-style chairs. The others freeze as Peaches #2 becomes Diva Peaches. She speaks directly to the audience throughout the scene. She is an off-balanced, seemingly very stereotypical character, reminiscent of Billie Holiday.

DIVA PEACHES: My parents say I was born depressed. That I came out crying—haven't stopped since. They tell all my doctors, "She burst into tears as a baby just to see the sun rise, like she upset to live another day. We had nothing to do with it." And they didn't. The way I see it—I'm inherently insane. I understand myself all too well. The way I see it, my soul is made up of the part of Black folks that is sad. Now, everyone has a little sadness in they soul—but Black folks!? Come on, now. You see, I have all their sadness. And that has made me crazy.

So, I became a blues singer.

(Laughter erupts onstage as the remaining Peaches and Progress Man/Homie become the chorus, patrons in a juke joint in the thirties/forties, reprising the bluesy-jazzy "Ain't Long.")

HOMIE *(Approaching Peaches #3)*:
It's been too long since I seen you.
My, my, my! It's been mighty *too* long!

PEACHES #1:
Chile! Well, how you doing?
I ain't think you was gon' make it this week.
You know with your husband and all . . .
Where *is* your husband?

(At the mention of a husband, Homie stops his advances.)

PEACHES #3:

> Chile, well, he ain't here, that's for sure.
> But I told myself I had to make it!
> At least *one good* time this week!

PEACHES #1 AND HOMIE: Amen, sister, amen!

DIVA PEACHES: I became a blues singer. Singing them songs that let you know it's somebody else feeling tired as a dog after walking miles and working for nickels all day. A jazz diva. Singing them songs that got folks 'round the world coming to my little shack lookin' for some "cul-cha." The Diva Peaches. Singing them songs that so hot they make you sweat till you burst, baby. And that's just from me opening my mouth. Songs about lovemaking, about low-down, dirty blues. Songs that no *good* Christian girl should be singing at places where no *good* Christian girl should be on a Saddy night.

(She sings "Care about Nothing." She's an amazing performer, a club favorite. The patrons go wild, joining her as she sings.)

> Loving you, holding you
> All the good things carefree lovers do
> I wish I didn't have to care about nothing
> But your love
>
> I'm tired of working, my feet are hurting
> My hands are raw down to the bone
> But when I get weary, thinking of you deary
> Makes me long to come home
>
> When I'm scrubbing floors and feeling mighty blue
> I just thinks about scrubbing on you
> I wish I didn't have to care about nothing
> But your love
>
> You cleaning for Mr. Charlie? I'm running 'hind him, too
> When all I wanna do is run straight home to you
> I wish I didn't have to care about nothing
> But your love
>
> Hey! This world can feel so low
> And darlin' that's no lie

Long days, hard nights
Making me lose my mind
But when I think of your loving
And what you do for me
I gets to take a break from misery!

My back is aching and my knees are bent
Try'n' to make a dollar outta fifteen cents
I wish I didn't have to care about nothing
But your love!

(Speaking somewhat winded from her energetic song performance) You understand? Needless to say, I thought for sure I was going to hell cuz being Black sho'nuff meant being Baptist. If you were Black and didn't pray to Jesus—you must be touched in the head. So, I tried it.

(The actors are no longer club mongers, but are now avid churchgoers. Homie has become the Preacher Man and he leads them in a gospel-style rendition of "Work On, Pray On.")

PREACHER MAN *(To Peaches #3)*:
It's been too long since I've seen you.
My, my, my! It's been mighty *too* long!

PEACHES #1:
Chile! Well, how you doing?
I ain't think you was gon' make it this week.
You know with your husband and all . . .
Where *is* your husband?

PEACHES #3:
Chile, well, he ain't here, that's for sure.
But I told myself I had to make it!
At least *one good* time this week!

ALL: Amen, sister, amen!

(Diva Peaches tries to fit in as the Preacher Man begins his sermon. The women are highly emotional and shout and fan themselves as the Preacher Man delivers a very passionate sermon.)

PREACHER MAN: I was walking down the street the other day and ran into one of the elders in our congregation. She say, "Pastor, I sho' need you to pray for me. My bills are long overdue and seem like no matter how long or how hard I work they don't get no better."

So I say to her, "Sister, you gotta have faith and trust in the Lord. Yes, sister, 'cause the faith of a mustard seed can move a mountain." I say, "Yes, ma'am. God has not given his people the spirit of fear and don't you fret over your payments. God will see you through. You got to step out without knowing there's a ground beneath you—just 'cause you got that faith that somethin' be there when your feet land!"

"Pastor, Pastor," she say, "let me see if I understand what you sayin' about this faith." She say, "The other night, Pastor, I went to bed without a dime to my name. I knew I had to be at work the next morning. But, ain't have a nickel to catch the bus and at my age, I cain't be walkin'." Are you with me, Church? She go on, "So I went on to sleep, woke up, put on my work clothes, yessuh, and ate me some breakfast knowing I ain't have a penny to catch the bus. Pastor, I set out to that bus stop without a piece of lint in my pocket—and lo and behold here come Miss Sally from down the street, I ain't seen in years, driving by that bus stop. She yell out the window, 'Chile, You still workin' cleanin' Miss Whatchmacallem house?' I say, "Yeah." She say, 'Well, chile, I'm right next do' at Miss so-and-so—get off that bus stop! Come on here and let me give you a ride!'"

"Pastor! Pastor!" she say, "is that the faith, Pastor?" I say, "Yes sister!" Amen! Hallelujah and glory to God!

(Everyone freezes at this climax of the sermon. Diva Peaches steps out of the picture and speaks to the audience.)

DIVA PEACHES: After that, and I swear to this, I was walking down the street in the city and I stopped and begin to pray to Jesus and the Holy Spirit and nem, like Black folks supposed to. And it didn't work. Tears filled my eyes. But, I didn't give up. I started to pray and sing like Black folks supposed to. *(Singing:)*

> Lord above, save me now
> I have strayed
> And I'm lost now
> I have prayed
> And I'm crying now
> Lord above, help me along the way.

But as I was singing I didn't feel nothing. I was just straight-up lost like in a dream. Standing in the street like a dummy, trying to feel. And doing all that ain't do me no good.

I said to myself, "Sistergirl, Honey-child, Lady, Diva Peaches! You searching for something else! And it's out there. But until you find it, stick to your blues, baby!" And maybe it's just me. I know what Black folks supposed to do and I know I must be crazy with all this Black folks' sadness in my soul, calling myself searching for something else. But, listen. I was born depressed. When I was a baby, I wept with the rising of the sun. Now, I can't drown in all that weeping water. I gotta keep on keeping on.

(The lights fade for a transition. The ensemble sings a milder, more melancholy reprise of "Care about Nothing." They are workers at the end of a long day. As they change into nightclub outfits, the song evolves into an up-tempo soul tune. All dance joyfully in stylized, soulful movements and freeze mid-motion. Progress Man, who has taken on the persona of the Pimp Man—think Goldie in The Mack*—speaks to the audience.)*

scene 4: blue peaches

PIMP MAN: Welcome to the House of Big Pimpin' and Gold Diggin', the House of the Bump and Grind, the House of the Good Times! Can you dig it, bay-bee? This the place people come after long days of apron-wearing, blue-collar-uniform-wearing, got-to-pay-my-bills kinda gigs. The place them no-good rags get thrown to the side and people come looking fine to boogie down! The place li'l White couples come a-peeking in the window wondering how people so broke can be so happy. Can you dig it, bay-bee? This the only place people can come to feel free.

(He snaps and the ensemble comes to life again, but now the mood has mellowed. It is very late. Late enough for everyone to have sobered up to the reality of work tomorrow and to the reality of their lives not being as they had once dreamed.)

BLUE PEACHES: Sleep don't come easy.
PEACHES #2: And years later, sometimes, I still sing the blues.
BLUE PEACHES: I used to say it was 'cause of them parties my daddy had when I was growing up. I would sleep through those parties and dream some crazy dreams with those party songs playing as the soundtrack.

(Pause. Then, like a confession or a secret:)

I want to lose my mind.

PIMP MAN: I want to experience a carefree existence. Where I can be care-less about everything and only care about myself. I marvel at peo-ple who can do that cuz, for the life of me, I can't figure it out.

PEACHES #2: How is it so easy for people to forget that they know so lit-tle and to drown themselves in worldly possessions and to laugh about things like getting drunk and drugged up?

PEACHES #1: I have yet to find the humor in drunk people.

BLUE PEACHES: I want to lose my mind.

PIMP MAN: I heard once that the heart has a brain, a memory. And I know I believed it. 'Cause I know my heart and my mind be working together. If I took my heart's mind out and put it aside, I like to think that my heart would come as close to stopping as possible, without me dying, and I could get some good sleep then, boy. I'd rest deep like the blue at the bottom of the ocean.

PEACHES #1: How long you think it would take to reach as deep as the blue bottom of the ocean?

PIMP MAN: I don't know.

PEACHES #1: I've never been there.

BLUE PEACHES: I jumped once.

PEACHES #2: What kind of fool would jump into the ocean without knowing how to swim?

BLUE PEACHES: I know I must've been crazy. I don't remember breathing at all.

PEACHES #2: I have never known fear quite like the fear of being in the ocean. Just me, Peaches, one of God's creations, and the ocean, Blue, one of God's *huge* creations.

PEACHES #1: I think I would just float. Not do a thing to keep that ocean from pushing me from this side of the world to the next. Maybe find carelessness for myself. I wouldn't fight it. I think I would just float.

BLUE PEACHES: I tried, but I couldn't. When I was in that water, I remem-ber the exact moment it dawned on me that there was no bottom beneath me for miles and miles. I wanted to scream, but I was barely keeping my head above water. I thought of drowning and where would my body go? And then, just like that! *(Snaps)*

(To the audience:)

I thought of the slaves who were murdered and thrown overboard into this very ocean. And what the slaves must have felt to throw themselves overboard! And the slaves in the Caribbean who leaped off those island mountains into the sea—that being the only way they could have control over their lives. I opened my eyes under water and thought of how their heavy bodies must've eventually sunk to the bottom. I was thinking about how much I could learn about my past and my history, if, I could just let myself, Peaches, give in to the ocean, Blue, and end up at the bottom. I'd know what it was like . . . And if someone was to gather those bones one day, they wouldn't be able to tell the difference from my bones and that of the Africans at the bottom of the ocean.

PEACHES #1, PEACHES #2 AND PIMP MAN: I want to lose my mind.

BLUE PEACHES: That is *my* fantasy! Just every now and again so I can sleep. 'Cause it keeps me up and it keeps me serious. I had a boy, my cousin, who figured out how to lose his mind. But, he couldn't just lose it and get it back when he wanted. He had to go out and find it.

There I was standing in my Texas, state-flower, blue-bonnet outfit, when I remembered the story of that boy, my cousin, who swam in the Louisiana swamp water for two days straight looking for his mind 'cause his mama said he must have lost his mind if he thought he could speak to her that way. That his mind must be running around in the Louisiana swamp somewhere. My costume itched around the back of my neck and when I looked up at the sky, I saw that same blue that matched the blue of that boy, my cousin's skin when they found him floating in the swamp more than half dead. But, by some miracle he wasn't dead. And weeks later when he could talk and see, he smiled and said to his mama, "Mama, I found my mind. It was blue like your hair floating at the very bottom of the swamp, just running away from me. But, I followed it day and night till it returned to me and got me to floating on top of that swamp. It was lost, Mama, but now it's found." That mama held that boy, my cousin's face in her warm hands. As blue tears welled up in her eyes she softly sang. *(Singing:)*

Baby if I could, sing you the blues
It wouldn't be sad at all
For when I look at you
I do see blue
Deep like your eyes, like your face
Blue like the sky, like the tears I cry . . .

ENSEMBLE:

Like a melody that lingers on
Like the echoes of an unforgotten song
When I look into your eyes
Suddenly the world seems simple and true
When I look at you . . .

BLUE PEACHES:

> Baby if I could, give you peace
> It would be as sweet as you
> For you are like the sea
> Just as deep, just as free
> Like your eyes, like your face
> Blue like the sky, like the tears I cry
> When I sing to you, my baby, ahhhh . . .

ENSEMBLE:

> What have I got to lose
> If I just jumped one day?
> I'd only lose my mind
> If I could, if I could . . .
>
> What have I got to lose
> If I just jumped one day?
> I'd only lose my mind
> I don't think I want it anyway . . .

BLUE PEACHES:

> Baby if I could, find a way to let go
> It wouldn't be sad at all
> Forever would I dream
> Oh, if only I could be
> Deep like your eyes, like your face
> Blue like the sky, like the tears I cry
> When I sing to you, when I sing to you
> When I sing to you, my baby . . .

(The song has grown into an ensemble number, reinforcing the connection between all of the Peaches. Blue Peaches works herself up so that at the end of her verse she is even more weary and yet, somehow, more hopeful.)

scene 5: love-chain peaches

The lights fade for a transition, then come up on Progress Man. He mimes pulling a heavy load at the end of a long rope. When he gets to the other end of the stage he yanks the rope and one of the Peaches stumbles in. He yanks in the other Peaches in a similar fashion. Each of the other women already onstage helps to pull the next. We find that they are tied, "chained," to the

peaches

rope. *The color of fabric around their feet matches their head wraps. They are the Love-Chain Peaches and they are pulled onstage in order from lightest in complexion to darkest. Once they are all onstage, we hear a lock get bolted as if the Peaches are in a prison. Progress Man plays their guard. The Peaches speak to each other and the audience, but start with a slow, tired song, "Say a Prayer for Me," bemoaning their position on this chain.*
    Singing:

PEACHES #3:
    Lay my burdens down

PEACHES #1:
    Try'n' to set me free

PEACHES #2:
    All I'm asking is that you—

ALL:
    Say a prayer for me!

    Turn my inside out
    Try'n' to set me free
    All I'm asking is that you
    Say a prayer for me!

(They repeat the chorus a few times before Homie interrupts.)

HOMIE *(Frustrated)*: Hey, hey, hey! Shut up! Fix yourselves up! Now, I swear, if I hear that song one more time from y'all . . .

PEACHES #1: Can't help it.

HOMIE: Come on now, Peaches. You all supposed to be big ol', strong ol', sturdy ol', angry ol' Black women! Don't you have anything else to talk about besides needing a man?

PEACHES #2: Shut up, you! *(Then, to the other Peaches)* He's right. We did say we wasn't gon' talk about this no more. I'm sick and tired of being sick and tired.

PEACHES #1: Maybe we should try it.

PEACHES #2 *(Loudly, so Homie can hear)*: Okay! Let's talk about something upbeat and happy.

HOMIE: At least talk about men in a good way.

PEACHES #3: So you want us to lie . . .

HOMIE: Can't you at least change the tune?

PEACHES #1: But we'd still be here because all folks still ever talk about is how so-and-so got good hair, still going around pinching babies' noses.

PEACHES #3: There's this one sister farther up on the chain who says she's bi-racial, but, I got a cousin lighter than her who ain't mixed. Plus, I seen her parents and they Black as you . . . *(Realizing)* and me! Why she lie like that?

PEACHES #2: Because the brothers I know don't even look twice unless you light enough or half White or half Filipino or half Puerto Rican or half something. And this is the year 2007! *(Change the year accordingly)*

HOMIE: Here we go again . . .

PEACHES #2: I feel like I be walking into the Cotton Club back in time somewhere 'cause I'm too dark and nobody pays me any mind.

HOMIE: You can't blame a brother for having a preference. Some like 'em tall. Some like 'em short. You wouldn't be complaining if a brother liked fat women! Some like 'em light. And some like 'em . . . like you.

PEACHES #1: It's like we're at the bottom of the food chain except it's the love chain. *(To the lighter Peaches)* And ain't no love down here at the bottom of the love chain.

PEACHES #3: The brothers I know got me trapped into the role of the tragic mulatto. Ain't Black enough or too bougie. I'm just stuck. It's like I have to fight for the right to be a Black American. Like I'm supposed to jump at the opportunity to be something "more." Ain't being light-skinned "more" enough?! Somehow I always felt that since I ain't have to worry about my color, *(Embarrassingly, glancing toward the others)* since having this skin was my ticket to beauty . . . loving myself should be a breeze, shouldn't it? Well, it ain't. It ain't enough. So, for the record: No! My family ain't from Puerto Rico! Ain't from Brazil! Ain't from no island! I don't know if I got Indian in me. And hell no, my mama is not White!

HOMIE: So whatchu gon' do about it except complain.

PEACHES #1: I wish someone could tell me what to do. Give me the solution. Tell me how to ignore it all, accept myself and be content down here at the bottom.

PEACHES #2: I'm guilty. I possess a slave mentality. I try to fight it—I do. But do you know, for the life of me, I can't bring myself to date a dark-skinned man? Much less an African!

So now, here I am, the first time in my life thinking I could fall for a White guy. He looks at me with such awe, like I amaze him and take his breath away. A Black man has yet to look at me with such awe. He smiles at me and hugs me like he wants to swallow me and never let go. And I, temporarily, lose myself in him. He kisses me and holds my hand and I feel tingles and curiosity. He looks at me, seeming to wonder why he likes me so much. Knowing that if I was a White girl, thick like this, he would think I was fat and disgusting. And I want to ask him, "Why do you like me?" Better yet, I say to myself, "Why do I like you?" Because none of the Black guys think I'm pretty 'cause I'm not light-skinned with long hair. And a voice inside is telling me that I could never marry him.

But I'm saying, should I pass up the opportunity to love him for a minute? Should I give up the chance to be cherished? 'Cause maybe God is sending me my package in wrapping I didn't expect. And then I think of my little girl. I mean, maybe if her complexion ain't quite like mine . . . And her hair ain't quite like mine. I see her: Black and proud. Tall and fine. Black and beautiful. Just not too Black.

But then, when I close my eyes and see me together with him, I start seeing chains and whips and me abandoned with my little Yellow babies. Me like Sally Hemmings—a lifetime of slavery with a White man who sees me not for the woman I am, but as some exotic fantasy. And I can't do it. So when he asks me out again I say no, 'cause surely he got some crazy thought in the back of his mind, too.

PEACHES #1: I need me a man with some color. That's what I tell myself. So I started dating a Nigerian. He showed me pictures of his sisters and said I reminded him of the girls back home. Later, though, I realized he was crazy. He kept comparing me to his last girlfriend who was White, and that was it for me. I can't see what he could possibly want with me, all the while reminding me of how I'm so much more "difficult" than his last girlfriend. And then I remembered that nearly all of Africa had been carved up, placed under colonial rule, and infected with the same Eurocentric crap that we have to deal with. And I understood why the brother was crazy.

Sometimes, I think about Africa and I know that with all the colonization that has terrorized the land, it's not half the dreamland I want it to be. But, I still think of it that way. I dream to myself, *If I was there, I could feel beautiful.* I've spent hours in front of the mirror telling myself, "Black is beautiful, girl. Girl, Black is beautiful. Black is Beautiful, girl. Girl, Black is beautiful, and you such a pretty Black girl." Yet, if Black is so beautiful, why is it such a fight for me to believe it. I mean, if I had pitch-black skin and pinch-short hair—would I be noticed at all? When they colonized the Africans they really did a thorough job. I used to dream about

Africa as being the homeland. But now I think, Why would I want to go there only to deal with another version of the same baggage I grew up with? The slave mentality, the colonized mentality— what's the difference?

PEACHES #3: My ex-boyfriend said to me:

PEACHES #3 AND BOYFRIEND: "Aren't there any Black girls who are just nice?"

BOYFRIEND: Without all that attitude and eye rolling? Just a nice girl.

PEACHES #3: Whatchu mean *nice*? Is your mama *nice*? Can't nobody be *nice* all the time!

BOYFRIEND: See! That whole attitude right there. Getting all mad.

PEACHES #3: First of all, yo' mama. Second of all, ain't nobody mad. Oh, I see, you want me to front. Give you some fake smile and say, "Coming dear," when I really feel like saying, "Get it yourself." Nice like that? Sorry baby, I gotta be me.

BOYFRIEND: See?! See?!

PEACHES #3: See, what?!!

BOYFRIEND: Calm down! Want me to get you some water?

PEACHES #3: Naw, I don't want no water! I am complicated! *(To audience)* Sometimes I get real sad. And it scares me 'cause I don't feel like I deserve to be as sad as I get sometimes. I don't want to feel guilty, ugly or unwanted. I am complicated. *(Back to him)* Can't I just express myself without you accusing me of having an attitude?

BOYFRIEND: Can't you just express yourself without having an attitude? *(To audience)* Black women, man. And I'm trying to be nice to the sister.

PEACHES #3: So I said, "I don't want you to be nice. I want you to be sincere."

(Boyfriend exits.)

(To audience) Look. No one ever told me that nappy hair is bad. No one ever sat me down and told me that light-skinned girls are prettier.

PEACHES #1: No one ever warned me that Black women have an international bad reputation. But these are things I learned nonetheless. Who knows? Maybe my great-great-great-great-grandkids won't have to deal with this chain.

PEACHES #2: But, going from unnatural to natural is a long, hard process. And Lord knows I'm not there yet. I'm getting there and once I make it there, God willing—

PEACHES #3: I'll find somebody who looks at me all kinked up . . .

PEACHES #2: My skin even darker from chillin' in the sun . . .

PEACHES #1: And he will say, "Yes, you are beautiful."
ALL: "Please come to me just as you are . . ."

(The lights fade to black as the Peaches exit, singing an inspirational reprise of "Say a Prayer for Me.")

scene 6: progress peaches

Lights come up on Progress Man alone onstage, dressed in black.

PROGRESS MAN: Last night, I dreamed about a revolution led by a bunch of Black women who shouted, "Peaches and Progress!" And they talked too much. I say they talked too much, but, I tried to listen. I let my defenses drop and I started listening. This wasn't some, "I'm Black and I'm female, so I'm double oppressed" kinda jazz. This was some hardcore hit-you-in-the-soul kinda blues. They wasn't trying to hate on their Black brothers or anybody else. They was tellin' their stories, tellin' it the way it is. The situation that society has forced on them was no illusion. It wasn't something that was just in their heads. These weren't no I'm-gonna-get-you-sucka type of broads. This was some stuff that made me question myself as a Black man living in a world full of barriers, where me and Peaches are trying to find a way to fight back and come together. But I ain't got no power or control over her pain. So, she's hurting and I'm hurting. So, I'm angry and she's angry. And now, I think to myself, "This is some messed-up stuff!" Talk on, Peaches. Somebody's bound to listen. I say they shouted, "Peaches and Progress!" Watch out!

(Progress Man raises a Black Power fist to welcome Progress Peaches #2 and #3, who enter dressed in black, marching. This is a rally scene, a protest, a college-campus demonstration, a community meeting, the precursor to a freedom march set in the present day. They all speak directly to the audience.)

PEACHES #2: Who are we?
ALL: Peaches!
PEACHES #2: And what do we want?
ALL: Progress!

(The ensemble performs "Who Na?"—a call-and-response chant based on Black-girl-hand games. They each take a verse to introduce them-

selves in the scene, changing the lyrics slightly from what is below (i.e., exchanging the word "revolution" for "progress," "teaching," "lyrics," etc. Progress Man switches the words to accommodate his gender saying, "Progress is my name" and "coolest cat" or "coolest dude," for example. They are very serious throughout the chant. The scene is high energy, urgent.)

CALL: Who Na? Who Na? Who think they bad?
RESPONSE: I DO!
CALL: Who Na? Who Na? Who think they bad?
RESPONSE: I DO! I think I'm bad cuz:

> Peaches is my name
> And revolution is my game
> So take a sip of my potion
> And do it in slow motion.

CALL: Unh! She think she bad.
RESPONSE: Baby, baby don't make me mad.
CALL: Unh! She think she fine.
RESPONSE: Fine enough to blow your mind.
CALL: Unh! She think she cool.
RESPONSE: Coolest girl in every school!

(Once everyone has had their turn saying a verse, Peaches #2 steps forward, center, as if she's stepping up to a podium. The others spread out, standing behind her.)

PEACHES #2: If you've come to hear Black girls who have the solution . . . you've come to the wrong place. If you've come to see Black girls smile and "lie to you, make it sound fly to you". . . you've come to the wrong place. If you've come to hear Black girls apologize for their confusion and anger . . . I say again, you've come to the wrong place.

As a Black woman, I feel like everybody around me is telling me to get over it. *(In a Latina accent)* "Hey, Mami, slabery was a long time a-go!" Get over it. *(In an African accent)* "Eeehhh, dis is not a Black-and-White iss-yew! What is Black?! That is so limiting!" Get over it. *(As an African American, Northeastern or Southern hip-hop-generationer)* "Yooooo, honestly? I'm not even so much worried about White people, na'mean? Slavery is in the past. It's done. I love this country. What I'm really worried about is all these people walking around here with beards and scarves and whatnot. The

Moo-slums, the Taliban, you know. Try'n to rob me of my freedom. That's what I'm really worried about." Get over it. *(In a White, Valley-girl accent)* "Uuummmm, Peacheeeees, when I look at yeeeeeew I don't even see you as being Black. I meeeeaaaan, this is the new millenium, color doesn't matter anymore." Get over it. But, I can't.

We are still searching for the solution, we can only use our truths to make a point. We always Black, we often confused, and we sometimes angry.

I saw on the news that today in America one in every four children born is bi-racial. And I laughed. *(She laughs)* HA! And I thought, *So?* After slavery aren't we all a bunch of half-breeds and mulattos and mutts and whatnot? But see, don't nobody wanna talk about all that—NOOO! Unh-uh! Don't nobody wanna really get down to the nut of thangs and talk about the multiracial people that's been in America since there was an America. Multiracial 'cause they was raping and killing folks!

Isn't it funny how people try to make the effects of slavery solely an African American problem? Talkin' 'bout, "I'm from the Caribbean—that's not my story—I can't relate." Talkin' 'bout, "I'm from Africa—that's not my story—I can't relate." Done lived in America all they lives or left home when they was 'bout three! Talkin' 'bout, "I can't relate." Gon' tell me, even though every woman in their family still bleaches their skin: color is an African American problem! "Oh, I'm from Europe. We love multi-culti! We don't even know what racism is!—that's not my story—I can't relate."

And isn't it funny how people are so ready to claim the blood of everybody else, except for they African ancestry. Proud to say somebody French, Portuguese, Spanish! Proud to say somebody Irish! Proud to say somebody British! Ooooh all the talk now is so nice. "Oh, we're mixed. Oh, we're bi-racial. Oh, we're multiracial." Ain't it nice? I'm mixed too! Get over it!

PROGRESS MAN: Our stories follow in the tradition of Malcolm X, Huey P. Newton, Fannie Lou Hamer and Assata Shakur . . . any other Black person on any given day. Genetically speaking, my great- or grand-so-and-so from here or there was a White rapist! And don't nobody know they name or nothing 'cause the coward just slipped through the window *and* when he finished he went to sleep next to his ol', pale-face wife *and* got up the next morning *and* whipped a few slaves before heading out to work. Civilized?

PEACHES #2: America was a country full of White rapists and murders! The legacy of America's founding fathers?

PEACHES #3: Rape and murder!

PROGRESS MAN: How about that? Walking around here talking about civilized! Walking around here talking about American freedom and democracy as an example for the rest of the world!

PEACHES #3: Walking around here talking—

PROGRESS MAN: Throwing out Declarations—

PEACHES #2: —and Proclamations! Got the nerve to be declaring war and then turn around and declare a peace talk.

PROGRESS MAN: Got the nerve to be declaring evil.

PEACHES #3: Well, I'm declaring a state of emergency!

PEACHES #2: A state of emergency like a big rain coming, your house under sea level and you with no way out!

PEACHES #3: Emergency like hundreds of Black bodies suffering in the Southern heat waiting five days for water!

PROGRESS MAN: In the most powerful country in the world. In the country we all love soooo much.

PEACHES #3: Said I'm declaring a state of emergency today! One of protest!

PROGRESS MAN: One of resistance! We building a new house—

PEACHES #2: And if you're not ready—

PROGRESS MAN: If it make you scared—

PEACHES #3: If it make you tremble—

ALL: Then move! Get out the way!

PEACHES #2: I confess. I will never be a patriot.

PEACHES #3: I am a revolutionary.

PROGRESS MAN: I like progress and truth.

PEACHES #3: America has a list of crimes against humanity that it is guilty of and built upon. Children, don't believe what your history books say! It's a scam, a setup, a booby trap—

PEACHES #2: —To make you sleep.

PEACHES #3: I say it's a trap designed to make you sleepwalk around this world thinking that everything is okay! Like a puppet, a doll, a dummy—

PEACHES #2: —And we can't sleep!

PEACHES #3: Ain't got no time to sleep! I'm here to tell you that we can no longer talk nice! Mustn't we speak plainly about our past in order to learn from it?

PROGRESS MAN: And I'm glad folks of different races love each other and all. We need that, too. I'm not promoting the angry Black woman. I don't know a Black girl who is *simply angry*. But, we can't ignore the truth. We can't sleep. That's not intelligent! That's not intelligent!

PEACHES #3: I've come home because I've forgotten what it means to be Black. Prior to five or six years of age, I have no memories of White people. This is a fact I've rediscovered and found most excitin' and intriguin' once I went away. It was one of those days where everything that went wrong in my day was involved with some White people. On the way to my morning class, some White psycho bumped into me on the street and called me a nigger—just out of the blue! As I walked into my class, twenty White faces turned to look at me make it to my seat. In my dance class, some White guy thought that his imitation of a Black dialect or slang was not only funny, but showcased just how comfortable he was around Black people. You know, "Yo, my nizzel, fuh shizzel! Wuz up, wuz up! Yo, dawg, dat's mad ghetto!" When I told him that he wasn't funny, he asked me why Black girls always got attitudes. On the subway, this White boy and his clan of Asian and East Indian and Puerto Rican homeboys laughed at one of the homeless men on the train saying, "Yo, dat niggah's crazy!" I, apalled, stood in protest with tears in my eyes, only to find that I was old-fashioned. Didn't I know that the word "nigger" could be said now without giving care to the history and experience attached to it? Didn't I understand that *they* went to all of the underground hip-hop concerts and knew the lyrics to every song on Biggie's *first* album? Plus, hadn't I heard "that nigga on MTV" even say that it was "one love" for everybody to use the word "nigger" nowadays? If anybody knew something about the word nigger, *they* did. And then there's the White girl at work—who reminds me on every possible occasion that her ex-boyfriend was Black—told me that she wanted to marry a Black man because they make pretty babies! I was so weary with White people's presence and me being Black within their presence that I just stopped on the way home, stood in the middle of the sidewalk and imagined myself as a child in my all-Black world. I reminisced on a time when it never dawned on me that my parents had to go to work every day and deal with White people. I rejoiced at remembering a time in my life when White people were nonexistent, invisible and irrelevant. As children, we didn't care! We didn't care if the White folks didn't understand the dynamics of our world! We had been so used to them being irrelevant in our lives that we felt no need to alter our reality for their approval. But, then I thought, *What does it mean to be Black?* Did my childhood represent Blackness, or my life now? I got confused. So, I came home.

PEACHES #2: Here she come!

(They all chant a short verse of "Who Na?" Peaches #1 enters to bass-heavy theme music with an undeniable Southern-rap rhythm. She is Big

cristal chanelle truscott

Mike's Peaches. She is adorned with shiny costume jewelry like a stereo-typical "ghetto girl." She sits and catches her breath before speaking. She sounds like a stereotypical ghetto girl.)

BIG MIKE'S PEACHES: This is the story of me and Big Mike: my babies' daddy.

So, you know I had an abortion when I was fifteen, right? Some fool said he loved me and I was so stupid, I believed him. Hm . . . Guess I was the fool, huh? Know what my definition of a fool is?

Believin' that no matter how many sorry brothers
they say are out there
only the good ones will be with me.

That was me, child. Believing only the good ones will be with me . . .

And then I was a double fool for listening to some old-bitty White nurse telling me that an abortion was the best thing. I was fifteen! I look back on that, I say, "How she gon' know what's best for me? She ain't even much know me!" And that abortion give me nightmares to this day. All the babies I got now, and still some nights, I lay up thinking about that one baby.

So anyway, it messed with me and I decided the next time I's gon' have sex was when I got married. And here I am, twenty-four years old, with four kids, all by myself.

I hadn't planned on getting pregnant for at least another ten, twelve years. But, I met Big Mike when I was sixteen and he was eighteen and he said he loved me and he wasn't lying. My mama said if he loved me for real, he'd respect my decision to not have sex till I got married. I knew she was saying right and I told him that.

So, we got married three months later and lived in this small apartment in the projects. My parents liked to died. And I got pregnant the next month. Oooooo, you know my parents liked to died! Mama say I got pregnant faster than the Lord allow. Oh, and don't you know when I first got pregnant, I didn't even want to be having no babies. I was sixteen! Ain't been married but a month. I wanted me and Big Mike to have some years to ourselves before we had twenty-something years worth of kids. But, the doctor say, "You gon' have a baby 'less you do something about it." And I'm like, *(Defiantly)* "Oh, well. I don't know what to tell you." 'Cause there wasn't no way I's gon' have another abortion.

And I ain't know what Big Mike would say. Everybody say a man think a woman trying to trap him in the marriage, but I ain't wanna trap Big Mike—I love him. But, I was scared. So, I told him while he was in the bathroom. I say through the door, "Big Mike . . . I'm gon' have a baby." And Lord, Big Mike got so happy, I ain't even much hear the toilet flush! So, I let myself be happy 'cause he was and we spent those nine months happy together. I went to school and worked at Walmart. Big Mike had already graduated and was workingwiththisoilcompanythroughthisprogramcalled-Inroadswhereyougotocollegeandworkatthesametime.

So, then Li'l Mike was born. He was a big baby. Look just like his daddy, except he got my nose. But, he was a real laid-back baby—he get that from his daddy, too. Sometimes we'd wake up in the middle of the night scared that we missed the baby crying. But, we'd go in there and Li'l Mike would just be chillin', smiling at whatever. He was a real laid-back baby.

Anyway so, two months later, I got pregnant again. And you know my parents liked to died. Mama say I get pregnant at the drop of a hat, she say I get pregnant so fast, she say I get pregnant if Big Mike even much look at me sideways. *(Pause)* I sho'll do!

This time we named the baby Theo, like on *The Cosby Show.* I always loved that name, especially since Theo was so cute. So, when the baby came out with all these dimples, looking all cute— he had to be called Theo. Now, he whine more than Li'l Mike. So, when I would be in the kitchen cooking, I'd sit him on Li'l Mike lap. Li'l Mike would sit so still, like he didn't want to hurt him none. They looked so funny, both of them looking up at me. But, Theo wouldn't whine a bit.

I'm sorry. I know this s'posed to be a story about what hap-pened with me and Big Mike. But, I cain't help but talk about my kids, you know? 'Cause it's like, they my babies, you know? I don't know how other mothers feel. But, for me, it's like, when you have that first baby, you just get filled up with so much love you don't know how you gon' have enough left over for the next one. But then, you just get filled up all over again no matter how many babies you got.

So, Big Mike going to college to be an engineer and I ended up finishing high school at nineteen instead of eighteen 'cause I had bed rest for a li'l while with Theo. Li'l Mike was two years old and he could already say his ABCs. I read to my kids all the time like my mama did me. I like to show them stuff. So, Big Mike say, "Why don't you be a teacher?"

So, I did.

That's what I started to do at the community college: Ele-mentary Education. But, we both only going part time, 'cause we got two kids andwegottaworkandpaybillsandnoscholarshipallthe-financial-assistance-in-the-WORLD can cover all that. OK?!

Then, I turn twenty-one and me and Big Mike celebrate five years. And Lord, I got pregnant again. This boy we named Kentoo after Big Mike Daddy who is Ken, Jr. So, we named the baby Kentoo—like "Ken-also," "Ken-as-well." Everybody think it's a African name. But, it's like this: Ken*too*. Not: Ken*tu*.

And anyway, Kentoo been loud since the day he was born. He used to pull himself up on his crib and shake it and holler—waking everybody up with his bad behind. But, the minute his daddy came around the corner, he just get to laughing and smiling. Oooh! He love his daddy. You know how every child got they own special connection with they parent? And Kentoo just got happy every time he saw his daddy. Now, Big Mike and Li'l Mike can just sit together and do nothing but stare at the wall and be content. Theo, too. Not Kentoo. He always want to be playing. He's not as laid-back. He like to wrestle and holler and he love for somebody to chase him.

Anyway, so six months after Kentoo came, thank God I got pregnant with a girl. But you know my parents liked to died. Mama said I oughta have my tubes tied, that I'm a baby machine. So, we named the baby Rosa Elizabeth after my mama 'cause my mama got to be the best lady I know. Now, Rosa, the baby, is crazy! Big Mike call her Ro-Ro, 'cause when she first started sitting up, she would scoot herself like this . . . like she was rowing her butt. Big Mike love that li'l girl.

(The ensemble begins to softly sing in Spanish, a passionate, Tejano music–style love song underneath her story: "Cuando estemos juntos es una realidad como te necessito, como te quiero." She is taken by suprise and pauses a second to listen to them before speaking again.)

Oh, that's my song. The first time I heard that song, I liked to died. She saying how her man is like the only one for her. And how him and his love is the 'cause of all the joy and pain in her heart.

(The ensemble stops singing.)

When I was sixteen, I wanted to write Big Mike a letter to tell him how much I love him, but I was scared. So, I wrote it in Spanish. Big Mike don't know a lick of Spanish! So, I wrote:

"A Mike Grande" . . . *(She begins to sing:)*

Mi amor, solo tú
Eres mi amor
Por todo mi vida
Aunque su amor
Como me duele
Quiero verte y escuchar tú voz

(The ensemble joins her.)

Cuando estemos juntos es una realidad
Como te neccessito
Como te quiero.

(By the song's end, she is lost in her own world of love and memories.)

So, he wrote me back:

All right then, Peaches. So let's get married.

And so we did.

They found Big Mike dead, shot in the head, in a ditch on campus last year. And I liked to died. Don't nobody know who did it. They say it's just some random "hate" thing. Everybody tell me, "What you gon' do now without your husband?" And I say, "No, not my husband. My 'babies daddy.'" Some kinda way, saying it like that make it easier. People got the nerve to say to me, "Who gone marry you now with four kids?" Like I know! Ain't like I planned to be by myself with four kids.

So, Big Mike gone and I say I cain't live in Texas no mo'. I packed up me and my four kids and we come to college. My parents like to died. Mama say, one thing about me, I always do what I want. I say, yeah, ever since that abortion I gotta do what I know is best for my kids and for me—not what somebody else say . . . So, it's this college that got housing for people with kids. I told them, "I got four. And I'm all by myself." I told them all about Big Mike. They said, "Come on—if you ready for progress."

And so I did.

(The opening music begins to play and the lights change. The Peaches take their opening positions, this time joined by Progress Man, and speak to the audience.)

ALL:
>
> My name is Peaches.
> I've recently been wonderin'
> how I came to be
> like
> why I think
> and feel the way I do
> and why carelessness
> has never been an option
> for me.

(Blackout.)

THE END . . . FOR NOW

Cristal Chanelle Truscott is Founding Artistic Director of Progress Theatre, a touring ensemble-theater company. She is a graduate of the High School for the Performing and Visual Arts in Houston and is currently a Ph.D. candidate in Performance Studies at New York University. She is Assistant Professor and Theatre Program Coordinator/Chair at Prairie View/A&M University in Texas. In addition to *PEACHES*, she is also the author of *'MEMBUH: Confessions of the Only Generation*, and co-author of *Notice Me*, which was presented at The New York International Fringe Festival. She is working on her next two plays, *The Rain* and *Shahadah*, both scheduled to premiere as part of Progress Theatre's touring repertoire in 2009. Cristal has been a guest lecturer and speaker at universities and arts programs nationwide, including San Francisco State University, University of Houston, Spelman College, NYU's Tisch School of the Arts and Columbia University. Her work has garnered recognition and grants from the Ford Foundation, Theatre Communications Group, Gates Millennium Scholars, National Foundation for the Advancement of the Arts and the National Performance Network, among others. She has served nationally and internationally as a guest artist in conferences such as "Future Aesthetics: Hip-Hop and Contemporary Performance" in San Francisco in 2003 and "Diversity Dialogues," a project led by the Leadership Conference on Civil Rights Education Fund to foster understanding through diversity-based discussions (in 2006 this project partnered with the U.S. Embassy in the Netherlands).

As a playwright, Cristal blends academic and pop-culture conversations, striving ultimately to be of some assistance to efforts toward peace, freedom and progress.

Contact Cristal through: www.progresstheatre.com

the no black male show

by carl hancock rux

author's statement

Writing *The No Black Male Show* began growing up in the New York City foster care system with a biological mother who was diagnosed paranoid schizophrenic and institutionalized all of her adult life, and an older brother who died of AIDS in a city-run hospice. It grew out of realizing that I came from generations of men and women who were economically disenfranchised and dependant upon a governmental system of assistance—living in the margins of society and, for the most part, voiceless. In my own desire to see myself as a unary subject, I tried to consider my *voicelessness* (thus, the nameless protagonist of this performance piece is always holding a script, and cannot find words to explain himself that do not already exist on the page). What emerged was a query into a centuries' old discourse on identity politics and its historical context. This process of investigation inspired my curiosity and compelled me to want to see the underside of things. As an artist of color, I am perpetually disturbed by the small number of works developed for theater that are culturally relevant to people of color. In order to contribute to the future of American theater, in my own small way, I thought it necessary to write a conversation (instead of a play) comprised of poems and essays—because it was the only way I knew how to try to capture my own continuousness: that reach for inclusion, aesthetic integrity and social relevance. My vulnerability. As a multidisciplinary writer whose work is often described as "nontraditional," I see myself as belonging to a long tradition of nontradition—an artistic continuum of looking at history as it was shaped and reshaped, and as it informed the politics of my *human* identity. The personal investigation that became *The No Black Male Show* became the last of many plays I used as a map to place myself in the magical urbanity I was rooted in, with its African American traditions framed by Greek mythology, jazz and hip-hop music. My concentration has shifted (so to speak) beyond the realm of self-confession, but my work still seeks political asylum and will always be a meditation on attaining freedom and incorporating freedom into my creative impulses—the only portal through which I escape reality—and, at the same time, find it . . . and, sad to say, this is the closest I have ever come to understanding my "black maleness."

production history

In response to the Whitney Museum's 1994 biennial art exhibit, "Black Male Show," *The No Black Male Show* was initially written as the poem "Hell No Won't Be No Black Male Show Shown Today" (published in the author's *Pagan Operetta*; recorded on the CD *Rux Revue*, Sony Music, 1999). The performance version of that poem attempted to tragicomically address racist/sociological studies and decades of overlapping riffs on the personal and political experience of the hypothetical black male figure.

A staged adaptation of the poem was initially presented by The Kitchen in New York City in May of 1999 as *Pagan Operetta*, directed by Talvin Wilks. It was further developed in 2000 as *The No Black Male Show* at the Penumbra Theatre Company in St. Paul, MN. It was later presented by The Foundry Theatre (Melanie Joseph, Producing Artistic Director) at The Public Theater's Joe's Pub.

The Foundry Theatre's world premiere presentation of *The No Black Male Show* was scheduled for the Edinburgh Festival on September 12, 2001, but was canceled following the events of 9/11. The Foundry Theatre then toured their production of *The No Black Male Show* in 2001–2002 at Trinity College (Hartford, CT), Portland Center for the Performing Arts/Hollywood Theatre (Portland, OR), Bryan University Center at Duke University/Sheafer Theater (Durham, NC), The New WORLD Theater/University of Massachusetts (Amherst, MA), The Andy Warhol Museum (Pittsburgh, PA) and CENTERSTAGE (Baltimore, MD), with the following production team: direction was by Carl Hancock Rux (based on initial staging by Talvin Wilkes); the lighting design was by James Overstreet, slide installation was by Felicia Megginson, movement was by Valerie Winbourne and original music was written and performed by Jason Finkleman. The cast: Black Male was played by Carl Hancock Rux, Woman in Gown was played by Helga Davis, Woman in Slip and Shawl was played by Valerie Winbourne and the Muse-Ishan was played by Jason Finkleman.

The song "Don't Go to Strangers" was written by Redd Evans, Arthur Kent and Dave Mann, copyright ©1954, EMI Music Publishing. Reprinted by permission.

characters

BLACK MALE, victim.

WOMAN IN GOWN, classically trained singer and pianist in the manner of Black Patti (born Sissieretta Jones), sometimes lapses into blues or torch songs, inclined to sharp wailing; also Game Show Hostess, Concert Pianist, Ghost of Aunt Emma and a West African prostitute.

WOMAN IN SLIP AND SHAWL, hyperintellectual academic; also battered maternal figure possessed by the Holy Ghost and a West African prostitute.

MUSE-ISHAN, Eurasian male figure with primitive musical instruments.

prologue

black existencia: waiting in the dark

When the dark comes, we are forced to remain in it. Then the vibration of metal striking metal—resounding quietly until a pool of evening light expands itself onto the clearing of earned space. The Muse-Ishan stands before cymbals, sticks, drums, various objects of metal, bowls of grain, apothecary jars, etc. He makes somber sounds. Two faint spotlights rise slowly; the Woman in Slip and Shawl leans against one wall; the Woman in Gown leans against another. Both are expressionless.

WOMAN IN GOWN *(Authentic necromancy; singing)*:
>Build your dreams
>To the stars above
>And when you need
>Someone true to love
>Don't go to strangers
>Darlin', come home to me
>Play with fire
>Till your fingers burn
>And when there's no place
>For you to turn
>Don't go to strangers
>Come on home to me . . .
>
>Make your mark
>For your friends to see
>But when you need
>A little more than company
>Don't go to strangers
>Come home to me . . .

WOMAN IN SLIP AND SHAWL *(Paraphrasing Aimé Césaire; with melancholy)*:
>For sure the rebel is going to die
>No flags

83

Not even black ones
No gun salutes
No ceremony . . .

For sure the rebel is going to die
The best reason being that
There is nothing more to do . . .
The season of burning stars
Is now at hand.

(Some poor light is cast onto some poor figure—in formal attire and tightly knotted shoes. The Black Male sits upstage of the Muse-Ishan. A DJ mix of questions:)

VOICE-OVER:
Tell me about your mother . . . please
Tell me about your father . . . please
Do you own a gun?
Tell me about hip-hop.

(The two women repeat these questions with the voice-over until the Black Male speaks:)

BLACK MALE *(Half-spoken, half-sung)*:
The call is tribal
The march is angry
The faces sharp
When my eyes
Opened this morning
I didn't see no sun
I looked out onto
The blinding dark
The night's fierce blade
What place is this?
And darkness cut deep into my sight
Split the canvass coat of my protection
Vision stabbed.

I spilled my blood and water across the floor
Like rushing waves
Opened my mouth and screamed
Echo-canyon high
Mountains cry

What place is this?
The abyss of nothing's happening—ness . . .
Wait to hear your soul drop to the bottom . . .
Falls for a lifetime.

My silhouette is cut on the bias
Appliqué to an evil white-night moon
Grin . . .
An evil white-night moon—grins
Can you hear my sister praying?
How come the veil is draped across her looking glass?
Dare she ask why there's trouble in this land?
I can't stand to hear her tears no more
Valleys gash like tribal marks
Down her cobalt cheeks . . .

first course of the black male discourse

The DJ mix of questions resumes. The Black Male stands with his back against the wall, unaffected. There is an outline of his body scrawled in chalk behind him. New DJ mix of gospel, basketball, hip-hop, TV sitcoms, cut and layered over each other, filling the air. The Woman in Slip and Shawl takes a seat before the Black Male. She plugs her ears with cotton and waits for him to initiate the conversation. The Woman in Gown takes her seat in front of him, plugs her ears with cotton and waits for the Black Male to do something she can applaud. They both cross their legs, fold their arms. The Muse-Ishan stands comfortably in the clearing of space he has earned and watches the Black Male. They all do. Every now and then the Black Male adjusts his jacket, pinches the crease of his trousers, unaware of the chalk outline. He looks to them for approval. Nothing. He eggs on the Muse-Ishan to play something. Nothing. The sounds build. The Black Male is engulfed in layers of language, does nothing about it, even the sounds are deafening him. The women, impatient but prepared, re-set their chairs facing the audience, retrieve a tea service and curl up in their chairs—a comfortable morning–talk show repose. Occasionally they will turn to the Muse-Ishan but their conversation is with each other and the audience. They pour the tea. The sounds fade as they blow into their cups.

WOMAN IN SLIP AND SHAWL: If we must discuss the so-called existential
    "Black Male/White Male" thing—
WOMAN IN GOWN: On the existential Black Male/White Male thing—

BLACK MALE *(From his seat upstage)*: On the Black Male/White Male thing (with all due respect to the Black Female/White Female thing).

WOMAN IN GOWN: Frankly, I am not interested.

WOMAN IN SLIP AND SHAWL: If we must discuss the Black Male thing—

WOMAN IN GOWN: Which, of course, leaves no room to discuss the Black *Female* thing—

WOMAN IN SLIP AND SHAWL: Operative words being *thing—hers— female—*

WOMAN IN GOWN: *Black.* Which is *much* more interesting—

WOMAN IN SLIP AND SHAWL: But if we cannot discuss—

BLACK MALE: We are *here* to discuss—

WOMAN IN GOWN: The so-called Black Male/White Male thing—

WOMAN IN SLIP AND SHAWL: Then we must discuss—talk about how we see.

WOMAN IN GOWN: Quite frankly, I am *not* interested.

BLACK MALE: I *am* . . .

WOMAN IN GOWN: No, I really mean it.

WOMAN IN SLIP AND SHAWL: We must talk about how we see, and the linguistics of that discourse, because—

WOMAN IN GOWN: Because—in order to discuss how we see the Black Male thing—

WOMAN IN SLIP AND SHAWL: That discourse must employ a metaphoric vernacular—

WOMAN IN GOWN: Regarding race.

WOMAN IN SLIP AND SHAWL: Right, and we must concede that race in America (according to the pejorative perceptions of the relevant majority) has been fractured into only two relevant denominations of being—

WOMAN IN GOWN: Black and White.

WOMAN IN SLIP AND SHAWL: Right.

WOMAN IN GOWN: Crude.

WOMAN IN SLIP AND SHAWL: This inaccurate minimalist vernacular employed by the relevant majority regarding race identity primarily acknowledges only these two denominations of being.

WOMAN IN GOWN: Inaccurate.

WOMAN IN SLIP AND SHAWL: The populous American tongue gets tied when challenged to conceptualize or validate anything beyond conservative gender roles, sexual preference, political affiliation or race reality.

(The Black Male joins them. There are only two chairs. He squeezes politely onto the edge of one of the already occupied chairs. He attempts a comfortable pose for the audience. He tries to pour himself a cup of tea. The teapot is empty.)

BLACK MALE: This is not to say that identity and alternative definitions of identity have not inspired hip slang, slogans, expletives, catch-phrases and nicknames that have entered into the American polyglot—

WOMAN IN SLIP AND SHAWL: But attempts at formalizing new linguistic practices for a preeminent mainstream tends only to employ inaccurate minimalist jargon acknowledging subdivisions of relevant identity.

WOMAN IN GOWN: Shouldn't we ponder when and by whom Whiteness was purchased and assimilated into and when and by whom Blackness was imposed upon? Shouldn't we question the politics of who is, at present, White, and who is, at present, Black, and shouldn't we identify those ethnic groups who, upon arrival in America, were recognized as and stigmatized as Black and remain Black without any possibility of ever attaining Whiteness?

WOMAN IN SLIP AND SHAWL: Yes. There are for example, people who appear to be of European descent or who are partially of European descent who consider themselves to be Black—

WOMAN IN GOWN: And people who are of European descent who do not appear to be of European descent—

WOMAN IN SLIP AND SHAWL: But who consider themselves to be White—

WOMAN IN GOWN: But are not *accepted* as White, by a certain populace.

BLACK MALE: And there are people who are of European descent—

WOMAN IN GOWN AND WOMAN IN SLIP AND SHAWL: White.

BLACK MALE: Who actually *appear* to be of European descent—

WOMAN IN GOWN AND WOMAN IN SLIP AND SHAWL: White.

BLACK MALE: But consider themselves to be—

WOMAN IN GOWN AND WOMAN IN SLIP AND SHAWL: Black.

(All pause to consider what they have just said. The Woman in Gown and the Woman in Slip and Shawl slurp their tea.)

BLACK MALE: But I have not encountered the latter.

WOMAN IN SLIP AND SHAWL: If we are to agree that identity formation—who we are—relies heavily upon the role of the other—who we are not—then we are forced to think about how we see ourselves . . . perception.

WOMAN IN GOWN: And quite frankly, we are all too preoccupied.

WOMAN IN SLIP AND SHAWL: Race is an invention (for purposes of colonization) used to make a distinction between how the *humane* figure sees the *inhumane* figure.

WOMAN IN GOWN: Too preoccupied to continue to pay attention to marginalized identities.

WOMAN IN SLIP AND SHAWL: The perceived image of race is based on individual (or collective) sight.

WOMAN IN GOWN: America's too preoccupied with Manolo Blahnik shoes.

WOMAN IN SLIP AND SHAWL: Race boils down to what you see and how you see yourself—appearance . . .

WOMAN IN GOWN: I'm too preoccupied, what with the decline of American theater . . .

BLACK MALE: Or how you are seen—

WOMAN IN SLIP AND SHAWL: —a set of appearances—

BLACK MALE: Detached from the place and time in which it first made its appearance.

WOMAN IN GOWN: Not to mention the decline of American opera and Broadway musicals, and with that, I ask you—what's left?

WOMAN IN SLIP AND SHAWL: Your failure to perform as a Black Male is our failure to detach ourselves from our inherited perception of you.

BLACK MALE: Thus I may have been unable to perform simply because at that moment I was unable to perceive myself . . . in this room.

WOMAN IN GOWN: The truly dying breed, the *truly* dying species is the classically trained diva of yore—

WOMAN IN SLIP AND SHAWL: You may have been unable to perceive yourself in this room because you were being witnessed . . .

WOMAN IN GOWN: Who finds herself in twenty-first-century America standing outside in the cold, waiting on line, warming up her five-octave mezzo-soprano just to audition for background vocal work for some hip-hop star!

WOMAN IN SLIP AND SHAWL: Therefore in this room you have no relationship with yourself, you have only a relationship with those of us who witness you.

BLACK MALE: And those of you who see me.

WOMAN IN SLIP AND SHAWL: A different relationship.

BLACK MALE: Because?

WOMAN IN GOWN: Because we're all TOO PREOCCUPIED TO CARE!

WOMAN IN SLIP AND SHAWL: No, because those of us who witness you may not see you at all.

WOMAN IN GOWN: I have my own preoccupations. I'm still learning to pronounce words like Pashtun, Tajik and al Qaeda.

WOMAN IN GOWN: But, nonetheless, as far as the Black Male thing goes, you have been given a stage on which to perform your identity.

BLACK MALE: I'm not sure . . .

WOMAN IN GOWN: My husband is too preoccupied with next year's property taxes, up or down, will they or won't they?

BLACK MALE: I'm not sure what stages are for: lights, curtains . . .

WOMAN IN GOWN: On finding a decent contractor.

WOMAN IN SLIP AND SHAWL: To perpetuate illusions . . .

WOMAN IN GOWN: Buying some decent air space—

WOMAN IN SLIP AND SHAWL: To compel us all toward false air, false light, false language . . . all chief components of the race concept.

WOMAN IN GOWN: Too preoccupied with our annual international travel plans—I MEAN, WHERE DO YOU GO?

BLACK MALE: What I would have liked to have done is a dance, or a poem, or maybe taken some questions from the audience but all of a sudden . . . there was this terror . . . this fear that time was spinning on its axis and the Earth was retreating into some ether, or ephemeral region of disbelief . . . and suddenly, all that I had prepared to do, all the stories I was prepared to tell at that moment . . .

WOMAN IN GOWN *(To the Black Male)*: Because you were just too preoccupied . . . me, too.

BLACK MALE: With what?

WOMAN IN GOWN: With what? With . . . with . . . which country is terrorizing which. With . . . you know . . . the holidays—I'm going absolutely NUTS trying to sort out greetings cards, making three separate piles for Ramadan, Chanukah and Christmas—God forbid you should get them confused—especially these days.

WOMAN IN SLIP AND SHAWL: Which is to say?

WOMAN IN GOWN: Which is to say, it's all TOO MUCH. I came all this way, ball gown, primitive musician and authentic Black Male figure in tow—to do WHAT?

(Their words fall out of their mouths, into silence. The Muse-Ishan plays his gongs. They cover their faces with cardboard minstrel masks stapled to flat sticks. A DJ mix of their prior conversation swells as they assume several positions throughout the space, remaining in a calm pose for a period of time before assuming another. They do this for a time, their words now swinging on particles of dust. Then they remove their masks and sing from the encroaching darkness:)

ALL:

> If I could black like Eminem
> Oh Lord maybe then . . .
> If I could black like Britney Spears
> Oh Lord no more tears . . .
> If I could be black like that
> Like that . . . Oh Lord . . .

(They fan themselves beneath the weight of heat, a hot plantation walk. The Woman in Slip and Shawl exits and returns wheeling a lectern on

stage. The Woman in Gown retreats to the grand piano, adjusts her gown at the bench, and flips through sheet music. The Black Male is unsure of where he is supposed to go or what he is supposed to do at this moment, so he stands there, looking stupid. The Woman in Slip and Shawl struggles to lift an enormous leather-bound book covered in dust onto the podium. She flips through its crumbling pages, settles on a passage, dons a pair of reading glasses and looks to the Woman in Gown who strikes a violent chord from the first theme of a concerto, then proceeds with a delicate tinkling of keys.)

primitive or savage music: an illustration in retro-afro-futurism

WOMAN IN SLIP AND SHAWL: "Primitive or Savage Music" from *The History of Music* by Waldo Selden Pratt, copyright, 1907.

(Reading:)

> Although most savage music is crude and to us disagreeable, its interest for the student is considerable. By noting how it arises, how it is used, and with what it is associated, we gain insight into the essence and relations of the musical impulse . . . It has been thought that ideas of harmony or part-singing are impossible for the savage mind. But it appears that some tribes in Africa and Australia do sing in parts and even attempt concerted effects between voices and instruments. Such combinations, however, are *rare* and do not show any *real system* . . . The widespread combination of song with dancing, mimicry, and poetry, as well as with religious exercises, *challenges* attention. The painstaking care in fashioning instruments is impressive and instructive. The *naive* experiments in scale-making suggest the probable sources of modern theory. The analogies between the musical efforts of primitive adults and those of civilized children have a bearing upon current pedagogy. For the critical student of either history or aesthetics, therefore, the facts of savage music are valuable.

(The Black Male exits. He returns wheeling a lectern onstage, dons reading glasses and hurls a big dusty book onto the lectern. He flips through its crumbling pages, settles on a passage and gestures toward the Muse-Ishan as he reads from the book. The Muse-Ishan demonstrates his instruments as they are mentioned in the following text:)

carl hancock rux

BLACK MALE *(Reading)*:

> Clappers of bone or wood are frequent, and various hollowed tubes and the like that can be beaten. Castanets of shell or metal are often found. Everywhere rattles and jingles abound, made of bunches of pebbles, fruit stones or shells (occasionally of a human skull filled with loose objects). All sorts of gongs or tam-tams occur, made of wood, stone, brass, copper, iron; these sometimes appear in sets, so that rude melodies or harmonies are possible. The varieties of drum and tambourine are endless, all characterized by a stretched head of skin over a hollow bowl or box, the latter being usually a gourd, a hollowed piece of wood (as the trunk of a tree) or a metallic vessel. They are sounded either by the hand or by sticks. Much ingenuity is sometimes shown in devising signals and intricate tattoos, and drums are *often* used in combination.

WOMAN IN SLIP AND SHAWL *(Vehemently)*: Excuse me! In *primitive* conditions, music is *first of all* a social diversion or *play*, affording an outlet for surplus animal spirit, stimulating emotional excitement, and helping to maintain muscular and nervous energy—

BLACK MALE *(Abruptly correcting her)*: While it is *true* that external nature supplies *suggestions* of primitive music, such as the sighing and whistling of the wind, the rippling and roar of falling water, the cries of beasts, the buzzing or calls of insects and the songs of birds—the influence of these on *primitive song* is *apparently* slight.

(They proceed to talk over each other as the Woman in Gown plays furiously, racing through her sheet music. In response, the Muse-Ishan builds his primitive percussion to a reverberating rage.)

WOMAN IN SLIP AND SHAWL: Singing and dancing are *always* conspicuously social—a center of interest for perhaps a whole village or *tribe*. The craving for popular activity in these ways often leads to stated gatherings of a festal character, the ceremonies usually being specifically associated with an occupation or event, as with *hunting*, agriculture, worship or *war*, or with birth, sickness or death.

BLACK MALE: Herbert Spencer argued that song is primarily a form of *speech*, arising from the reflex action of the vocal organs under stress of emotion (as a cry follows the sensation of pain). More likely is the hypothesis that music is derived from some attempt to work off *surplus energy* through *bodily* motions, to coordinate and decorate which rhythmic sounds, vocal or mechanical, are employed, and that what was at first only an accessory to dancing was finally differentiated from it.

(The Muse-Ishan and the Woman in Gown have long stopped playing. She removes her glasses and stands next to the Black Male and the Woman in Slip and Shawl, who continue to argue as they present their theses.)

First of all, beee—atch, the traditions—

WOMAN IN SLIP AND SHAWL: Bitch?

BLACK MALE: —the traditions of many races recount the importation of instruments or musical ideas to men by the gods!

WOMAN IN SLIP AND SHAWL: Did he just call me a—

(The Woman in Gown proceeds to stand between the Black Male and the Woman in Slip and Shawl; she sways and hums a steady dirge.)

BLACK MALE: These myths are significant, not as historic statements of fact, but—

WOMAN IN SLIP AND SHAWL: You don't KNOW me!

BLACK MALE: But as an idea of music as—

(The Muse-Ishan tries to restrain her; a Jerry Springer moment.)

WOMAN IN SLIP AND SHAWL: *HE DON'T KNOW ME TO BE CALLIN' ME NO BITCH!*

BLACK MALE: Maybe some form of music is found in every part of the uncivilized world, from the islands of the southern Pacific 'round to the Americas—

WOMAN IN SLIP AND SHAWL: Don't you eeeeeeeever call me out my name!

BLACK MALE: —and from the equatorial zone far toward the poles . . .

WOMAN IN SLIP AND SHAWL: I got your pole right here! He don't know me!

BLACK MALE: As testimonies to the strange potency and charm residing in musical tones, these speculations are not especially fruitful. It is true that some form of music is found in every part of the uncivilized world—

WOMAN IN SLIP AND SHAWL: You ain't seeeeeen uncivilized . . . you don't be . . . no . . .

(The Woman in Slip and Shawl falls under the spell of swaying and humming. The Muse-Ishan returns to his table. The Black Male is still talking when he realizes the two women are standing on either side of him, swaying and humming a steady dirge. He removes his reading

glasses and joins them. They hum in unison, then break into harmony: first a somber moan, then a classic aria, then a hip-hop flow, then hand claps and field hollers, repeating the same lyrics.)

BLACK MALE, WOMAN IN GOWN AND WOMAN IN SLIP AND SHAWL *(Singing)*:
>Hell No
>Won't Be No
>Black Male Show
>Shown Today.

(They hold the final note until all breath leaves their bodies and they collapse into one final chain-gang exhalation. They bow gracefully to the audience. The lights transition to a moody blue. The Woman in Gown sits on top of the grand piano and crosses her legs. The Black Male moves to the other side of the stage. The Woman in Slip and Shawl takes a seat upstage in a circle of light. The Woman in Gown breaks into a jazz scat. The Woman in Slip and Shawl appears to be quietly enjoying the jazz scat. She closes her eyes and basks in it. The Black Male returns to his space at the wall. He speaks slightly above the scat:)

BLACK MALE: I think Archie Shepp played hambone hambone where you been in our living room the night faces and fists melded melliflu-ous melancholy madness onto red-river carpeting—spurt, splash, torrent falls, gushing reds, primeval screams crashing through vodka spittle, sharp tenor sax and subjective alto, trumpet, trom-bone, hambone bass and Roger Blank drums . . . blank . . . drums . . . blank . . . Shepp's lyricism lurking behind fichus and forlorn fruit and rhythm patterns lined in gold fringe, clutched, clutched in, in our living room, in *Where you been*? arrangements scattered from kidney-shaped, cherry-wood coffee table and Camels sleep-ing in red-river woven carpeting, caravans of Camels and Kools and vodka and blood and Shepp and rhythm . . . I think *Garvey's Ghost* came to play with me between Charlie Brown's sheets to the percussion of belt-buckle slaps and cracked wall mirrors and ripped Chinese watercolors, or was it *Mendacity*?

WOMAN IN GOWN *(Singing)*:
>Mendacity . . .

WOMAN IN SLIP AND SHAWL *(Whispering to herself)*: Mendacity . . .

(Uncomfortable beat for all.)

BLACK MALE: Either way, the party was in my pillow, where cutouts held court with *Right On!* magazine centerfolds, conversation was had, freely, and maybe Junior Walker interrupted for a moment, or might have been, then again, I think, it was . . . no, yes, it was Mendacity, it was Abbey Lincoln who sent herself into my restlessness and jazz frenzy and comic book high, and quivering and quake and not sure now what the silences mean after Johnnie Walker Black Black Black came crashing down to the harmonic freedom and improvisation of Roach and Mingus and Hawkins and Dizzy . . . Dizzy . . . Dizziness . . . I know Jimmy Garrison summoned a nature boy to come my way, we entertained battering and long fingernails broke against leather strap, against cheek and ass and eye, I played to Jimmy Garrsion's plucking, sucking my thumb in corner circle rhythm patterns, *Brilliant Corners*, creative post-bop, Monk's *Brilliant Corners* a hiding place, while ass whoopin's are taking place, like what seven year olds like me supposed to get for stealing or lying or the kind maybe you hear women who can sing—

WOMAN IN GOWN *(Singing)*:
     I fall in love too easily—

WOMAN IN SLIP AND SHAWL *(Lighting a cigarette, a private lament)*:
     Too easily . . .

(Another uncomfortable beat for all.)

BLACK MALE: Women who can hang tough with *Willow Weep for Me,* and take a swing, take a swing, a swing and a hard-hitting fast blow down crashing fruit and floral patterns and primeval screams through vodka spittle, the kinda ass whoopin' maybe women who sing supposed to get after they done tried to do *Afro Blue* but you don't hear about broken nails and Jimmy Garrison and split lip and Eric Dolphy and swollen cheeks against red-river roads where Camels and Kools caravan away from cherry-wooded areas, spilling themselves away, like the long and vibrant notes of *Yardbird Suite*, with the sweet repose of Holiday on—

WOMAN IN GOWN *(Singing)*:
     There is no greater love . . .

BLACK MALE AND WOMAN IN SLIP AND SHAWL: . . . Not in your living room.

(Percussion builds, softly. Scat resumes. The Woman in Slip and Shawl closes her eyes, tries to stay within the safety of music.)

BLACK MALE *(Loosening his tie, air boxing)*: Jamming . . . jamming . . . jamming . . . they don't tell you about this in record jackets, what to expect when Booker Little sings on that trumpet, when Carlos Valdez gets to cong, cong, congaing, the beat, to beat, to beat, the beat, the beating taking place in the circle of frenzy, in your living room, and there are no sequins for the diva, no boas, no rhinestone tiaras, no pencil-black eyebrows arched in pride across her forehead, or gentle shadows softly sleeping above the lid of her falling eye, her falling eye in sweet repose, no straightened hair illuminating lights and gels and gobos, not in your living room, just Charles Tolliver's "Plight" to her modern-dance ballet, rond de jambe of the knee, to the fall, to the fist, straight back, and lip split side turn, ever so gracefully, ever so soft, and hard, and swing, and bop, and bam, and pow, and Dizzy . . . dizzy . . . swelling cheeks, weak alto sax, strong bass . . .

(The Black Male bobs and weaves. Beat. Scat halts.)

I think it was Etta James screaming—

(The Woman in Slip and Shawl repeats with him, hands covering her face.)

BLACK MALE AND WOMAN IN SLIP AND SHAWL: JAMES . . . JAMES! JAMES! JAMES!

(Beat. Scat resumes carelessly.)

BLACK MALE: . . . Or maybe not . . . or maybe it was just the rustling of the knees and elbows, and the match stick struck across the board, and embers, and smoke rising, and flames, lifting broken body beaten like how, beaten the way seven year olds like me supposed to be beat, or maybe if you Abbey Lincoln and sing that good, maybe if you can do primeval screams to Max's drums, and then there was nothing there . . . and then nothing . . . no voice . . . somebody hollered one last time and I can't recall if it was Grachan Moncur with Sonny Rollins, and Joe Henderson, but I think maybe it was the silences, and Moncur's "Intellect" that came up next, in our living room, with nothing there . . . no voice . . . I think it was the silences . . . finger-turning rotary dial . . . door shut . . . locked

. . . running water . . . or was it ? . . . no, I'm sure it was Moncur . . . who played with me . . . unveiled trombone taking me up in gentle long notes and tickling vibes, texture and shape, and safe brilliant corners to suck my thumb . . . I think it was the silences . . . next . . . I think it was the silences.

social and mental traits of the negro
or aunt emma's zuni recipe for soul transition

The Woman in Slip and Shawl recovers from her stool, takes a moment. The Black Male recovers, takes a moment. The Woman in Gown proceeds to the lectern, dons her eyeglasses.

WOMAN IN GOWN: From *Social and Mental Traits of the Negro* by Howard W. Odum, copyright, 1910.

(Reading:)

> The Negro woman is not infrequently the head of the Negro family . . . Negro men who are regularly employed are at home little of the time, and those who do not work regularly are more of a hindrance than assistance . . . Many Negro men loaf about the home, depending upon their wives and children to support them, while they work a little here and there and abuse the family . . . It will thus be seen that there is little orderly home life among the Negroes . . . Sometimes an entire family consisting of father, mother, large and small children occupy the same rooms. Nor do they ventilate, and especially when any of the inmates are sick they are loath to let in the fresh air. Many superstitions constrain them to endanger their health by foolish practices . . . Consequently there is less hope of recovery in case of serious sickness, and more opportunities for sickness to grow. In the day, at night, when sick or when well, the Negroes have no conditions for inspiring love of home or for health of mind and body.

(Photographs of rural landscapes are projected. Shadows of a woman reflected on the walls of wood shacks. A boy. His mother. A ghost.

Downstage there are three old, sturdy chairs. The Black Male sits between the two women. Listens. They all do. A DJ mix of boiling water, clanking pots and pans. The Black Male now has the subtle countenance of a twelve-year-old boy. The Woman in Slip and Shawl removes her shawl and places it in her lap. Folds it, unfolds it, drapes her head with it, repeats. Pauses. Mumbles to herself, giggles. The Woman in Gown is stoic and centuries old. She leads the boy and his mother in recalling recipes for soul survival.)

(Husky whisper) Yes?

BLACK MALE: August. Sunday. Nine A.M.

WOMAN IN GOWN *(Husky whisper)*: Celery . . .

BLACK MALE AND WOMAN IN SLIP AND SHAWL: Seven sticks.

WOMAN IN GOWN: Garlic?

BLACK MALE AND WOMAN IN SLIP AND SHAWL: Seven cloves—save some for altar space.

WOMAN IN GOWN: Pork sausage . . .

BLACK MALE: Made immediately after—

WOMAN IN SLIP AND SHAWL: —the death of the beast.

WOMAN IN GOWN: Cayenne pepper.

WOMAN IN SLIP AND SHAWL: Seven dashes.

WOMAN IN GOWN: Bell pepper.

BLACK MALE AND WOMAN IN SLIP AND SHAWL: . . . From someone else's garden.

WOMAN IN GOWN: Fresh tomatoes.

BLACK MALE: . . . From your own garden—

WOMAN IN SLIP AND SHAWL: —Crushed to the consistency of blood and pulp.

WOMAN IN GOWN: Fresh chicken livers?

BLACK MALE AND WOMAN IN SLIP AND SHAWL: Store the body of the bird for later consumption.

WOMAN IN GOWN: Onions . . .

WOMAN IN SLIP AND SHAWL: . . . sliced in seven rings—

WOMAN IN GOWN: Then chopped.

WOMAN IN SLIP AND SHAWL: Three tablespoons of all-purpose flour . . .

BLACK MALE: Bay leaf—

WOMAN IN GOWN: Save some for altar space.

BLACK MALE: Salt from your tears . . .

WOMAN IN SLIP AND SHAWL: Seasoned with the blood of your last flow.

WOMAN IN GOWN: Sweat?

BLACK MALE AND WOMAN IN SLIP AND SHAWL: Seven dashes.

WOMAN IN GOWN: From?

WOMAN IN SLIP AND SHAWL: From the last breast to give last offspring suck.

BLACK MALE, WOMAN IN GOWN AND WOMAN IN SLIP AND SHAWL: Gather ingredients into the tips of your fingers . . .

WOMAN IN SLIP AND SHAWL: On the day of the death of your first son.

WOMAN IN GOWN: Store in a cool place.

BLACK MALE: On the morning of his internment . . .

WOMAN IN SLIP AND SHAWL: In the presence of your son who still breathes . . .

BLACK MALE: Combine ingredients in one-gallon cast-iron pot.

BLACK MALE, WOMAN IN GOWN AND WOMAN IN SLIP AND SHAWL: Simmer.

BLACK MALE: Pour into an unwashed bowl last used for the last meal served before—before . . .

WOMAN IN SLIP AND SHAWL: The day of death.

WOMAN IN GOWN: Wait.

BLACK MALE: Return to cast-iron pot.

BLACK MALE, WOMAN IN GOWN AND WOMAN IN SLIP AND SHAWL: Stew.

(Beat.
   The Woman in Gown makes the slightest noise ever so often with her breathing. The Woman in Slip and Shawl continues to fidget with the shawl, alternating between crying and laughing, acknowledging an unseen presence making conversation in her ear. The boy speaks:)

BLACK MALE: Brother lay dead in a box. We sit living in a box. Inherited house. Zuni, Virginia. A Southern box, facing Northern light, with one window. One soulless chair. A bed for quaking. A stove. No music. Bland food. Ghosts give recipes for soul. I be nothing, unrecognizable child, watching television. Waiting for the hour when Father and Mother take my hand to kiss the cold face of Brother. I be without my self today. Brother, he be fixed, hushed. Waiting for the hour when the spirit divorces itself from the flesh. Hebetudinous young man in slumber. Hands crossed, palms face down. White suit. Flower. Quiet. Asleep in apostolic holiness . . . across the ditch . . . just outside the window. Waiting for roar of tears and thunder of clap and stomp and, "Save me, Lawd! Hep me Jeezus!" Father be drinking Wild Turkey too early this morning, staring out of window—impatient with Mother's disjointed scurry. He be drinking Johnnie Walker Black when Wild Turkey finished, and cursing her nonsense to himself, and cursing her cooking. Father likes to believe he can control his emotions. "This is the Northern way," he has informed us all. He and me, we wear identical suits and shoes, and parted hair. We wait, like the apostles on the Mount of Olive. Mother, she be skittish, jumpy, tremulous woman in fear. Mother be dressed early this morning; hair controlled and arrested in pins and net, perfectly pressed black suit trying not to fall from thinning frame. Legs want to move. Want to shout. Throw themselves up and out again, like they did in the days of birth pains. Stockings say *no*. Say *quiet*. Say *still*. No soul. Don't lose it. Feet try to move, try to pound heel into wood floor, try to grieve like other women. Women who can't care about how their panties show when they fall over pews and drape themselves over caskets. Patent leather pumps rationally ask *why*? Request sensible steps. Careful walk. From here to there. No throwing out of voice or flinging up of hands. No Holy Ghosts. Ignore the quake and quiver and tremble of hand. Mother likes to believe she can control her emotions.

BLACK MALE AND WOMAN IN SLIP AND SHAWL: "This is the better way,"

BLACK MALE: she says to Father in agreement.

(Beat.)

"Wife?" Father asks in perfect pitch through drunken slur, "are you do-doing all right?"

BLACK MALE AND WOMAN IN SLIP AND SHAWL: "Yes,"

BLACK MALE: Mother replies in normal octave,

BLACK MALE AND WOMAN IN SLIP AND SHAWL: "yes, I am. Thank you."

BLACK MALE: "Have you f-finished?" Father asks, poised and sure with unsteady stance, "have you finished pr-preparing?"

BLACK MALE AND WOMAN IN SLIP AND SHAWL: "Not yet,"

BLACK MALE: Mother replies in soft tone and broken heart . . .

BLACK MALE AND WOMAN IN GOWN: "not yet."

BLACK MALE: Mary outlived Jesus. Sometimes mothers outlive their sons.

WOMAN IN GOWN: Yes.

WOMAN IN SLIP AND SHAWL: Sometimes mothers do.

BLACK MALE: Aunt Emma outlived four. Lost—

BLACK MALE AND WOMAN IN GOWN: —one to fever, one—

BLACK MALE: —to a woman's tumultuous husband. One to—

WOMAN IN GOWN: —homemade whiskey.

BLACK MALE: One to an angry union of men. Aunt Emma outlived four and called on Jesus till she heard from—

BLACK MALE AND WOMAN IN GOWN: Mary.

BLACK MALE: Mother says Aunt Emma closed her eyes one morning and died in this house. In the chair where Father sits on the day of the internment of his eldest son. Father says the dead are dead for good. Mother says Emma's six-foot frame rushed out into the fields of Zuni, Virginia—barefoot—with her machete in her fists, and slaughtered hogs and picked her vegetables from around the yard, and massaged the necks of sleeping chickens so she could slit their throats. Mother says Aunt Emma prepared a stew for revival and changed her garments. Let God change her name. Aunt Emma's been dead now some twenty-five years. She left this house in Mother's name. Father calls it his. Father, Mother and Brother migrated South, bringing with them boxes of Northern ways. I was not yet. That was before now. I have met Aunt Emma before. Years after her death. She is here today. Even now. Ignorant and uneducated sister of Mother's grandmother, born to former slaves and Sha'lako shamans. Aunt Emma stands in doorways and looks at Mother from mirrors. Looks over her shoulder as Mother prepares the stew. Says:

BLACK MALE AND WOMAN IN GOWN *(As Emma; husky whispers)*: Dis whut be yo' transition now. Ah pray tuh Jesus, hear frm Mary. Make da stew. Dip yo' fanger in da pot—you be speakin' in tongues aftah while. Tarry some, you be speakin' in tongues aftah while. Ah outlive fo'—you got one in da basket, but ya still got one waitin' tuh be a man. No soul wiffout dis kine sacrifice, dis kine rituah.

BLACK MALE: Aunt Emma, in bloody linen and sweat-soaked head rag, six-foot frame, with the hands of a man, looks at Mother and listens to her careful speech, and Northern ways.

BLACK MALE AND WOMAN IN GOWN *(As Emma)*: Heh . . . ya need tuh dance tuh da coon shouters! Delta blues . . . Niggah blues . . . Leroy Lasses White can hep ya— Call on 'em! Call on 'em! Albert King, Mamie Smith, Charlie Patton, Son House— CALL ON 'EM! Did ya add da innards o' da hog to da stew? Ya 'member to stir whif ya las' flow? Transitional. Change ya gawments, girl. Dat'll be all right. Yep . . . Dat'll be all right . . . change y' gawments. Transitional . . . yep.

(The Woman in Gown, fighting back tears, hums softly to herself.)

BLACK MALE: Mother hums a gospel song for the first time in years, listening to ghosts for instructions, stirring all the while. Father drinks gin and tonics now and stares out of one window. Brother lay silent. Still. Brother left this house some four years ago. I was eight. Mother says he could not contain himself here. His spirit restricted by bloodstained walls and shattered glass spittle spewed from fraternal throat. Danced out the door and up the hill, with busted eye and broken hip. He died somewhere in the hills . . . free. He died for our sins. We all smell of chicken livers and tears and garlic and blood. Father curses Mother's foolishness through tight lips, and Mother sings spirituals louder from tight lips, and Brother sleeps quietly, face drawn back with tight lips, and I say nothing of the smell in this house. I say nothing. Aunt Emma finds the records, piled away some many years. She spins 78s and guides

Mother's hands as she stirs the stew. Mother laughs to herself a little. Makes the stew for the day of internment. Hopes for transition. Resists lack of control. About these things Mother knows nothing. The music plays. Emma says:

BLACK MALE AND WOMAN IN GOWN *(As Emma)*: Big Bill Broonzy curse Ray Charles for gospel voice and blues rhythm. Heh . . . I say combine de two!

(The Woman in Gown begins to clap her hands and hum to a steady beat. A conjuring.)

BLACK MALE: Mother serves the stew. Aunt Emma blesses the table from behind Mother's eyes.

(The Woman in Slip and Shawl hums pleasantly to herself, a hint of laughter sometimes, masking deep wounds.)

Aunt Emma, she hovers over us like some great warrior bird from the Southern mesas flying at dusk, singing tribal chants and summoning Ma Rainey to bless us all. We eat in silence, except for Emma's blues wail. It is small and private. The stew is thick and smells. We eat in mourning, except for Mother's laughter.

(The Woman in Gown gets louder as she increases the intensity of her claps and rocking. There is a slow build throughout the following.)

When the cedar bowls are empty, with no trace of flesh or soup or spit, the table is cleared and the cloth is cleaned with water bile.

(The Woman in Slip and Shawl gives herself over to the humming and clapping, then resists, pulling back.)

Retiring to the chair facing the window that looks out over the hill, Father drinks and grumbles and curses. He walks toward the kitchen as Mother places the clean white sheet carefully over the dining room table. Mother is naked—has discarded the suit and shoes.

(The Woman in Slip and Shawl lets go, pours out. Intense build.)

She rends the tablecloth in two. Emma lays out the pattern for new garments. Instructs her hands to cut and rip. To sew and fold. Garments of white, ragged and free. Flowing cottons and head rags. Long skirts and ruffled blouse. Mother drapes herself in grandiloquent silence. Emma's hands pick through Mother's hair. Hair unbound. Hair singing and stomping in percussive wails. Chorus of braid and bush. Clapping.

(We hear the intense voice of his father over the noise.)

Father wants to get to the church where Brother sleeps. To—to say things to the corpse he never said to living flesh. To grieve and hurt and break and bend, without a flinch or winking eye. To dance and scream and blame himself without a sound or stir or failing gate. But his wife—his wife takes her time and wastes the hours. Changes her garments and laughs too much on the day of their son's internment! His wife has not asked him—she has *not* asked *him* about *his* grief! About *his* apathy toward this thing called life and death. She has not asked why he could not touch or look upon the thing that was once his son. The boy integral and elegant in all his manner. She has never inquired *once* why he must sometimes break his holy vow! The loss of control, the beating away of beauty when it is present all around him! *No!* She does not *care* about him, the living! She spends these hours with *no* concern for the economics of time! Stands in silly attire—and now the waiting and too much drink will surely challenge the steady calm he has worked *so hard* to maintain today. Father says:
  (Standing, fist raised, a roar bouncing off the walls) "WHAT THE FUCK YOU WEARIN'?"

(Pause. Reverb.)

"YOU DONE LOST YO' MIND?"

(Pause. Reverb.)

Mother says nothing. Hair singing and stomping. His tone familiar. Her feet, still and quiet. Father says, "People comin' from outta town, you gon' shame me? You gon' EMBARRASS ME by wearin' RAGS?"

(Pause. Reverb.)

Mother says nothing from tight lips. Does not make a sound— only percussive wails come from scalp and root. Nigger blues. Leroy Lasses White. Coon shouters singing from her tangled bush. Father says, "Get holdta yourself! *Comb* your hair! Turn *off* dis music, early in da morning! You tryin' to make me act a fool! I know what you up to! You gonna *tell* people it's my fault the boy left—huh? *My* fault he died young—huh? *My fault!*"

(Silence. Reverb.)

Mother says nothing. Tight lips loosen. Mother sings. Just sings and moves. Mother's hair is dancing. Her feet are bare. Ingredients for the post-funeral collation meal are placed on the table. Father curses and father yells, "*My* fault I lost my job! *My* fault we had to move back down here, in *your* aunt's house! My fault the boy never listened to me! Can only be *one man in a house!*"

(Silence. Reverb.)

I say nothing . . . I see nothing . . .

(A boy again:)

Aunt Emma's palms veil my mouth and eyes . . . Aunt Emma folds me into an unmade bed . . . my head resides on the pillowcase and I am fully dressed in black suit and black shoes and tie . . . on my back . . . like Brother . . . asleep . . . aware . . . deaf ears to slaps and crashing glass . . .

(He sits back, eyes closed.)

Brother dances for me from the dark of Aunt Emma's palms, integral, in all his elegance . . . and fragile ways.

(Sudden darkness. Light on faces.
DJ mix of boiling water, clanking pots and pans.)

WOMAN IN GOWN *(Husky whisper)*: For sores inflicted by someone who wants to take your power?

BLACK MALE AND WOMAN IN SLIP AND SHAWL:
    The lard of male hogs (one pound)
    Spignut (half a pound)
    The extract of dandelion (one ounce)
    The seed of lobelia (one ounce)
    Turpentine (one ounce)
    Beeswax (two ounces)

WOMAN IN GOWN: Make into a salve . . .

BLACK MALE AND WOMAN IN SLIP AND SHAWL: . . . and apply until the
pain subsides.

WOMAN IN GOWN: For bleeding at the nose?

(Uncomfortable beat for all.)

For bleeding at the nose?

BLACK MALE AND WOMAN IN SLIP AND SHAWL: Take birthroot, and cranes-
bill—pulverize and snuff into nostrils.

WOMAN IN GOWN: For hysterics?

BLACK MALE AND WOMAN IN SLIP AND SHAWL: Take a portion of mountain tea, white root and unkum root. Pound them and make into
pills with Canada balsam and yellow poplar. Take two with water.

WOMAN IN GOWN: For spitting blood?

WOMAN IN SLIP AND SHAWL: Two spoonfuls of nettles.

WOMAN IN GOWN: For dizziness?

BLACK MALE: Peel garlic—

WOMAN IN SLIP AND SHAWL: Dip it in honey . . .

BLACK MALE: Put into ear . . .

WOMAN IN SLIP AND SHAWL: With a little black wool.

WOMAN IN GOWN: For the trembling of hands?

BLACK MALE AND WOMAN IN SLIP AND SHAWL: Mugwort soaked in water.

BLACK MALE: Wash hands—

WOMAN IN SLIP AND SHAWL: While singing to Morgana King.

(Transition: soft morning light coming through stained glass.)

BLACK MALE *(Still a boy)*:
> one corpse
> one red velvet room
> one lithograph of Jesus and sheep
> seven mourners wailing
> one ancient woman on the organ
> one thousand songs

Mix and stir, and shake hands and heads. View the body, speak
well of the soul.

(Beat.)

White night. Milky glare. To the left of me, women in straw and
plastic fruit holding pocketbooks and clean white handkerchiefs.

This brownstone has been abandoned by the spirit of rhythm. Brick and damp wood exposed. Walls strong and flat, brass candle-holders and red velvet things draped over platforms and stands. To the right of me Mother is blackened and bruised and smiling. Father does not share the front row. He waits in the back, by the door—just in case the walls cave in. Men in shiny polyester shake strong hands and speak in loud whispers while the organ plays itself a dirge. Brother is the fairest of them all. Reminding me of a pigeon, dead just outside the door—where the hard white pavement meets the foundation of gray mortar. A gravesite for broken neck, and severed wing. Still, beautiful gray and beautiful white feathers are guided by evening gale forces, moving even though the twisted body is still. There is movement in stillness. Movement, still. Brother looks like that to me. All words come from folded hands across the chest. All holy songs come from his painted lips. Can anyone else see the body moving? Aunt Emma leans into me.

WOMAN IN GOWN: You speak. Gon' on.

BLACK MALE: I have nothing.

WOMAN IN GOWN: Gon' on. Make it right. Reach. Resurrect. Sew up the pieces. Make it right. Cup the fragments. Make 'em one thing.

BLACK MALE AND WOMAN IN GOWN: Whole.

(The Woman in Gown rocks and claps in four/four time, summoning spirits.)

BLACK MALE: Brother's face sings:

(Singing:)

Canaan, I'm on way, and I am well able to posses the land!

WOMAN IN GOWN: Gon' on!

BLACK MALE: It is finished. The word made flesh. The eulogy was performed by me, from my seat.

(The sound of the preacher's cadence comes through.)

Brownstone walls echo a jazz fusion. Classical violins are played by spirits like fiddles. Feet pounding into hardwood floor.

(The Woman in Slip and Shawl gets caught up in the ceremony.)

Ghosts march up and down the aisle chewing tobacco and dancing with their thighs and stomachs. The room is fragrant with cayenne and pork, and Mother's hands throw themselves up and out again, like they did in the days of birth pains. Legs move up and down. Shout precious memories into the carpet. She drapes herself over pew and casket while women in fruit and flower lay white sheets across her legs and fan her face. Quake and quiver and tremble of hand.

(Beat.)

The lid of the casket is closed. Father stands in the back, by the door, calling out: "Wife! Wife! You doing all right? Wife? . . . You . . . doing . . . all . . . ?"

(The Woman in Slip and Shawl, still caught up.)

Quake and quiver and tremble of hand.

(Lights change. The kitchen.)

> mackerel fish (cut open and cleaned)
> one tablespoon of olive oil (save for anointing every member
>   of household)
> medium leeks (seven)
> spit (three times)

> Let cool, then serve. Be cool, then serve. Warm hands in the steam. Rub together until you feel the friction. Until you feel the spirit. Until you feel the soul return to your body. Serve yourself first . . .

WOMAN IN SLIP AND SHAWL: Let the guests serve themselves.

BLACK MALE: I be waiting for people to come to the house after they leave the burial ground. Father removes his coat and sits quietly, his foot tapping to rhythm. Brother sleeps in a box underground. This house changes. Aunt Emma dances in blood-soaked smock. Mother holds her hands up in the air, feet stomping into hardwood floors, lips loose and rolling words—unintelligible. Intellectual language between her and the ghosts. The fish is waiting for invited mourners. She speaks in tongues. Father waits for the walls to cave in around us. Brother's body ascends. Carried off in the arms of Eddie Kendricks. Garments, new and flowing—garlic and olive oil and cayenne on our faces. We sit, living in a box, with one window— walls turning. Changed. There will always be music, and seasonings, and free-flowing garments. No shoes. From now on. Mother's steady rhythm and rapid dance dent parquet floors. The walls cave *out.* Open air. We sit, living in open air. Changed. Father drinks and smokes with trembling eyes to Otis Redding and waits for redemption. Mother holds onto a doorknob to sustain herself, and dances. Bopping head tilted toward rapid feet. There will always be music and free-flowing garments in this house. Open air. Aunt Emma bustles up a path toward Zuni dirt roads. A bird's secret dance through ancient mesa-top ruins, amid song and prayer and sacred recipe. Ending this offering. Native Negro woman with man's hands, bestowing blessings on us all, moving . . . up the hill . . . bloody linen skirts traversing to a six/eight pulse.

(Lights fade to black.

A projection reads: COMMON CONTEMPORARY PREOCCUPATIONS OF THE AFRICAN AMERICAN WITH AFRICA.

The Woman in Slip and Shawl proceeds to podium. The Woman in Gown exhibits cards. The Black Male makes maps across the outline of his body.)

WOMAN IN SLIP AND SHAWL: Common Contemporary Preoccupations of The African American with Africa:

1. The Ankh: An Egyptian symbol of life and prosperity.
2. The Pyramid: An Egyptian architectural structure.
3. The Dreadlock: A process of matting, coiling or twisting the hair into cylinder-like locked positions. Most effective with Negroid hair, but occasionally appropriated by other cultures and races. Most often this style of matting dead hair follicles with living hair follicles is fashioned with the assistance of numerous Negro hair products, also a pre-occupation of the Negro; most popular products being beeswax, African Hair Pride Pomade, Dax or any hair product containing shea butter.
4. The African Mask: Self-explanatory.
5. Mud Cloth or Kinte Cloth Textiles: Patterns thought to come from West Africa, printed onto woolen or cotton fabrics.
6. The Eye of Osirus: Also an Egyptian symbol of prosperity.
7. Africa: The continent.
8. African heritage, origin and a return thereof.

WOMAN IN GOWN *(Proceeds to the podium, reads from an index card)*: According to *Blacked Out Through Whitewash* by Suzar Epps, 1999:

Based on the evidence of recent findings, modern white science has officially declared that *all* of present humanity came from one race . . . the black race—the oldest race. Scientists have unearthed the ancient bones of a black African pygmy woman who is indisputably the mother of humanity . . . a woman who lived twenty thousand years ago and left resilient genes that are carried by all of mankind. This overwhelming evidence shows that Africa was the cradle of modern humans. The story the molecular biology seems to be telling is that modern humans evolved in Africa two hundred thousand years ago . . . therefore white skin is a form of albinism.

Frances Cress Welsing, author of *The Isis Papers*, argues that the albino Caucasian "came into being from blacks, born of coal-black parents. This albino gorilla named 'Snowflake' has platinum blond hair, white or pink skin and blue eyes." Similarly, according to Suzar, "Other scholars theorize that Africans who migrated to Europe and were caught in the Ice Age gradually lightened until their genes mutated to adapt to the scant sunlight, thus producing a race of whites."

(Lights change. Dirt roads of Ghana, West Africa. The women vanish behind a scrim. The Black Male proceeds to the podium.)

BLACK MALE *(As himself)*:
>Jesus
>Is changing winding sheets
>In New York
>A final kiss on
>Unleavened head
>The flesh embarrasses.

One. The sun: a puissant flame circumnavigating; the sky: magenta acquiescence surrounding; the ground: terracotta watercolor omnipresence; Kwabina: cool, cobalt skins pulling through azure shadows and smiling, holding my hand up hills and over ditches, over the cool calm of the ocean waves and sugar waters, little girls with licorice hands yelling *sankara* from the side of the road, load of fresh fruit balanced on top of their heads. The dead are calling from Suruwi waters where daughters dance to the drum. Kwabina and me, we hitchhike to Ashieman, in the car of men and red leopard upholstery moving too fast down dirt roads. Kwabina's girlfriend lives in the marketplace of Ashieman, near a kerosene lamp, in tin-and-cardboard condominiums, spilled oil and roosters screaming. We weave, he and me, through alleyways and over sewer ditches to find her. Florence: sorrel-blush dappled with citrine hues. I think she is asking him for money, and he is asking her for touches. Ashieman is an old woman in vapid dress and platitudinous mask. Ashieman is perfumed in goat meat and hickory and yellow yams tonight. Florence is happy for two-hundred cedis and the touch of cobalt pulling through azure blue shadows. Ashieman is asking why I come to this earth with glamorous ideologies and mystic expectations. He and me, we move too fast down upward hills. In Legon, I trade poems with A-level students, and Kwabina is happy to receive a music box from a Milwaukee woman who once played Desdemona to his Noble Savage. She has sent him a couple of dollars and a photograph of herself. She is plain, I think. She is old, in drab jeans and shirt, and wide, flat ass and damaged hair. Damaged skin stretched stretched across sticks of bone to dry. She has sent him a letter reminding him of her visit last year, her first time on this terracotta earth, her first time having this earth in her, and she has sent him an application to Milwaukee Technical College, and money, and pictures of her hueless face smiling in front of a daisy yellow porch. She has enclosed an opaline-mirrored jewelry box from Woolworth's or Pathmark or someone's garbage can, and it is ugly, very ugly, like her, and I am angry for the memory she holds of red clay soil, cobalt and azure between her pointed knees. Ugly angry. Kwabina tells me he'll fill out the application to Milwaukee Technical College and send it to her, not this year, maybe next year, not now, maybe then. And he'll bring drums with him to Milwaukee, from Kumasi's wood-carving village, and he will sell them for at least one hundred Milwaukee dollars each, and he will be rich, he says, because there are no drums from Africa in America anywhere, and it means nothing that his father's blood covers the floor in Kumasi, and it means nothing that Kwabina cannot read and he cannot write and he has no mother except for the apathetic hands of Ashieman and cast-iron fingers scraping Elmina's ocean floor. He will move to Milwaukee, not this year, maybe next year, not now, maybe then, and he will bring drums with him to Milwaukee, drums from Kumasi's wood-carving village, and he'll sell them for a lot of money, because there are no drums from Africa in America, and he will be very rich and very famous, for bringing these drums, and then he will retire in Freetown and become a chief and I will, if I want to, also become a chief, in a neighboring village, and we will be Christian, and we will always race down upward hills holding hands, and by then Florence will be out of his mind, because she only wants money. There are no drums from Africa in America. Anywhere. He will forget about Florence: citrine-dappled blush . . . she only wants money. There are no drums in America from Africa anywhere. None. No drums. There will be three children, one boy, two girls, not now, maybe then, and when men come to his home to ask to marry his daughters, they will offer gifts and good wine . . .

Ashieman walks slowly away from me, spitting up blood carrying seven suckling corpses from her tit, and I am ugly angry very ugly, and I am: a thick asphalt gray; and he is: looming blues washing up poppy orange, and there is: no sky right now, and no drums . . . from Africa . . . in America . . . anywhere . . .

(Stands beside Muse-Ishan, linked arm in arm.)

Two. He and me, we play tricks on white faces in Nkrumah circle. We hold hands and walk up to white faces and I speak gibberish and Kwabina tries to interpret and the white faces are confused and upset because they can only understand French, German, the King's English, and they are white faces turning red, opaline masks bleeding, and I speak gibberish and Kwabina tries to interpret, his hand in mine, and they demand French, German, The King's English, and syllables strung haphazardly roll from my tongue, tongues as ancient as Hittite dances, rapid and loud, and clear, like storefront basement sonatas, eclectic dialect, ecclesiastical phraseology, anti-ecumenical phonetics, talk, talk, talk, loud, to shouting opaline masks, and they scream, speak French, German, the King's English, and I break, I break inside, break my jumbled dialect, break up my fallowed ground, disrupt my holy tongues, and I scream back, Ga Twi Fanti Ga Twi Fanti Ga Twi Fanti . . . their language, not your language, not my language?, their land, not your land, once my land . . . not my land . . . not my . . . land.

(The women, visible behind the scrim, have become silhouettes of nude bodies walking through trees. Endless walking. Girlish laughter and whispers amplified over drums. The Black Male speaks with trembling recollection:)

Three. Her carrion, damp, shiny, bulbous-black, dusky dirt, painted earth of eyes and dead of night, hill of iridescence, lips and lid of colors, dun, dark, darken. Impervious face of mirrored earth, thick, black as coal, kohl black, wash of pink and red and baby blue pale across the terrain of obscurity. Smooth face, inviting earth, quake and quiver of cheek and sucking lips, eclipse of lash and rising brow. White hands marauding her dusky earth, nipples wedged between fingers, white faint fingers touching crevice of land, wet, black as coal, kohl-black inviting earth. Milwaukee-white hands, King's English hands, milky-white fingers, fingers pallid, cold, bleached hands traveling, frost moving across sable penumbra, sooty dark, resplendent earth. She leans in with knees crossed and toes crammed in heels. Fake ore of gold, foreign and fashioned into something of nothing, lynched and hanging from her lobes. Imitation stone of paste catching no light, dead, buried above the ground of her hands, no light, dead on third finger. German Rastafari leans in, touches ass and sips gin from her bottom lip. Blond roots meshed into sickly turds of apple green. Tresses falling over shoulder, caught in bulbous constellation. Red, black, green thread entwined and roped around his waist, pale, sickly blue eyes and blond lashes, marauding her neck and thighs and shiny ass, then leaving change, consuming last of beer, and taking hand— and taking her, away from Nkrumah circle, through crowd of vendors and kerosene light, from the sound of yelling voices and open call, up the road, on foot, foot on terracotta soil, to tiny field, not far away, out of the circle, just left of here, on foot, foot on earth, earth in his hands, and finger in then lay it down, and pull it up, and bend it down, and rend the veil, the veil twain, pallid stake pushed into dusky earth, and steady motion and rock-and-roll, and Motherland is on her knees, frosty fingers in, fake gold swinging off, corpses dangling from ancient ears, and nothing like this, dark and wet and smelly too, on Mien Stein Strasse, or cobbled hill. Blond snakes fall over face and now stand up, saliva mouth, and scrotum breath, now on two feet, feet on the ground, terracotta soil, and open hand receives the bills and folds them into a shoe, and she smoothes back her plastered locks, fried and sheened, and spits out the taste of pubic hair, then returns to the circle, where we wait . . . we wait our turn, to reclaim this land.

Four. He and me we share the fish and share the beer and Motherland, who sells herself and the fruit thereof, and I am holding a breast in my mouth and fingering the ass and he is inside her and we are sweating. Azure shadows. Crimson lipstick spread across a blaze mouth. Calloused hands kneading big thighs fragrant with come and spit. He and me we share the motion and rhythm and money for her willingness and she is impatient with the stabbing and the spanking and the biting, and she does not dance to our percussion. We have not paid enough for two. To come a second time and I am on my back feeling yearnings and she is on my stomach feeling nothing, and Kwabina is behind her feeling impervious, and the moon is a voyeur masturbating beneath a sheath of sky, and he and me, we share perversions. Fried hair. Cherry-fire broken nails digging into terracotta earth, and I say, I want, I want the, I want the, give me the, my turn, to have, the, yes, I want, I say, I want it now, speak it now, I want—French, German, the King's English! I have not come yet and I demand, give me my turn, to have the, I want it now, I have come to be baptized, I have not come, and I have come to be baptized, and she says, pay first, and lights a cigarette and says, pay again first, and Kwabina grabs a fistful of grass to wipe himself off. Her dress hiked up still, fried hair escaping from behind her ears and neck, the blues jazz whistle of early day and the hum of sleepy-eyed skies, land where my fathers must have died, over a bed of nails. Here. And I am not enough inside. I want to push in and be and call it a place and make my bed and stay but she has no place inside herself for me, has not made room for me or him, or the white mask threaded with blond locks, or any of us, who want a home inside herself. She laughs at my teary eye and heaving breast and erection spilling from zippered pants, and she has not made a place inside herself for me or him, or any of us.

He and me we share the cigarette and the hands and she finds another face in Nkrumah circle and he and me we share our hands and the hills and the sky and moon, and Ashiemen is an old woman over us in vapid attire, laughing at the sun: a flame circumnavigating through a magenta sky. The ground: terracotta soil omnipresent. Kwabina: cool cobalt skins through azure shadows. I am a thick asphalt gray. There are no drums from Africa in America anywhere. No drums . . . Not anywhere.

(The show lights come back up as at the beginning. Voice-over of a DJ mix of questions. The Woman in Slip and Shawl takes her camera and snaps photos of the Black Male. The Woman in Gown plays the piano and sings her aria.

A projection reads: HELL NO WON'T BE NO BLACK MALE SHOW TODAY (DUE TO TECHNICAL DIFFICULTIES).

The Black Male looks out over the audience. He backs away.)

(To himself) Huckabuckin' . . . The ghosts are huckabuckin' 'round your bed at night, masturbating you empty, demanding rent and laughter and food-stamp tithes . . . each morning no mercy, each noonday no cool to calm your village fear . . . you be marginalized

on Fulton Street, vomiting upwind into the face of your Latino buddies who welcome you back from your European tour with beer and blow . . . you all be composing broken bilingual dramatic and lyric verse 'bout Bakongo slaves singing ancient freedom and resistance songs from the silver mines of Zacatecas and the sugar plantations of Veracruz building themselves a new land—cuz you and your Latino buddies know we the same nigger . . .

(A chant, back against the wall:)

> We
> Speaking one same nigger
> Language in the
> Same nigger
> Neighborhood.
>
> We the
> Same descendants
> Of the same souls
> From across the water
> Brought back
> Together
> In urban nigger realities
> And the niggers
> Who don't know we
> All the same nigger
> Are the niggers
> Who can't speak nigger
> Bilingually
> And that's a damn shame cuz if all of us
> Who the same nigger
> Spoke the same nigger language
> We wouldn't have to be the nigger
> Somebody made us
> We could be our own nigger
> A new nigger
> Who's one nigger
> Living the same nigger urban reality
> And then and only then
> Can niggers who think they ain't
> Niggers at all and don't want nuthin' at all to do
> With nigger music
> Nigger poetry or niggers period

Well until they learn bilingual nigger
They can't even have
Conversations with niggers
About no longer being niggers or
Perpetuating that word
Nigger . . .

(Frantic writing on the blackboard:)

WARNING: Li'l Kim iz not at home waiting for you in thong and lipgloss with Foxy Brown, who is also not at home waiting for you— They do not call you to discuss their reinvented ideas of black blue-collar contemporary feminism in popular culture and its influence on Versace and Prada.
WARNING: The slam judges don't know the difference 'tween a sestina and a simile.
WARNING: This may be hazardous to your health.
WARNING: Broadway is only interested in you posthumously.
WARNING: Publishers aren't buying books about nuthin' but your tragedy.
WARNING: The record companies want to buy you and your publishing rights with free Hilfiger gear (for the poem your father died for), want to mix it to machine-drum samples that drown out the verse—want uninformed theory about revolution. Want to edit all terse language that may offend the money people. They want to dress you in spandex, put a glock and a blunt in your hand and stand you under a Phillip Morris sign onstage at a bar mitzvah bash. They want your *black* ass, not your *black* art . . .

(To himself again:)

And you be dreaming of dying naked in Andy Warhol's arms . . . *huckabuckin'*. The ghosts *are* huckabuckin' 'round. Huckabuckin'. The ghosts are huckabuckin' 'round your bed at night.

(A final prayer in final fetal position:)

Eli, Eli, lama sabachthani?

No show. Not today. No show.

(Lights fade to black.)

END OF SHOW

Carl Hancock Rux is a former resident artist of Mabou Mines and the Ebenezor Experimental Theater festival in Lulea, Sweden. He is the recipient of the 2002 NYFA Prize, the 2002 NYFA Gregory Millard Playwright in Residence fellowship, an NEA/TCG Theatre Residency Program for Playwrights fellowship, the Bessie Schomburg award and CalArts' 2003 Herb Alpert Award. Rux's poetry, plays, fiction and essays have been published in numerous anthologies, and he is the author of the *Village Voice* Literary Prize–winning collection of poetry, *Pagan Operetta* (Autonomedia Press), the novel *Asphalt* (Simon & Schuster/Washington Square Press), and the OBIE Award–winning play, *Talk* (TCG Books). His plays and performance pieces include *Song of Sad Young Men, Chapter and Verse, Geneva Cottrell, Waiting for the Dog to Die, Singing in the Womb of Angels, Smoke, Lilies and Jade* and *Mycenaean*, among others. He wrote the book and libretto for the operas *Makandal* and *The Blackamoor Angel*. Rux has also written and performed his poetry for several dance companies, including the Alvin Ailey American Dance Theater, Jane Comfort and Company, Urban Bush Women and Bill T. Jones/Arnie Zane Dance Co. He is the Head of the MFA Writing for Performance Program at the California Institute for the Arts. He lives in Los Angeles and Brooklyn.

cautionary tales

free jujube brown!

by psalmayene 24

author's statement

Free Jujube Brown! was written during a creative fury that lasted about two weeks. It was early 2002 and I would go into the bedroom of my Columbia Heights apartment in Washington, D.C., close the door and wait . . . I would wait to be inhabited by the characters/spirits/people that would eventually end up saying their pieces in my play. I would usually end up on my feet, walking and talking in character, and then go to pen and paper to record what was being uttered. My wife didn't know what I was doing. It was indeed an exciting exercise of trust and faith as I did my best to allow the play to unfold on its own while I interfered as little as possible. What materialized was a "collage" of characters, each with his own story and version of the truth, with the character of Jujube Brown as the unifying through line. I have intentionally not connected all the dots in the play. The dots exist, but I leave it up to each audience member's faculty of perception to shape how s/he experiences the play. Aesthetically, I wanted to challenge myself to use hip-hop-based movement in universally accessible ways that supported the story. To that end, I focused on making the transitions between monologues seamless, with the emphasis on continuity. Looking back at the play now, I consider some of the topics that emerged: the gauntlet of police brutality that too many in the African American community still have to run through, the current state of hip-hop culture, stereotypical images of African Americans, the complexities of "black" cultural identity and the intricacies of racism. My hope is that other people consider these things too, albeit through their own prisms. Peace.

production history

Free Jujube Brown! is a prequel or, in hip-hop terms, a "remix," of a two-person piece titled *The Hip-Hop Nightmares of Jujube Brown* that was produced by The African Continuum Theatre Company in Washington, D.C., written by Psalmayene 24 and Toni Blackman and directed by Jennifer Nelson, with music by DJ Munch. *Free Jujube Brown!* was written and choreographed by Psalmayene 24 and directed by Kamilah Forbes, with music by DJ Munch. It received its world premiere at the NYC Hip-Hop Theater Festival in June 2002 and was subsequently produced at D.C.'s Hip-Hop Theater Festival, the Bowery Poetry Club, the Nuyorican Poets Cafe, Diaspora Flow at Pillsbury House Theatre, the French Embassy, the National Black Theatre Festival, Elegba Folklore Society, The Kennedy Center, Kalamazoo College, Virginia Commonwealth University, Sol & Soul at Warehouse Next Door, the 2004 Cincinnati Black Theatre Festival, The Metropolitan Ebony Theatre Company, Bay Area Hip-Hop Theater Festival, West Virginia University, The African Continuum Theatre Company and, most recently, with Musefire Productions at the District of Columbia Arts Center in March 2007.

notes

A "pop" is an isolated/flexed movement that often belongs to a larger movement idea. The "bogle" is a Jamaican social dance that was popular in the early 1990s.

Certain celebrity names and/or social references may be replaced with ones more relevant to the current time.

Prop pieces include (any other objects referred to are mimed):

One cube (approximately 16" X 16" X 16")
One off-white sheet (approximately 48" X 63")
One pair of "blind-man" sunglasses
One *Free Jujube Brown!* CD by DJ Munch

this is not the story

The stage is bare except for a cube in the center of the playing area. A sheet is on the floor to the right of the cube. Music comes in, a short, soulful hip-hop/blues lamentation. Our performer, the Dreamer, enters from stage right. The Dreamer walks over to the sheet, picks it up and drapes it over his body, then prays silently. The Dreamer then turns, his back to the audience, tightens the sheet around his body and goes to sleep—still standing. The music fades out. A spare electronic beat that gradually grows in intensity and fervor begins. Moving as if in a nightmare, the Dreamer turns to face the audience, pops out of the sheet and thrusts it to floor. He looks around suspiciously and takes a few steps downstage into a bathroom. He examines his eyes in a mirror, feels his facial hair, turns on the cold water and grabs his toothbrush. With his free hand he grabs the toothpaste and twists the cap off with his teeth, spits it out, squeezes some toothpaste onto the toothbrush and puts the tube back on the sink. He pops brushing his teeth. He rinses off the toothbrush, puts it back, rinses out his mouth and splashes water on his face. He turns off the water. He grabs a tie from the left of the sink, assesses it, pops tying it. He grabs a suit jacket from the right of the sink and pops putting it on. The Dreamer then pops reaching down to grab a briefcase from the floor to the left of the sink. He looks in the mirror one last time, walks left until directly downstage of the cube. He's on a subway platform, looks into the distance for the subway train. The train arrives and the Dreamer steps into the subway car. He grabs an over-head handle, showing the movement of the train through the bouncing and swaying of his body. The Dreamer acknowledges a passenger to the left, then one to the right, then indiscreetly sniffs his armpit while grabbing the handle. (His reaction says, "Damn, forgot to put on deodorant.")

At this point the first recorded Voice-over comes in:

VOICE-OVER 1: This is not the story of a gun totin', blunt smokin', rhyme spittin' wannabe rapper.

(The Dreamer turns upstage and takes a seat on the train [the cube]. He puts the briefcase down, takes out a book from the pocket of his suit jacket, leafs through the book to the middle and begins to read. He yawns.

Voice-over 2 and 3 come in:)

VOICE-OVER 2 AND 3: This is not the story of bitches an' hos, niggas and pimps, players and hustlers, or ballers and shot-callers.

Nor is this the story of rednecks and crackers, spics and chinks, fags and dykes, or Jews and gentiles.

(During this voice-over, the Dreamer's head drops in sleep. The Dreamer then rolls to the left side of the cube, goes to the floor, backspins, then jumps up into Kid 'n' Play/Charleston-type movement with mock-Sambo appeal. Voice-over 4 comes in:)

VOICE-OVER 4: This is not the story of coonin', samboin', Uncle Tomin', Mammy playin', shuckin' an' jivin', or watermelon-rind chewin'.

(The Dreamer freezes into a Black-Power, right-fist-in-the-air picture. Voice-over 5 comes in:)

VOICE-OVER 5: And this is not the story where the black sidekick saves his white buddy's life and his buddy gets all the women.

(During the voice-over, the Dreamer ballroom dances around the cube, spins his partner, and waits a few moments for his partner to spin back into his arms.
Voice-over 6 comes in:)

VOICE-OVER 6: This is not an interracial love story.

(The Dreamer goes straight into a pose that looks like a hanging [his right hand holding the noose]. He holds this pose for a few beats. Then he picks up the sheet, wraps it around his body like a headdress and veil, and moves across the stage.
During this Voice-over 7 comes in:)

VOICE-OVER 7: This is not the story of black women degrading, disrespecting and complaining about the shortcomings of black men.

(The Dreamer stops downstage and transforms the sheet into a baby cradled in arms.
Voice-over 8 comes in:)

VOICE-OVER 8: This is not the story of a black man who is scared of work, scared of love, scared to be a man and scared of The Man.

(The Dreamer then drapes the sheet over his head and body to represent a wedding dress. He moves across the stage.
Voice-over 9 comes in:)

VOICE-OVER 9: This is not the story of a black, seventeen-year-old, pregnant, welfare muva with five babies' fathas.

(The Dreamer then turns upstage, takes a few steps, stops, and does a bridal bouquet toss into the audience.
Voice-over 10 comes in:)

VOICE-OVER 10: This is not the story of any one of those babies' fathas.

(The Dreamer then immediately puts the sheet over the cube and proceeds to caper back and forth across the stage, mock-rapper style [flailing his arms, grabbing his crotch, and the like].
Voice-over 11 comes in:)

VOICE-OVER 11: And this is definitely not the story of a white rapper, who grew up in the 'hood, and goes platinum.

(Voice-over 12 comes in:)

VOICE-OVER 12: This is the story . . .

(The Dreamer speaks the rest:)

THE DREAMER:
>Of a person who happens to be young, gifted and African American
>This is the story of his journey through life
>This is the story of his imagination
>This is the story of his hopes and dreams
>This is the story of his fears
>This is the story of all that he has chosen to be in this very moment
>All that he has chosen to be in this very moment
>This very moment . . .

(This last line is repeated as the Dreamer does a frenzied popping movement that transforms him into a young Jujube at play, making a siren sound while reenacting a car chase.)

garbageman

We see a young Jujube playing cops and robbers.

JUJUBE: Hey, Tat-Tat, come here.

Whatchu want Officer Johnson?

Tat-Tat, didn't I tell you whenever you talk to me to take your hands out your pockets?

But I ain't do nothin', Officer Johnson.

Shut up, shut up, boy. Oh, what's this you got here: a gun and some crack. You goin' under the jail now, boy— Officers get him!

Hey, whatch'all beatin' me for? Whatch'all kickin' me for?

Disorderly conduct!

Now here come Mama: "Juju, get your butt in the house. You know they put little black boys in jail for bein' nosey. How many times do I have to tell you that? You know a hard head makes a soft behind. Now get ya butt in the house right NOW!"

Shoot, you ain't have to beat me, that's child abuse. I'ma call the cops on you.

(Jujube turns on a TV and video game and begins to play.)

It don't even matter because I ain't goin' to no jail. I ain't goin' to jail 'cause when I grow up I'm gonna— *(To video game)* "Die! Die! Die!" *(Back to self)* Shoot, when I grow up I ain't goin' to no jail 'cause I'm gonna be a garbageman. I wanna be a garbageman because garbagemen are big and strong and they smile more than anybody I know. Garbagemen be havin' fun, they be whistlin' at the pretty ladies and stuff sayin', "Hey baby how you doin'?" *(As a woman responding)* "All right, Mr. Garbageman."

Plus, garbagemen are important because if they don't come pick up the trash, your house would stink. They more important than the people you see on TV, 'cause the people you see on TV, you go up to the TV and go "click," *(Turns off TV)* they go away. But if you go up to the garbageman and go "click," he'd probably beat you upside the head and say, "Boy, whatchu doin' that for?!" But the garbagemen aroun' my way are friendly and congenial—I learned that word yesterday—and they laugh and joke while they pick up the trash. Ooo, I wanna do that when I get older. Me and my friends Ray-Ray and Lakesha, we would have fun doin' that! Wait a minute. I never seen a girl garbageman before. I wonder if girls could be garbagemen? Lakesha proly could. She could be the first girl garbageman. And she could drive the truck and I could ride on the back. *(Stands on the cube)* "Come on Lakesha, drive the truck! Stop the truck! We gotta pick up the trash. *(Jumps off cube)* Fill the truck. Fill the truck!" And after we do that, we'd be free for the rest of the day 'cause everybody know that after garbagemen pick up the trash in the morning, that's it, they done. I don't know what garbagemen do after they pick up the trash. I know they gotta empty the trucks out. Shoot, they proly take they sons fishin' or go play pool. Or maybe . . . maybe they go to an island. Yeah, they fly out to some island where only garbagemen get to go: "Garbageman Island"!

(A succession of magical "eureka" bells are played as young Jujube stands on top of the cube.)

And they have lions there, happy ones, not like the ones at the zoo. And big, gigantic video games. And no belts—so nobody could get an ass-whupin'. And all the Now 'n' Laters you could eat. The Now 'n' Laters grow on trees. And no garbage. Whatever would be garbage just disappears into thin air. And they go to this island every day after work and then they fly *(Jumps off the cube)* back early in the morning just in time to pick up the trash. And that's why garbagemen be lookin' so happy when they work 'cause they just got back from Garbageman Island. Yeah, and that's why I ain't never goin' to no stupid, stinky, ugly jail when I grow up, 'cause I'm gonna be a garbageman. But if I'm not gonna be a garbageman then I'll settle for being a writer.

(Jujube goes to the cube and sits, grabs a notebook and pencil and begins to write.)

I like to write. My favorite writers are Amiri Baraka, Langston Hughes and Pablo Neruda.

(He stands up in front of the cube and recites:)

> Freedom is just frosting on somebody else's cake and so must be till we learn how to bake.

(He sits back down on the cube.)

That's Langston. I like him 'cause he write like he talkin' straight to me.

(He goes back to writing, stops, looks at what has just been written.)

Mama say that sometimes the stuff I write is too grown to be comin' out my head. But it's not, 'cause it's what I feel.

(Jujube gets up and lays down downstage right of the cube, continues to write for a couple beats, then stops writing.)

And sometimes I write what my imaginary friends tell me to write. They're all around here. They talk inside my brain. And they talk a lot so I have to write a lot. One of 'em told me what to write yesterday, but I still haven't figured it out.

(Jujube goes back to writing in his book and we hear a recording of the sound of writing. Jujube's writing movement becomes bigger and bigger until his whole body is "writing." With this movement young Jujube, who is transforming into Revolutionary, makes his way around the upstage side of the cube while getting sunglasses out of his pocket. He starts miming a blind person walking with a cane. He goes downstage right, folds up his cane and puts it into his pocket.)

whatever it takes

REVOLUTIONARY: Brothers and Sisters, I have organized this meeting here tonight at *(Says name of venue)* to build a support base for our brother Jujube Brown who has supposedly shot and killed a police officer. Now, I'm not going to get into a debate about whether or not I think Mr. Brown is innocent or guilty because that is not what we are here for. And furthermore, to cut to the chase, anyone who thinks that brother Brown is guilty can ever so discreetly excuse themselves right now. So that those who believe in Freedom can continue to chisel our way through the Stonehenge of Oppression and make our way to the Great Pyramid of Liberation. Nobody's gonna stare at you, or call you names, or Molotov Cocktail your home. You can leave right now. Anyone? No one? Well then, my people, it gives me a great sense of pride to have all of you here tonight. And I sincerely hope that each and every individual here over-stands the kind of focus that it's gonna take to free one of our most popular political prisoners here in AmeriK-K-K, Jujube Brown, who, as a young boy, used to go to my father's church with his mother every Sunday. Now the question is: what must we do?

And the answer tonight is, as it was last night, as it will be tomorrow night, and every night forevermore—the answer is: whatever it takes. Whatever it takes, brothers and sisters. If it means marching, well then we must march. And I'm not just talking about down these main avenues and boulevards, but through these side streets and in the residential neighborhoods of suburbia as well. If it means sitting in, we must sit in. At the courthouse, universities, outside of these concerts and sporting events—wherever. If it means logging on to our website, www.freejujubebrown.com, and building and dialoguing with others of a like mind, then we must do that. We also have T-shirts and posters and mugs available for sale on the site, which I encourage you to buy. We also take donations—hint, hint. I, myself, have been working 'round the clock, reaching out to all sorts of high-profile individuals in all arenas for their camaraderie. People like the Reverend Al Sharpton, the Reverend Jessie Jackson, Bill Clinton, Michael Jordan, a few of these one-name wonders like Oprah and Bono, Tiger and Puffy, and a host of others. *(A cell phone rings)* Now y'all know you ain't supposed to have your cell phones on in here. Come on people, turn off your phones. Whose is it? Oh, it's mine. Excuse me. *(Answers cell phone on hip)* Free Jujube Brown! Hey, Puffy, what's goin' on?! I mean "P. Diddy," my bad, my bad. Congratulations on being in *A Raisin in the Sun* on Broadway—Sidney Poitier, watch out. Yeah, that's right, me plus two for that guest list tonight. Pass the Courvoisier. Look, lemme call you back. *(Puts cell phone away)* We have a major benefit concert planned for the end of next month. I'm in the process of writing a book. Spike Lee has approached us about collaborating on a movie. Believe it or not, even a toy manufacturer has approached us about making a Jujube Brown doll. Now that may be taking it a bit too far, but if it has to come to producing an action figure in order to get the type of attention and support that this brother needs, well then so be it. Whatever it takes. And if it means that you keep your eyes on the lookout for our clothing line, Free Jujube Clothes, coming out next spring, and our new debit card, and our new Free Jujube Brown! ring tone—well, then you can do that too. So I want everybody here to join voices, and repeat after me—and use sound power so that we can chant down the walls of Babylon: "Let Freedom Ring!" *(Audience repeats the phrase)* "So We Can All Bling-Bling!" *(Audience repeats)* Come on y'all, "Let Freedom Ring!" *(Audience repeats)* "So We Can All Bling-Bling!" *(Audience repeats)* Last time, "Let Freedom Ring!" *(Audience repeats)* "So We Can All Bling-Bling!!!" *(Audience repeats)*

(The writing sound is played again as Revolutionary does a quick melting transition into Mr. Pollack, while taking off his sunglasses and putting them back in his pocket.)

peace and quiet

Mr. Pollack, elderly, goes to the front door of his cleaners to investigate a commotion and opens the door.

MR. POLLACK: What in Christ name is goin' on out here? Oh, it's a march. A march, huh? Huh? *(To one of the marchers)* No, I can't join your march, I got a business to run. But if any a ya need ya clothes laundered, I'm the best cleaners in town, the oldest one too. Huh? Yeah, I know who Jujube Brown is. He usta come to my cleaners. Oh, I see now. Ya marchin' fa Jujube Brown. OK. All right. Look, I would love to stay out here and revolutionize witcha, but I think I'm gonna close up shop for a little while, take an early break, take my medicine. But good luck witcha marchin'. Power to the people. Free Kobe Bryant! He's not locked up? She dropt the case? And Nike gave him back his endorsement deal too? He'll rape somebody else, thank you, good-bye.

(Mr. Pollack proceeds to hastily shut and lock his door. He pulls down the door blind and peers cautiously from its side. He speaks directly to audience:)

I'm not gonna take any chances. You know they rioted after they killed King. Sure. Burned down and looted their own businesses. God only knows what they'll do to mine. Damn shame what that kid done did. Nobody really knows what the exact circumstances were, but one thing we know for sure—a police officer is dead. He was such a good boy. Every Saturday, reliable as the sun risin', he'd come in here to pick up him an' his mother's clothes for church. He'd say, "Hi," take a mint or a butterscotch candy from off the countertop—the customers love those—he'd gimme his ticket, I'd get the clothes, and it was, "Thank you, Mr. Pollack, have a good day. See ya next time." I never had any problems from him, notta one. But to tell you the truth, I don't entirely fault him.

(He takes papers and marijuana out of his pockets and begins to roll a joint.)

Oh no. Kids have a lotta influences these days: TV, the streets, their peers. But by far the biggest one is that music that they listen to, that hip-hop stuff. Yeah, I blame hip-hop. *(Lights up the joint, takes a hit, coughs)* Oh, this is for my glaucoma. I was talkin' to one a my customers about my eyesight and he pulled me to the side and he said, "Hey, I've got some stuff that could help you wit' that." So, I tried some a the stuff, for the first time in my life thank you very much, and whadoyouknow, he was right. But yeah, that hip-hop's a doozie. Like ya got that one rapper guy. The guy wit' tha loud voice? The guy who curses a lot. You know the guy I'm talkin' about. C'mon, c'mon, c'mon, c'mon. Lemonade! Lemonade, wit' the cop-killer song—no, no, it's Ice-T, that's his name. I knew it was a beverage. Ice-T, Ice Cube, Ice Tray—who can keep up wit' these guys. But anyway, he's tellin' kids to go out there and kill the first cop you see. So of course you're gonna have kids who listen to the crap enough times, they get brainwashed, it seeps into their sub-conscious mind, which really controls you, and they actually go out there and do it. Then you got this group of 'em, *(Puts out the joint in an ashtray on the counter behind him)* a gang. They call them-selves the N.W.A. Now the "N" stands for the N-word. I don't say that word. But it's Enns Wit' Attitudes. Why would you wanna call yourself that? That's no example for the little ones. Martin Luther King, Jr., my hero, fought against stuff like that. You didn't hear him sayin', "I want all the enns, and the mics, and the wops"—No! He didn't say that, he said, I want the blacks, the whites, the yel-lows, the reds, the browns, the purples, the blues, the greens, all colors, get your asses on a mountain top and sing, at the top of your liberal lungs, "We Shall Overcome." That's a beautiful song. That's somethin' that the kids nowadays could stand to listen to. But kids today are of a different breed. Especially the black ones. Not that I'm a racist or anything but I just call it like I see it. The black kids nowadays are like matches. Sure, they might look harm-less, but if you strike them enough times they will ignite, and one match can burn down a cleaners or a city block or a police precinct. They got a lotta rage pent up inside. So I just give 'em their space. Figga I'm not gonna be in the wreckage when they explode. Like the other day, one a my regular customers, Tomeka, black girl, mid-twenties, professional, pretty girl, comes in with her hair braided in two pigtails—one on each side of her head. She looked like a freakin' Indian. So I say, "Hey, Pocahantas, how ya doin'?" And she gets all pissed off and says, "You're the third white person to say that to me today and I don't appreciate it. Why is it that white people feel like they can just say whatever pops into

their mind without any regard for how other people may feel?!"
And I said, "Sweetie, sweetie, sweetie—no. Tomeka. Tomeka sweetie,
I apologize. From the bottom of my heart. I am sorry." And she
said, "Yeah, you are sorry—all a ya—just sorry." And I didn't say
nothing else to her after that. But I could feel myself gettin' real
hot. So hot my palms started to sweat, shortness of breath, my
head felt like it was gonna pop right off my shoulders. I get panic
attacks—and she was givin' me one. Here it was. I apologize to this
girl for something I said that was supposedly so wrong and does
she accept it? Does she say, "Thank you"? Does she say, "Oh—well
he must not have meant it in a cruel way. I know Mr. Pollack, he's
a good guy." No. She says, "You're all sorry." Right to my face like
that's not supposed to bother me. And I was very upset, very upset
because I try my damnedest to treat all people like they're equal.
I mean it's not like I walked up to her and said, "Hey, nigger!
Howya doin'?!" I never called her nigger once, I didn't say that!!
But God knows that's how I feel sometimes!!!

*(The gravity of what he just said hits him. He takes a few moments, and
then peers through the door again. He pulls up the blind, unlocks the
door, opens it and steps out.)*

Oh good. They're gone. Finally, some peace and quiet around here!
Yeah, you march down somebody else's block!! Free Jujube Brown!

*(Mr. Pollack slams the door shut and a composed medley that includes
layers of violin, electronic keyboard, piano, drum and snare beats begins.
At this point Mr. Pollack transforms into various musicians in a movement piece that uses popping, fluid movement and mime to bring to life
the different musical sounds being expressed in the music. We see a violin, a piano, a trap-drum kit, turntables, an MPC and a studio mixing
board, all being played or operated. This movement section ends with
the emergence of Hip-Hop: twisted mouth, gnarled hand and hunched
body, sitting on the cube.)*

hip-hop

HIP-HOP *(With a slight British accent)*: No applause, ay? Yes, it figures. You
all probably expected me to come out here rhyming, spinning on
my head, beatboxing, and cutting 'n' scratching at the same time.
That ain't even my style, kids. You all don't know who I am, do
you? It's me, Hip-Hop, here in the flesh. Here to tell you about a

beef that I have, a major grievance. I'm feeling oppressed, I am feeling exploited, and I am feeling used. There are many people out there who have this perception of me, a very limited, close-minded impression of who I am. "Hip-Hop, he's too violent." "Hip-Hop, he hates women." "Hip-Hop, he's so materialistic." In my defense—and I'm using the word defense because I feel as though I've been attacked and put on trial by many people, especially the mainstream media—in my defense I'd like to say that too many people, particularly these so-called artists, have done and said things in my name without ever coming to me for permission. Without ever asking me how I felt about this, that, and the third, without coming to me to get a sanction for activities that are produced and presented in my name. Some of the biggest culprits of this are lyricists who have taken my tongue and mouth and twisted, distorted and lacerated them to the point where they are unrecognizable, and to the point where the vast majority of the world thinks that I, Hip-Hop, am nothing but a bigmouth who blows hot, polluted air across continents and overseas. I am more than rhymed syllables. I am a full body, a total organism with blood, bones, ether, soul. And I am thoroughly disgusted by the slanderous misrepresentations of who I am. I am being used, without my consent, mind you, to sell soda pop, clothing, music, alcohol, video games, fast food, presidential campaigns—I have never voted. I did like what Reverend Al Sharpton had to say, back when he was running for president, but the perm disturbed me. The perm bothered me—I wasn't feeling the perm. But getting back to the point—you name it, I've been used to sell it. Please make them stop. They are killing me. I used to be young and vibrant, fresh. My father, Jazz, warned me about this. He said, "Son, I hope things will be better for you than they were for me." And my grandmother, Blues, died with a broken heart, dreading what she believed would be the disastrous fate of her grandson. And Grandmother's greatest fears have come to pass. And all these people who claim to love me. Who say they can't live without me, who are "keeping it real" and "representing." Lies. I don't remember the last time someone came to visit me, called me, wrote me a letter, sent me an email. And it hurts. It's a fucked-up situation. But even more painful than that is the fact that there are people out there who blame me for what happened to Jujube. Who say that I've been influencing him and all these other wayward youth. Filling their heads with the idea that it's OK to shoot and kill police and the concept of gangsta-as-hero and bling-bling. I never said that. Bling-bling, no, never bling-bling. I cannot control what knuckleheads do or say in my name. Don't blame me. Look at that man or that woman and evaluate them. Do you blame the gun or the shooter? And for the record, I did not kill Tupac, or Biggie, or Jam Master Jay. I take those accusations quite seriously. I am no one's scapegoat, but that is what people are trying to make me out to be. And my brother, Rock 'n' Roll, says, "Hey, you're paranoid. Have a drink. Cool out." Unbelievable. It seethes me because Rock has lost his mind. Forgotten his roots. Going through some sort of identity crisis right now. But it's all copasetic because when it's said and done I still have control over myself and I know it. I have ultimate agency over my power. And it may just be time for me to make my exit. To take a final bow, let the curtains close, and retreat to the grand DJ booth in the sky. To say, for the last time, "Somebody say, 'Ho!' Say, 'Ho, Ho!' Now, somebody, anybody, everybody scream!" And then disappear. My cousin, Disco, did it. Went off to an undisclosed location in South America. He's somewhere in the mountains. He's living a stress-free life. Lonely but peaceful. Well, I just have one request before I do go. *(Stands in front of the cube)* The next time you hear a song that turns your stomach, or see a video that dehumanizes women, or one of your senator's wives starts complaining about hip-hop dilapidating the minds of the children, you just remember me, *(Begins transformation into a healthy Hip-Hop)* here, now. *(As healthy Hip-Hop in the Dreamer's natural voice)* This is hip-hop. I am hip-hop. Believe it or not in this very moment we could all be considered hip-hop. And I love you. I love you all. *(Transforms back into wizened Hip-Hop)* And I still love you.

(The sound of writing as Hip-Hop goes stage left and grabs a liquor bottle from the floor. He stands, transforming into Tat-Tat.)

tat-tat

TAT-TAT *(In an inebriated state)*: Look, I'ma tell you straight up, the FBI approached me about hangin' wit' Jujube and keepin' close tabs on him from between the time he got outta jail up to his court date. They basically wanted me to get some dirt on him in exchange for two things. One: they would drop some possession charges they had on me. And two: they would give me three hundred and fifty dollars. Shit, I told 'em, "Hell yeah. I'll do it, me, me! Sign me up, sign me up!" I know Jujube ain't no criminal. It's not like he gon' be out there stealin' cars and knockin' over Chinese carry-outs and shit. I just can't go back to prison, man. It's not good for my self-esteem. And that money's gon' come in real handy. I'm gon' smoke it. But it's not like I'ma bad, cold-hearted person. I feel compassion. It wasn't a easy thing me doin' that to Jujube. After all, I known him ever since he was a little hardheaded kid who usta be up in his window cryin' 'cause he jus' got his ass whupt 'cause he was outside when he wasn't supposed to be. Hell, I remember the time, right after junior high school, when he got that writin' scholarship to go off to that fancy prep school in Pennsylvania. And oh Jujube didn't want to go, didn't want to leave the 'hood, but his mama made him go. And I sure nuff remember all them times he would try to preach to me, "Tat-Tat, they're places around here that can help you, places where you can go so that you don't have to sleep out here on the street." And I would have to tell him, "Look, young blood, don'tchu worry about Tat-Tat. Tat-Tat gon' be all right. Tat-Tat gon' handle his business. You just make sure you get your education and make your dreams come true. Don't waste your time worryin' 'bout the folks aroun' here. And if I ever catch your ass doin' drugs I will kill you." I tell all kids that. I tell my own kids that because when I was a child I never thought I would grow up and be like this. No child dreams of bein', "Oh well, what do you wanna be when you grow up?" "I wanna be an alcoholic crackhead!" No, kids don't say that. It's a series of bad decisions that get you there and when you ain't got nobody to tell you north from south or east from west you can get real lost. So you can just call me the compass of the community. Kids, if you're headed in my direction—about face, run the other way. But ultimately, it's on you. Shit, I let people know I'm out here cuz a choice, and I will not be out here forever. I'm gon' go back to my career. I didn't pop out my mama's coochie lookin' like this. I'm a actor. Stage, TV, film, done all that. Been to Hollywood and everything—you may have seen me in something. But I got tired of the roles I was being offered. Slaves, pimps, crack-heads. So I told myself, I said, "Self, you will not be accepting any more stereotypical roles." And this is where that shit got me. But I'm blessed beyond belief because my wife's house is right up the street from here and I can go there whenever I want to. But, lucky for Tat-Tat, Tat-Tat ain't got to go to wifey's house for everything, because Tat-Tat has acquired a degree that enables him to survive out here in these streets. I have a Ph.D. A professional Panhandlers Degree. That's right, I carry my black ass right downtown an' solic-it funds. I got my regular customers, the tourists, every now an' again somebody'll drop a twenty on me, a fifty . . . "Oh, reparations." I do quite all right for myself. And I'm very disciplined. Because I never panhandle . . . *(Magically sobering up)* when I'm high. It's bad for business. When they see you clean and in good spirits they tend to give ya more money. The better off I look the more folk wanna help me out. You'd think it'd be the other way aroun', but it's not. Yeah, it's crazy. Don't make no sense. *(Aggravated, needs a drink)* Pardonnez-moi, s'il vous plaît.

(Tat-Tat turns his back to the audience, drinks, becomes intoxicated once again, then turns back to face the audience.)

Merci beaucoup. Yeah, these drugs are a beast, man. Me and my wife usta get high together. In fact, I turned her on to the shit. Never forgave myself for that. Then she went to rehab and cleaned herself up. I'm real proud of her. The kids were stayin' wit' my mother for a while, now they're back home. And soon we will all be one big happy family. Like the Cosbys. Well like the TV show, not like Bill Cosby for real, well because Bill Cosby be trippin' sometimes man!! See, cuz this ain't me. For real for real, this ain't me. I'm beyond all this. Tell ya the truth, I'm not even here right now because I visualize myself in a better place. I'm on the brink. I see it. The family: we're in a big gorgeous house in the Hamptons. Rolls Royce is in the driveway. We are in the dining room eating dinner. A crystal chandelier is glistening above the mahogany table while Miles Davis's *Bitches Brew* is wafting through the lower level of the residence, and I'm cuttin' pork chops. *(To his fantasy family)* Kids, how was school today? Wonderful, wonderful. Dear, how was work? Another promotion?! *(Irritated)* Fantastic. Well, mine was peachy. I didn't smoke any crack today.

(The fantasy has dissolved.)

I wouldn't wish this on nobody. I mean, I would love to stop, and I'm gonna stop, but it got me by the neck, the neck and the throat. Stranglin' me like some invisible monster that just don't wanna let go. I'm sorry, Jujube. The FBI made me do it!!

(A melancholy, piano-infused jazz/hip-hop musical piece begins. It starts with a DJ scratch, and the words: "Another public service announcement from this (Scratch) D (Scratch) J." As the music begins, Tat-Tat takes a final swig from the liquor bottle and tosses it. He proceeds to dance in a hip-hop-flavored drunken/high state with spins and

floor moves. He then mimes digging a grave and jumping into it. He comes out of the grave as if being attacked by an invisible monster while moving to the upstage right of the cube where he freezes as Nyabingi. The music stops.)

black angel

NYABINGI *(To a reporter; a Jamaican accent)*: Now which newspaper you write fi again? E-he. Look 'ere—you mus mek sure you quote me correctly, mon, because if you don't me gon' bus you bumbo ras head! A wha' you mean you can't guarantee dat? I don't care who de guy is in your shitstem who edits tings, I wan' my talk word fi word. Ah-right, good. Now you can turn on ya lickle cassette recorder. Jah! Ras Tafari. Greetings from the Most High. I remember Jujube from when 'im was a lickle youth bwai dung in a Washington, D.C., an' 'im yuse fi come outside an' sidung wit' me an' wit' my bredren them, wit' the Rastas. Bwai usfi watch us play football inade street. Now, what we call football unyoo call soccer. But it mek more sense fi call it football . . . *(The reporter interrupts him)* because you play wit' you foot. Yes, you're brilliant. Einstein. Anada stupid Yankee ting, but anyway, Juju use fi love fi jus chat with us, mon. An 'im yuse fi always ask questions, questions, questions. Ya know like, "Why do you wear your hair dat way, in de dreadlocks?" And, "How come it all right fi de police to carry gun but it not all right fi de people 'round here to carry gun?" And, "How come there's soo much money to build bombs but none to feed the hungry?" Yeah, Jujube was very inquisitive. Juju. Juju. Is a powerful name dat you know. In certain parts of West Africa— you know how you have voodoo in Haiti?—well dat is what dem call de same ting in parts of West Africa. Juju. In Jamaica dem call it Obeah. Dowg Sout dem call it "roots." Some people tink it evil but it nuh evil, it natural. Just depen' 'pon how you use it. But anyway Juju was a very bright pickni, mon, yeah. Bwai use fi come outside an' read 'im lickle story fi de Rastas dem. Him use fi love fi write and read 'im story. I remember one story 'im seh 'bout a black angel who came dung to de eart' fi a special mission. Now, all de plants an' trees an' flowers in every part a de world was wilting and dying. An' if any of dese tings was to survive de people would avefi tek seeds from dis black angel and plant dem. An' only dose who took de seeds and planted dem would 'ave enough fi dem an' dem family fi eat. So dis black angel went all 'round de world to different lands an' try him best to give people seeds but nobody would believe that this black mon was an angel an' that his seeds were magical. So, de ole eart' an' everyone on it perished. So, finally—bups—de black angel gwan back upa 'eaven, feeling dat he had failed God. And when 'im reach back upa 'eaven 'im ask God, and God was black, too, ya na. Quote dat. Him ask God, "Why didn't anyone believe me? Why didn't dey take the seeds?" And God said, "Life can be as simple as taking and planting seeds but many, many will die and never know this simple truth." And all of us were jus'—bottom jaw jus' 'it de ground, mon—boom. Can you imagine dis lickle bwai tellin' you dis? Dat story mek me tink a something dat Frederico García Lorca seh, the Spanish writer, him seh, "The poem, the song, the picture is only water drawn from the well of the people and it should be given back to them in a cup of beauty, so that they may drink and in drinking understand themselves." And dat is what dat lickle bwai did, him give back to de people in a cup of beauty. Dat bwai is a prophet, mon! And dat is why when I see 'pon tell-lie-vision dat Jujube 'ad shot a cop I was jus' . . . special lickle bwai, mon. It must 'ave been a setup—if it's even true. Same way like how dem did kill dat bredren dung in a Maryland—Prince Jones. Wicked, brutal police, mon. Me did write a song 'bout de bredren an' de people dem need fi know dees lyrics, mon. Come, raise ya recorda . . . well do you 'ave enough tape? Well ahright den, come.

(Nyabingi proceeds to sing "Prince Jones" a cappella:)

A cop killed Prince Jones not too long ago
Another brother took out, another war casualty
It makes it really hard for me not to have hate for po-po
'Cause under different circumstances, you know that woulda
    been me.

And now Prince Jones will never get to be a King
'Cause they took him out, way too early
But we're all prone to the same exact expiring
So just keep him people in your memory.

And don't unoo forget Amadou or Rodney King
And me, myself, and I, I been harassed by the boys in blue
And they say that everything is everything
Well if that's the case y'all, we gotta change more than a
    few because . . .

Now Prince Jones will never get to be a King
'Cause they took him out, way too early
But we're all prone to the same exact expiring
So just keep him people in your memory.

Ah-right, newspaperman, interview done. You can tun off your tape now. And mek sure you get me a copy a dat, mon, seen, ah-right, good.

(The sound of writing. Nyabingi pops bogle movement stage right into a freeze for Sasha.)

sasha

SASHA *(In a preppy manner of speech):* So I mean, dude, like what can I like not say about Jujube Brown? I am soo admiring and soo respecting Jujube Brown. He's like a brother to me. He's like a twin that I was separated from at birth and then mystically reunited with at the Evergreen School for Boys. I have never felt such an intense, profound, cosmic connection with anyone. Not my mother, certainly not my father, not even a human of the female persuasion. I fell in love with Jujube Brown. And it's not like I'm gay or anything. OK, so I've had a few weird dreams, but that doesn't count. He is my genuine soul brother and I mean that in the truest sense of the phrase. For starters, he's just an amazing writer. Grandson of Leo Tolstoy, cousin of the bard William Shakespeare, sibling of Alice Walker—he is indeed a member of the family of literary giants, slumbering no more, awakening to greet the new day with bright eyes, able hands and open heart. Genesis—from the very first moment Juju and I encountered each other at Evergreen, which is like this snooty prep school, we had an instant connection. And well, why shouldn't we? We were the only two young men of African descent there. And please, don't get confused. Let not the cadence of my speech throw you off. I am very clear about who I am. I've been to The Continent, Mother Africa, several times. My parents have been doing the whole Kwanzaa thing for years now, Kujichagalia. And I get pulled over and harassed by state troopers for no apparent reason. Like, yeah, I know who I am. Or at least who I'm perceived to be. The truth is me and Jujube come from two totally different solar systems. The planets that revolve around him share the axis of the ghetto galaxy. While the celestial bodies of my universe consist of particles of a more privileged makeup. Or, as Jujube would say, "Oh, so like you grew up around rich white people." Pretty much my whole life. But seriously, I've never even gone out with a Nubian Queen before. I don't even think sisters would be interested in me. Unless they were like Lisa Bonet, or Macy Gray, or Cree Summer, or someone like that because, I don't know, I guess I'm like a peculiar bird. *(Makes a bird sound with arms flapping)* I like doing things like that. I love doing that. And as a result I've been ostracized by my own people. I've been called Oreo, wannabe, white boy. Contrary to popular belief, many African Americans are ridiculously conservative—sexually, politically, culturally. Jimi Hendrix once got booed in Harlem until he started playing the blues, something that folks were familiar with. I bet most of them were ignorant of the fact that like African Americans are like the progenitors of rock 'n' roll. Learn your history, people—makes me wanna puke. And European Americans have treated me no better—yeah, sure, like everything's cool until it's time to go to Papa's country club. Then it's no haps, blackie. Fucking assholes. But with Jujube it was different. No expectations of me to operate within imaginary boundaries of "blackness." No demarcated social lines that I was pressured to stay behind. He accepted me for me. And for that I'll be grateful until the moon ceases to orbit the Earth. Digression. I know Evergreen was like a really drastic change for Jujube. And like most people who experience change, I think he was a little fearful at first. But after a while it seemed as though he was really beginning to settle into his skin. He got used to the bland food, the ignorant questions about hair texture. He even got used to the bugs. Then it happened. The accusation. One of the boys at school had died after using coke. And it was extra tragic because it was his first time doing it. He went into cardiac arrest and that was it. But the accusation came into play when Jujube was the first one to be interrogated by the faculty and the police. Now, mind you, Jujube wasn't even with the kid when he died, didn't do drugs of any sort, not even marijuana. Abbreviation. They eventually found the boy, Zack, who was selling the stuff at school, and expelled him. Yeah, I think a lot of people have a difficult time dealing with the fact that someone with blond hair and blue eyes is the person selling their kids drugs. Well, a week after that Jujube left Evergreen. Said he was going to New York to live with his father and brother, Peanut. And that was the last I heard from him. I wrote him a couple letters but no response. There is the possibility of me having the wrong address. Or maybe he just needed a clean break. Conclusion. Whatever the case may be, like I really, really believe that like people come in and then like go out of your life for a reason, so with that I say, "So long, dear friend, we shall meet again, in this life perhaps not, but we shall meet again."

(Sasha freezes and a lively percussive metal sound accompanied by a driving beat begins. Out of the freeze, Jujube's brother, Peanut, comes to life. He dances to downstage center and picks up two cans of spray paint and puts them near the downstage left corner of the cube. He then takes the sheet off the cube and spreads it out fully on the floor to the right of cube.)

the backdrop

PEANUT *(In a thick New York City B-boy accent)*: Ah-ight, so bus-it, bus-it. So the first idea I had for the backdrop for my brother's concert—the Free Jujube Brown concert—was like in big block letters in red, black and green, was to have: FREE JUJUBE BROWN. Wit' the "Free" in red, "Jujube" in black and the "Brown" in green. On some ol' everyday-Joe tip. You see it and you get it. It ain't nothin' to gaze at. It ain't nothin' to scope out. The performers are rippin' it, MC's spittin', breakdancers doin' they thing, while you gettin' the raw message in the background. But then I was like, naw—it's too literal. *(Sits on the cube)* So I was at the crib and I was like, word, let me set the type atmosphere that's gonna be conducive to my creativity. So I put on some KRS-1. Yo, Blastmaster KRS always does the job. His music is mad thought provokin'. *(Gets up from the cube)* So I was vibin' and "Boup-Boup, it's the sound a the police, Boup-Boup, it's the sound a the beast" was on, so I'm feelin' it and then it jus' came to me. I seen this kaliedoscopic prism a colors, shapes and rhythms. It started bubblin' from the soles a my feet, up through my legs, out the top a my dome-piece. I was like, word, here it is, I feel it. So bus-it, right, bus-it, you got this figure, it's a cop, and he got like the crazy scowl on his face, just lookin' real, like grrrr, like the wil' Busta Rhymes expression, an' he got his little nine or whatever in his hand. And then beside him, but much more voluminous, you got this portrait of Jujube in the bugged-out, ill Shaolin pose. But in his hands he got this massive pen, 'cause like he a writer of the spoken word an' that's his weapon. So the both of 'em are in this crazy battle-stance duel position, and they about to joust wit' they weapon a choice, nadamean. Yeah, yeah. But then I was like, "Naw, naw. The images might be too strong for citizens to judiciously absorb." So I was like, "I gotta flip it, I gotta change my environment." Cuz like, check it, "The creative personality never remains fixed on the first world it discovers, it never resigns itself to anything. That is the deepest meaning of rebellion." Anais Nin, word up. So I started pacin', 'cause like my process lives in my body. My process is mad visceral. My process is like . . . *(Does a short pop-infused movement sequence)* That's just how it comes out. Need to get out the house, go somewhere. Outdoors. So I left the crib. I ain't bring nuthin' wit' me. No Walkman, no markers, no paint. Had to get out free a aething. Although, I did bring a small hammer wit' me just in case anybody tried to get slick. So I hopped the turnstile, got on the Number 2 train, got off at Grand Army Plaza in Brooklyn, went to Prospect Park. Now by this time it was late, like one in the morning, so the park was barren. I ain't hardly see nobody—couple white people joggin'—it's a free country, do ya thing. So I make my way to the middle a the meadow and just sit down, *(Sits downstage of sheet)* look up at the sky. And I hadn't noticed until right then that it was a full moon that night. And, oh man, I could see stars too—more stars than I had ever seen in my life. So I'm sittin' there feelin' like I could jus' reach up and grab the moon and stars and pull 'em down beside me. And I thought to myself, Yo, this is the same moon and stars that people throughout the ages have gazed at: artists, poets, philosophers, revolutionaries. The same moon and stars that they've sat under pondering the meaning of life. The same shit they've looked to for solace and for inspiration. And at that very moment, when that realization struck me, I knew right then and there what I was gonna paint for the backdrop, yeah!

(A foreboding, pulsating beat that includes claps and shaker sounds is played. Peanut gets up and grabs spray-paint cans and begins to paint the sheet on the floor. This painting eventually turns into a physicalized interpretation of what happened on the day of the shooting. This is done with spray-paint motions and mime. A person is shown eating and offering another person food. A second person is shown refusing the offer and eating their own food. The first person has to take a piss. The second person does, too. They go to the bushes and urinate. A cop is in the distance, radios someone, and pulls out a gun and points it at the two men pissing. One of the men gets on the ground. A cop kicks the man, who swings his arms wildly at the cop. The man then finds a gun on the ground. The music stops. The man raises the gun slowly while standing up. We hear the sound of two gunshots. The man transforms back into Peanut and runs downstage left.)

the shooting

PEANUT: Ah-ight, so bus-it, bus-it. What had happened was, is that we wasn't botherin' nobody. We was chillin' at the park at a family-type picnic. Eatin' potato salad, macaroni and cheese, and fried fish. Anyway, me and Jujube had to piss so we went to the bushes. Next thing you know we hear this voice, *(As Officer Cavanaugh)* "Hey! What you boys doin' in them bushes?" I was like, "Fuck it look like we doin'? We takin' a piss. Whatchu jealous or somethin', 'cause my balls are bigger than yours?" So we was laughin', makin' fun of whoever it was, when they came runnin' towards us. It was Five-O, two of 'em, a male and a female cop. But at first we ain't know they was cops, we just thought they was some knuckleheads lookin' to start a fight. Then everything happened real fast. The lady cop got to us first, she pulled out her gun, knocked me down, and told me not to move. But Jujube was quick to the punch, he grabbed her up from behind and she dropped her gun in the bushes. She started shoutin' shit to her partner, he pulled out his piece and came running. Jujube turned around and seen this gun pointed at him. Then at me then him then me then him. The cop was talkin' shit man! He was sayin' how he was about to do, *(As Officer Cavanaugh)* "God's work." Then he got Jujube on the ground and started kickin' him. Then somehow, by some miracle, Juju found the lady cop's gun in the bushes, and I was like, "Shoot that mother-fucker!!" Then I heard two shots. And when I opened my eyes I seen Jujube standin' there like a man, glarin' down at the officer's bleedin' body. The cop missed but Jujube didn't. He shot him. Yeah, Jujube shot that cop. But it was me all the time tellin' Jujube we gotta stand up for ourselves. Oppressed people gotta rise up, man! Malcolm did it! The Panthers did it! And Jujube did it! But it all happened so fast. I ain't know if it was the revolution comin'—or what.

(Peanut mimes pointing a gun at the audience. The gun is then instantly transformed into a can of spray paint. The sound of hurried writing. Peanut frantically sprays to where the sheet was left. He then gets under the sheet and becomes Officer Cavanaugh.)

god's work

Officer Cavanaugh is lying on the floor under the sheet.

OFFICER CAVANAUGH *(In a raspy sandpaper voice)*: Don'tchu listen to doc-tors, you wanna know why, I'm a tell you why.

(He stands, the sheet dropping to the floor.)

I go to the doctor and he says if I keep on smokin' two an' tree packs a cigarettes a day, like I been smokin', I'm gonna increase my chances of dyin' an early death. And just in case you were wonderin', my voice hasn't always sounded like this. I got sick a coupla years ago. I had a fever, strep throat, I felt nauseated, the works, felt like I was gonna die, but I kept on smokin' every day. And after I got better, after about two weeks, my voice sounded like this. The texture of it changed completely. It's not painful or anything. I don't mind it and the ladies love it. Quick story, I was datin' this chick one time and we were ah . . . we were, you know . . . we were playin' hide the salami. And she asks me to talk to her. And I tell her, "Well, I'm not much of a talker. I'm more so into action, baby." Boom, boom, boom. I keep doin' my thing. And she says, "No, it's sexy." I won't bother you with all the loquacious details, but let's just say I was talkin' to her all night. Boom, bah, bah, bah, boom. Back to the doctor. I look at him an' I say, "Doc, I been a police officer for seventeen years now, my job is dangerous, every day I go out there on my beat I run the risk of losin' my life. Quickly, like that. *(Snaps fingers)* If I was a bettin' man, an' I'm not, never gambled a day in my life, but if I was the type a guy who was into statistics and rollin' the dice and numbers, I would say that I have a greater chance of dyin' by a bullet squeezed outta the gun a some hoodlum than by gettin' lung cancer." Doctor looks at me an' he says, "Officer Cavanaugh, you've made it to seventeen. You're probably safe. Quit smokin' cigarettes." I got shot the very same day I decided to quit smokin' cigarettes. But hey, that's life. I don't know, maybe I deserved it. In my day I busted a lotta heads. A number of 'em, many may say, were unwarranted. But my philosophy was, I don't need to see you doin' anything wrong. I'm representing karma at that point. I'm sure you've done something at some point to deserve punishment. We all watch TV here, right? Who do you always see in handcuffs lookin' down like this, *(Does the classic image)* hoodie over their head? Huh? Who, who, who? You know who. My mother, she got mugged twice. By who? You know who. Who are the most criminal-minded people in this country? You know who. So I figured I'd nip it in the bud, so to speak. There wasn't gonna be no roses wit' thorns growin' up outta the concrete to prick people around here. I thought of myself as a vessel working on behalf of the Almighty to balance the moral weight of the universe. I was doin' God's work and that's beyond the comprehension of man. God's work, you know, the type a thing where you see one or two black guys drivin' in a car, they don't look in my direction, stop the car, search the car, God's work. Three or more Hispanic guys in a car, look in my direction, stop the car, el licenso, el registrationo, search the car, God's work. Young hip-hop kid late at night, baseball cap backwards, pants saggin', diddy-boppin', stop him, frisk him, scare him, God's work. Group a black kids on the corner, loud, laughin', lovin' life, in a cipher doin' their freesyle thing, pull my gun, get 'em up against a wall, search 'em, if drugs, take drugs, lock 'em up, if no drugs, hit 'em wit' sticks, they retaliate, take 'em in for disorderly conduct, God's work!!! And that's the kinda thing that happened to that Jujube kid. I didn't mean no harm. I was jus' doin' God's work.

(A couple of beats. We hear a muffled and distorted gunshot that also sounds like the slam of a cell door as Officer Cavanaugh does a 180-degree turn. This is now the "older Jujube," with his back to the audience, in a prison cell. He walks around the cube. His hands feel the downstage bars of the cell. He goes to the cube, sits, then picks up a pen and pad of paper. Older Jujube experiences momentary writer's block. A recorded sound of paper ripping, a crumple, then a ball of paper hitting the floor as Jujube rips a page off the pad, crumples it, then tosses it. He writes a little bit. Frustrated, he rips off that page too, crumples it, then tosses it. Then he throws the pad and pen to the floor as we hear the sounds again.)

in prison

JUJUBE: It seems like just moments ago I was five years old dreaming about being a garbageman. And here I am now, in prison. But I'm fine the days I retreat into my own secluded mind. In one instant I'm here, in a cell, a cage, locked up like hair on a Rasta's head, then—poof—I'm somewhere else, someplace I've read about, like Madagascar, or the Himalayas, or Rio De Janeiro during Carnival. I'm laughing, I'm dancing, I'm swept up in the thrill of a celebration ritual. But sometimes I'm lured into a corner of my mind that deceives my better judgment. And always the same thing happens: Vincent van Gogh.

(For a quick moment we hear the sound of a record spinning backward.)

I end up in three separate van Gogh paintings. It always starts with my favorite one: *Rest from Work*. I'm right next to the man and the woman sleeping in the hay, not too far from two cows grazing. I take my shoes and socks off, feel the long golden strands between my toes, chill out, and watch the clouds as they shape shift. That's a kangaroo. And that's a platypus, laying eggs, and that's . . . Martha Stewart?! Then, an empty forty-ounce malt-liquor bottle, *(A hard-hitting, ominous beat with booming base begins)* syringes, crack pipes. It always happens. I can't control it. So, I get up and run and all of a sudden I'm in another painting: *Wheat Field with Cypress*. But this time it's worse. I look up: nimbo stratus cumulous shards of broken glass. Stop it! I look down, I look up: Tat-Tat. Go Away. I look down, I look up: Sasha from Evergreen. I'm not goin' back there. I look down, I look up: Officer Cavanaugh. He was fuckin' wit' me. Guns, blood, mistakes, a bottomless hole in the sky. I look down and begin to run again. Finally, I'm in *Starry Night*. I look up: no more clouds, just bright, glowing balls of heaven, swirling, turning, contorting, calling my name, churning: Free Jujube Brown! First at a whisper, then louder: Free Jujube Brown! Growing, multiplying painfully like cancer: Free Jujube Brown! Wailing: Free Jujube Brown! Free Jujube Brown! My ears weep, a sinful church steeple pierces the purple, black canopy of the earth and the moon is shining like the sun, blinding my eyes. I die here again and again and say I won't come back. I hate Vincent van Gogh. He murders me every starry night!!!

(The music stops and Jujube is sitting on the cube with his back to the audience.)

jujube brown

Jujube turns to face the audience, still sitting on the cube. He then desperately goes to pick up his pad and pen from the floor, sits back on the cube and begins to write violently. As he writes, a recording of Jujube's voice is played with a slight audio reverb effect:

JUJUBE: This is Jujube Brown here. I never wanted to be anybody's hero or icon or savior. My back's not strong enough for the weight of that responsibility. I am no shepherd who was sent to lead sheep over hills, through pastures and around mountains. My staff was built to be held by one hand. And please don't think me a selfish or ungrateful person. I do appreciate all that people have given me: the thousands of letters, the rallies, concerts, marches, radio shows and TV programs. None of it was for naught because I know that's what you needed to do for your spirits to be resolved.

(He stops writing, gets up and slips the pad under the front bars of the cell.)

But that's what it's about—the tranquility of your souls. Getting together for a unified purpose and protecting, fighting for and celebrating life.

(He removes his belt from around his waist, stands on the cube, adjusts the belt around his neck and ties the other end to a fixture on the ceiling of the cell. He is going to hang himself . . .)

It's not about any one individual but each and every individual themselves, who agree to come together in the name of a true humanity. If I get the electric chair today, what happens? If I was never born, what would've happened? And if I am free tomorrow, then what?

(He changes his mind. He unties the belt from the fixture and jumps off of the cube. He then takes the belt from around his neck and throws it to the ground, distressed. He grabs the downstage bars of the cell in the midst of a post-suicidal fit.)

All I'm saying is that I love the fact that people have gotten together to support me, but I don't need that. This is your creation, your fantasy, a cause that was desired so you could come together and feel oneness, that which you truly long for. And if all this needed to happen, so I could say this to you right now, then I guess this is what was supposed to happen.

(He takes a moment and steps away from the bars with a new realization. He goes to touch the bars and his hands suddenly go through them. The cell has disappeared. His prison is gone. He circles the stage in partial disbelief.)

I am free and so are you. We always have and always will be. Now get behind that and support that. Rally over that, because that's the truth, and that's all I have to say.

(He stops downstage left with the epiphany that this entire experience was all a figment of his imagination. Jujube is now the Dreamer. He takes in the audience for a few moments.)

closing piece

One hand of The Dreamer goes up to grab a subway car handle and the other hand holds a briefcase. He is back on the train as in the opening sequence. The Dreamer speaks directly to the audience:

THE DREAMER:
> So this was for the ancestors, the ones who came before us
> For those who sing in the church choir and those in the
>   school chorus
>
> For those who couldn't give a damn about a play or a book
> For those who get harassed by cops, and those whose lives
>   they took
>
> This was for those cops who are just tryin' to feed their families
> And for those politicians who write unjust and crooked policies
>
> For the children who are here and those still yet to be born
> This was for the sun that rises each and every morn'.

(He walks downstage right to where the bathroom was in the opening sequence.)

> This was for the animals, the land and the sky
> For those who have the courage and vulnerability to still cry

(He puts down his briefcase, takes off his jacket and tie and hangs them up.)

> For the mamas and the papas, the sons and the daughters
> For the dollars and the cents, the nickels and the quarters

(He turns on the faucet, grabs his toothbrush, applies toothpaste and brushes his teeth.)

> This was done to counterattack the belligerence of war
> For the haves and have-nots, the rich and the poor

(He puts the toothbrush back, rinses his mouth and turns off the faucet.)

> Done for the sake of tradition, the heritage of man
> Done to prove, once and for all, the creator has a master plan

This was done for those who study peace like it was science
Done for those who put their love to work like an appliance

(He goes to where the sheet is, picks it up and faces the audience.)

This was done for the sick and the healthy alike
For the heads who traveled here by plane, train, car, foot or bike

This was for those in heaven and those in hell
This was for your sense of taste, touch and smell

This was for the West Coast and this was for the East
This was for the beauty and this was for the beast

But most importantly, this was for the idea of changing what
   you can
And spreading a little bit of love throughout the land

(He drapes the sheet around himself like a robe.)

This was for you. Thank you.
And good night.

*(The Dreamer faces away from the audience, tightens the sheet around
his body and goes to sleep. We hear a reprise of the violin, electronic keyboard medley from the opening of the play.
   Lights fade to black.)*

THE END

Psalmayene 24, aka Gregory Morrison, is an actor, playwright and singer/songwriter. Originally from Brooklyn, NY, he currently lives in the Washington, D.C., area, where he is also the Master Teaching Artist and a commissioned writer at Arena Stage. Psalmayene started his professional performing career in 1992 with the hip-hop dance company *Subtle Motion*, which he co-founded. Shortly thereafter he became a principle dancer with the *Kankouran West African Dance Company*, which he performed with for several years. His hip-hop theater credits include writing and performing *Free Jujube Brown!*, co-writing and performing in *The Hip-Hop Nightmares of Jujube Brown*, choreographing the ensemble hip-hop theater play *Rhyme Deferred* and conceiving, writing and performing in the ensemble piece *Undiscovered Genius of the Concrete Jungle*. In 1999, Psalmayene was nominated for a Helen Hayes Award for his performance in *The Hip-Hop Nightmares of Jujube Brown*. Along with being featured in *Honey* magazine, he has appeared on HBO's *The Wire*. In 2005 he was the recipient of a grant from The Boomerang Fund for Artists, Inc., an organization that offers unsolicited grants to artists who demonstrate their talent and commitment to a life in the arts. Psalmayene's band, PS24, is currently the resident band at Washington, D.C.'s Busboys and Poets. PS24 has performed at New York City's S.O.B.'s, the Lincoln Theatre (Washington, D.C.) and The Baltimore Museum of Art.

Visit PS24 at www.myspace.com/ps24music. Inquiries about *Free Jujube Brown!* can be sent to psalmayene24@hotmail.com

beatbox

a raparetta

by tommy shepherd and dan wolf

authors' statement

Beatbox: A Raparetta (born in 1994) had a profound effect on our vision of how to create a hip-hop collective that could function simultaneously as a live band, a theater company and a team of performing arts educators. Today that collective is known as Felonious: onelovehiphop.

Beatbox: A Raparetta has gone through six major revisions, from a comic book-esque allegory about a sack of power corrupting a group of street kids, to an attempt at including all the elements of hip-hop culture into the story of two stepbrothers who have lost their parents and who are on the verge of losing their way.

Actor Carlos Aguirre and Director Gendell Hernandez had a profound effect on the evolution of the piece. Their insight into and opinion of the "raparetta" form always challenged us to be specific in our attempt to write rhymes that furthered story and character within the classic operetta form. They were instrumental in the creation of this piece as the cornerstone of our collective work together.

MAKE SOME NOISE!

acknowledgments

Charlie Bachman and Marie Garcia at Centerpoint Theater Group
Yuriko Doi, Chela Cadwell and Theatre of Yugen
John McCluggage, Karen Piemme, Alexandra Urbanowski, Bruce Elsperger,
    Nakissa Etemad and Timothy Near at San Jose Repertory Theatre
Santa Clara Juvenile Facility and Unit B-9
Marty and Frank Wolf
Billy Cohen and Colleen Kennedy
Kim Cook, Sean Riley, David Szlasa and Theater Artaud
Patrick Haynes and Fatbelly Productions
Steve Snyder and the Oakland Box Theater
Anna Maria Luera, Leah Chalofsky, Karla Robinson, Lila Maes and
    Rosa De Anda
Kamilah Forbes, Danny Hoch and the NYC Hip-Hop Theater Festival
Deborah Cullinan, Sean San Jose, Kevin B. Chen and Intersection for
    the Arts
Kim Euell
Gendell Hernandez, Carlos Aguirre, Keith Pinto, Dylan Mills, Tony
    Nazem, Taymour Ghazzi, Jessica Wolf, Nicole Antelo, Sulo Williams,
    Richard Reinholdt, Selena Allen, Emily Mills, Juliet Pinto and
    Yuri Lane
Headz worldwide!

production history

Beatbox: A Raparetta was first presented as a one-act on March 27, 1995 as part of Centerpoint Theater Group's Nebula New Stage Works Series (Marie Garcia, Artistic Director) in San Luis Obispo, CA under the title *Beatbox: A Lyrical Train of Jazz.*

The play was next presented in 1998 at Theatre of Yugen (Yuriko Doi, Artistic Director) in San Francisco. The cast included Dan Wolf, Tommy Shepherd, Gendell Hernandez, Carlos Aguirre, Tony Nazem, Taymour Ghazi, Nicole Antelo, Sulo Williams, Jessica Wolf and Richard Reinholdt.

In 1998 the play was workshopped as part of San Jose Repertory Theatre's New America Playwright's Festival (Timothy Near, Artistic Director) at Villa Montalvo under the Direction of John McCluggage, with dramaturgy by Buddy Butler. In 1999 and 2000 *Beatbox* toured to juvenile halls and correctional facilities throughout the South Bay in association with San Jose Repertory Theatre's outreach program: Red Ladder Theatre Company. The cast included Dan Wolf, Tommy Shepherd, Gendell Hernandez, Carlos Aguirre, Keith Pinto, Taymour Ghazi, Nicole Antelo and Karen Altree Piemme.

From June 2000 until January 2001 the play was workshopped at New Roots to Hip-Hop, a weekly showcase of theater and music hosted by the live hip-hop band Felonious. Since 2001 *Beatbox: A Raparetta* has been seen at the Oakland Box Theater, the Stern Grove Festival, Die Wüste Lebt (a theater festival for young actors and directors in Hamburg, Germany), the Cinnabar Theater and the fourth annual NYC Hip-Hop Theater Festival.

Beatbox: A Raparetta was produced by Wishbone Entertainment at Theater Artaud (Kim Cook, Executive Director) in August and September 2001. It was directed by Gendell Hernandez, assistant directed by Anna Maria Luera; choreography was by Keith Pinto, set and sound design were by Dylan Mills, lighting design was by David Szlasa, technical direction was by Sean Riley and musical direction was by Tommy Shepherd and DJ Raw B. The cast: Mikey Finch was played by Tommy Shepherd, Tet was played by Carlos Aguirre, Malloy was played by Dan Wolf, Jazz was played by Jessica Van Neil, Zac was played by Keith Pinto,

Parry was played by Elizabeth Gonzalez, Scat was played by Gendell Hernandez, Teacher was played by Karla Robinson, the Cop/Ensemble were played by Michael Barr, the Dancers were Jessica Wolf, Miles Kenedi and Jackie Badzin and the DJ was Rob Blach (Raw B).

characters

FINCH.

TET, his younger brother.

MALLOY, lives in the neighborhood, Tet's friend.

ZAC, professional dancer, just back from tour, Finch's friend.

DJ.

ENSEMBLE AND DANCERS.

note

Finch, Tet and Zac all play in the Ensemble in the first scene. They are "unfinished" characters until Malloy reveals them.

This is a play with rhythm that is intended to be on beat from beginning to end. Where text is spoken you should find the natural rhythm that moves the words along, but not necessarily on beat. Most of the play is rapped and you should find the rhythm within a 4/4 time signature, with either a DJ or a beatboxer. Each line of text/rap is intended to be matched with one bar of music or (1, 2, 3, 4). We use the 4th, 8th and 16th notes as starting points for some of the lines. Also, any time you see numbers inside the parentheses they represent where a beat exists but no text, i.e., "*(1, 2)* I broke you in half." These beats exist in the play's emotional peaks and are intended to enhance that tension.

Good luck!

place

The city. An alley.

time

Right now.

scene 1

The neighborhood. The mouth of the alley. Malloy sees a composition book. When he picks it up he begins writing this story as it unfolds in his imagination and before his eyes.

MALLOY: I seek a story / The battles and realized dreams of ancestry.

> Folk, fairy and fake tales make up you and me
> Which storyline do you belong to be, long to be?

> I seek the peoples' story / Beatbox and battle-rap cats from the streets.

> Folk, fairy and fake tales make up you and me
> Which storyline do you belong to be, long to be?

(Malloy grabs the composition book.)

ENSEMBLE 1 AND FINCH:
> Ladies and gents, dawgs, kittens and OGs
> Young Gs to backpackers, chip stackers, yo, just freeze.

ENSEMBLE 2 AND TET: We got a story to spread but don't be misled.
MALLOY: Characters that I show—
ALL: We put 'em up in our head.

(Zac hands Malloy a pencil.)

ENSEMBLE 3 AND ZAC: Still, people like you and me with human fate /
> Human situations, human love and human hate.
ENSEMBLE 2: Embark on this journey with us, participate.
DANCE ENSEMBLE: Laugh—
ENSEMBLE 1: Cry—
ENSEMBLE 2: Scream—
ENSEMBLE 3: Shout—

ENSEMBLE 1: Just don't discriminate.

> *(1)* We're in a world full of people where no one's the same
> Same thing different place with a different name.

ENSEMBLE 3:
> Clutching tight to her purse, holding tight to his case—

ENSEMBLE 2:
> Getting punched for your lunch money up in the face.

ENSEMBLE 1:
> 'Cause where there's money to get, there's money to be had.

ENSEMBLE 3 AND 1:
> Some don't need it—

ENSEMBLE 2 AND DANCE ENSEMBLE:
> Some want it real bad—

ENSEMBLE 3:
> Stealing Mom's TV for a half hit of crack.

DANCE ENSEMBLE:
> Hey!—

ENSEMBLE 1:
> Crossed so many lines you're always . . .

ALL:
> "Watch your back!"

ENSEMBLE 2:
> Can't get ahead—

MALLOY:
> Why!

ENSEMBLE 2:
> 'Cause you don't like your mug
> So you get liposucted and a new pair of jugs.

ENSEMBLE 1:
> And if it's not jugs it's Lugz , Sean Jean or Rockawear.

ENSEMBLE 2:

I got it at Ross 'cause they rock the cheap gear.

ENSEMBLE 3:

We got the happy-go-lucky, old-money folklore.

ENSEMBLE 1:

She got to suck and fuck for four walls and a door.

ENSEMBLE 3:

Day care.

ENSEMBLE 2:

Car note.

ENSEMBLE 1 AND DANCE ENSEMBLE:

Groceries from the store.

ALL:

People developing their craft in the art of poor.
War for you could mean peace for me
See people are people, why should it be?
It's a delicate thought to entertain.

MALLOY:

Still try to explain, you see, I seek a story.

ALL:

War for you could mean peace for me
See people are people, why should it be?
It's a delicate thought to entertain.

MALLOY:

Still trying to explain, you see I seek a story.

ENSEMBLE 1:

A world full of people where no one's the same
Same thing different place with a different name.

ENSEMBLE 3:

Good life good friends holding hands in the park
There's a softer side of life than what goes bump in the dark.

ENSEMBLE 2:

> Parents working nine to five so their kids ain't deprived.

MALLOY:

> I can't believe what some folks do just to survive
> But they keep it positive 'cause they're happy to live.

ENSEMBLE 1:

> Just to carry on their name and what their ancestors give.

ENSEMBLE 2:

> Could be a favorite antique or a fat wad of cash.

ENSEMBLE 1:

> The weight on the present what you got from the past.

MALLOY:

> You could be like—

ENSEMBLE 3:

> "I'm rich and I don't give a fuck."

ENSEMBLE 2:

> "Was poor and I don't give a damn."

ENSEMBLE 1:

> This heirloom may be a gem but you'd rather have them here
> again.

ENSEMBLE 3:

> And they will be.

ENSEMBLE 1:

> 'Cause people come and go.

ALL:

> That's life.

ENSEMBLE 1:

> Stressed.

ALL:

> That's the way it is.

ENSEMBLE 1:

Depressed.

ALL:

That's life.

MALLOY:

Fast-lane livin'.

ENSEMBLE 2:

Maintain that life.

ALL:

Keep fightin' for your light and you'll find your mic.

(On a four count (1, 2, 3, 4) the entire ensemble vocally creates the sound of a record being scratched on a turntable, accompanied by the DJ. Malloy is sucked into the story. On the one (1) of the next four count the entire ensemble begins to vocally create the sound of the alley morphing into the train station as the train pulls in. They morph into passengers on a train. Finch and Tet enter the train, followed by Malloy. Finch begins to beatbox for the passengers.)

TET: Yes, ladies and gentleman. How you doing this fine morning? We are gonna do a little something for you on the train on your way to work. So pull out some coins or dollars, whatever you have. Sit back and enjoy the show as we go to work.

(Tet and Finch begin to perform for the passengers. They walk up and down the aisle asking for money while beatboxing. Eventually the train slows to a stop.)

FINCH:

Thank you, ladies and gentleman, and remember, let my microphone bless you.

FINCH AND TET:

And don't let the cops arrest you! Peace!

(Finch and Tet collect money and jump off the train.)

MALLOY:

I seek this story
Stepbrothers with no mothers who fight to be free.

ALL:

>Folk, fairy and fake tales, me and you
>This is the storyline that we belong to.

MALLOY:

>You met Finch and Tet, the best beat in the West
>Simulate the DJ with their voice and their breath.

FINCH AND TET:

>Livin' the good life.

MALLOY:

>Till they were plagued with death
>Not their own but they had to lay their parents to rest.

FINCH:

>Now we fam', not in blood but in the head and the heart.

TET:

>We're the only fam' we got.

FINCH:

>We'll continue the spark.

MALLOY:

>So they lived to prove their parents' wisdom left its mark
>And they vowed to each play their part—that's how it starts.

>*(Malloy continues to write in his composition book. Tet and Finch are on the street. Finch teaches Tet some new sounds for eight counts. Zac enters.)*

>Guess who's back. *(1)*

ZAC:

>Zac the cat with the wild style.

ALL:

>Look who's back.

MALLOY:

>We haven't seen him in a while
>Back from a 'round world tour as a dancer
>Left it all behind he knew rapping was the answer

Came back for Finch and for fame and the block
The top-notch crew they used to rock nonstop.

FINCH, TET AND ZAC:

Living the good life.

MALLOY:

Never was there to see
Change came quickly.

MALLOY AND TET:

The train moves rapidly
Follow me.

FINCH:

Damn! When you get back?

ZAC:

Just now.

FINCH:

Look at that gear! You got paid.

TET:

(Playful) Sellout.

ZAC:

Shut up fool, I did all right.

FINCH:

Clothes and money don't mean your skills are tight.

ZAC:

You ain't too bright. Yo, I got skills.

FINCH:

Yeah you do got skills.

TET:

I got skills, too.

FINCH:

You can't hang with the real.

TET:

    That's fighting words.

ZAC:

    Why you always gotta fight.

TET:

    Then let's battle.

ZAC:

    Things never change, right?

FINCH:

    Yeah they do. Look at you kid, you living phat.

TET:

    Come on, bring the heat.

ZAC:

    Son, I'll swat you like a gnat
    You best have been practicing with a mouth like that.

TET:

    Yeah I been practicing and I'm pretty dope, in fact.

ZAC: Step back, step back, the greatest show on earth is about to start. Drop that beat Finch.

(Dance battle. Zac battles Tet with old-school popping style. Tet tries to come back at him, but then Zac goes again and crushes Tet. Tet is no match for Zac.)

FINCH:

    (1) It's your move.

ZAC:

    You can't beat that.

FINCH:

    What you gonna do?

ZAC:

    Where you at?
    You better do something.
    You're getting laughed at.

FINCH:

Bring that beat back; let's show them how to battle, Zac.

(The DJ drops a beat. Finch and Zac school Tet. They show him what it means to battle by doing one of their old-school routines. After the dance is finished, Zac and Finch begin to exit.)

TET:

(1, 2) I broke you in half
(1, 2) I'm the master of my craft.

ZAC:

Finch, tell your boy he better take a step back.

FINCH:

(1, 2) He's all talk with no attack.

TET:

(1, 2) I drop the ill formats.

(Malloy joins in.)

MALLOY:

(1, 2) You know, I second that.

MALLOY AND TET:

It's the R2-D Crew on the attack
We got the *(Each showing off)* one-two-three-four step on back.

ZAC:

(1, 2) Well look at that.

TET:

(1, 2) We'll take you flow for flow.

MALLOY:

Toe to toe.

TET:

Mano a mano.

MALLOY AND TET:

Bro to bro.

ZAC:

> Yeah, kids, you're so hot I should act like I know.

MALLOY:

> *(1, 2)* Rally up then, start the show.

ZAC:

> *(1, 2)* Boys, stop playing.

TET:

> *(1)* I got the scratch for the itch, now I'm blazin'.

FINCH:

> *(1, 2)* That's my peoples, stop hatin'.

ZAC:

> *(1, 2)* I pay it no mind.
> *(1, 2)* He always wanted what was mine.

TET:

> *(1, 2)* Watch your back every time.

FINCH:

> *(1, 2)* Watch your back every time.

TET:

> *(1, 2)* Now let's battle written raps.

FINCH:

> *(1, 2)* Something else to take you at?

TET:

> *(1, 2)* He'll get took, so turn back.

ZAC:

> *(1, 2)* Is that a fact?

(The beat stops. A tense exchange between Tet and Zac. Finch steps in between the two to cool them off.)

(To Finch) I gotta bounce anyway. I gotta go kick it with the family. We'll catch up though.

(Zac grabs his gear and bounces. Finch walks off with him.)

TET: What? Come back and battle me, punk.

> Where you running to? / You still can't beatbox like I do.

(Tet freezes.)

MALLOY:

> And who am I, Malloy, I'm just a neighborhood cat
> Tet's ace, we went to school, and met a long way back
> But to Finch and to Zac I'm just a shorty, that's all
> They let me roll with the crew, I'm just a fly on the wall.
> So this is what I see, these are my friends
> Writing this story with my pad and my pen
> Our life in rhyme, so press play after pause
> You'll get the effect, come on follow the cause.

(Finch reenters.)

FINCH:

> Ha, ha, ha, ha, ha, ha, I shake my face
> He walked away from you as if his time was wasted.

MALLOY:

> Can't walk away from Tet before you get raided.

TET:

> Zac's wack ass is highly overrated.

MALLOY:

> Rhyming and stealing.

FINCH:

> It's not a sport, it's for survival.

TET:

> He better hope his house is locked.

MALLOY:

> Bolt tight upon arrival.

TET:

> Your ally is my rival
> My title is survival
> Been doing it the while.

beatbox

FINCH:

But with no style.

MALLOY AND TET:

What up with that?

FINCH:

Snatching at whatever clings to claws
So watch your jewels, and while you do
Someone else has their paws in your stash.

TET:

I'll spin it right from the gate "watch-your-back money."

FINCH:

Every time watch your back.

TET:

Yeah, 'cause Tet's coming.

FINCH:

You're showing off with this flash—

TET:

I'm trying to flash a quick dash—

FINCH:

You won't attack—

TET:

I'll get scrilla by jacking Zac—

FINCH:

Jack Zac, what's that, get off that yo
It's nobody's fault but your own, sucker, you're digging this hole
Back off, shut your trap and get some shit on your own
You ain't even got a job so what you got you stole
I'm sick of doing shit for you, it's time to get your own
Take your ass to work, network, let's roll.

MALLOY:

Where?

FINCH:

>Out and about.

MALLOY:

>What?

FINCH:

>Take another route
>Use your hands and your feet and your eyes and your mouth
>*(1)* Go. Out and about.

(Finch grabs Malloy's pencil while he is writing.)

MALLOY:

>What's that?

FINCH:

>You know
>It's about going out and getting your own flow.

MALLOY:

>Out and about?

TET:

>Cash money.

FINCH:

>Now you know
>Out to get the dollars
>It's about clocking dough.

ALL:

>Out and about.

FINCH:

>Step back, about to blow.

MALLOY:

>Use your lips to break it down.

TET:

>Use your mouth to kick the flow.

MALLOY AND TET:

    Out and about.

(A woman passes by.)

FINCH:

    Act like you know
    Rally up, tally up
    Let's start the show.

(Finch stops her.)

(Actor can improvise) Showtime, my fine lady. We got something special for you.

(Tet kicks a beat.)

MALLOY:

    It's the R2-D Crew, on the attack
    We got the one-two-three-four right on track and relax
    Watch the vibe unfold
    You gonna dig what we do whether you young or old
    So step back on up, we won't slice or cut
    The flesh, we fresh, we just came to . . .

TET:

    (Scratches, raps part of the text) . . . tear shit up.

(She applauds and walks away. Finch stops her and says the next line over her shoulder to Tet and Malloy.)

FINCH:

    You see these people have hearts for us hustlas to pinch
    If they give a centimeter then you take an inch.

TET:

    Can you spare a dime, lady?

MALLOY AND TET:

    Cuz we're out and about.

MALLOY:

    Ma'am, a quarter would be nice.

MALLOY AND TET:

    While I'm out and about.

TET:

    You see my stomach's rather hungry.

MALLOY AND TET:

    When I'm out and about.

MALLOY:

    And I'm tired of eating mice.

MALLOY AND TET:

    They're always out and about.

TET:

    See there's a mean old man *(3, 4)*
    And his name is Finch *(3, 4)*
    And he's the kingpin of the alley *(3, 4)*
    And his backhand really hits. *(3, 4)*

MALLOY:

    You see he expects that we go—

MALLOY AND TET:

    Out and about.

MALLOY:

    Bring back some money for a meal *(3, 4)*
    And if we don't, he's gonna beat me.

MALLOY AND TET:

    So I'm out and about.

MALLOY:

    I have no choice but to steal. *(3, 4)*

TET:

    Do you understand what I'm saying? *(3, 4)*

MALLOY:

    Do you catch our drift? *(3, 4)*

TET:

    So go reaching for a dollar— *(3, 4)*

MALLOY AND TET:

    So this transaction can be swift. *(3, 4)*

    (On [3, 4] Tet and Malloy put out their hands, waiting for the money. The Woman reaches into her purse and gives Tet and Malloy each a dollar and walks away.)

FINCH: There, that's how you get it done.

    (Finch tries to grab the dollars from Malloy and Tet and they have some fun trying to keep it away from him.)

DJ/DRUG ADDICT: Pssst!
FINCH: Yo, I'll catch up with you later.
TET: What's the deal?
FINCH: I said I'll catch up with you later. Here, take this back to the spot.

    (Finch throws Tet his hoodie.)

Go.

    (Finch watches until he thinks Tet leaves. The transaction continues. Malloy watches from the shadows.)

drug addict ballet

Tet and the Ensemble, as the Drug Fiends, ooze onto the stage and surround Finch like a pack of ghouls. Finch conducts the freak show into a whirlwind of movement symbolizing the uncontrollable pursuit of the fix. One by one, the Ensemble scores from Finch. They are transformed by the drugs as they exit the stage.

FINCH:

        I run this life, still find myself alone
        In this, the place that I call home
        Alone, convincing myself that I'm content
        Yet my heart's contained by a chain-link fence
        It's like, I have children, I am their guide
        And I'm trying to guide myself at the same time

No one's teaching me lessons on the structure of life
I do what I do to keep a place to sleep at night
This shit won't last though, it's getting out of control
I know I'm not always right, that's an essence to behold
But time unveils this tale piece by piece, it will be told
Time unveils this tale piece by piece by piece because
I got what you want, I got what you need
I'll make your throat dry, I'll make your arms bleed
Hit this blunt, it'll blow out your lights
I'll tab you on the tongue and make you dance all night
I get ends when you be itchin' for whatever you're sniffin'
I try to slow my roll but these gurpers keep givin' and givin'
I know it's sinning, it's survival in the same
It's either push this dope and vacation from pain
Or be like the square never set up to gain; it's a question of
    how long not *if* you can hang
Simple and plain, bang, if you can't play the game
It's a grain you can't go up against, this subterrane
Movin' so fast you never know when to jump off the train
It's a damn shame, you see, I got what you want, I got what
    you need
But what do I need?

(Finch hands Malloy his pencil and urges him to answer the question.)

scene 2

Finch and Tet's apartment. Tet is making beats. Malloy is writing in his composition book.

TET:

    If we gonna beat Zac, you gotta practice with me.

MALLOY:

    Naw, dawg, you got it all wrong, we polished to a T.

TET:

    So what about the new shit? We gotta keep it fresh
    A step above the rest—don't you wanna be the best?
    We're the R2-D Crew, I thought you knew
    These Magnificent Two won't stop until we're through
    Live it, walk it, talk it man—

MALLOY:

Look at *you.*

TET:

Don't forget who you're talking to.

MALLOY:

I see where you're going, you got work on your mind
But for me, I'm doing something else with my time
So chill and relax, we made *some* money anyway
Besides this ain't even our practice day.

TET:

You so lazy.

MALLOY:

Look who's talking.

TET:

Man you crazy
I be rocking.

MALLOY:

The cradle. I don't see no crowds you been shocking.

TET:

The subway, the corner, up and down these city streets
I always get my piece seven nights of every week
I'm in my peak . . .

MALLOY:

Don't tweak, take a seat, I'm feeling you
Tonight I'm doing this, tomorrow we work it through.

TET:

And the day after that, till there's no time left
I always wanna work, you always wanna rest.

(Finch enters with a bag of groceries.)

FINCH:

What up, what up!
Damn, smells like a skunk up in here.

TET:

This lazy motherfucker's polluting the atmosphere.

FINCH:

Your dirty little hands, been in my stash?
If you got greedy, I'm a have to whup that ass.

TET:

We just took a pinch, we didn't go crazy
I wanna practice, but this fool got lazy.

FINCH:

You can practice tomorrow.

MALLOY:

Yeah, that's what I said,
Today we take a break, tomorrow we break bread.

FINCH:

You think you know it all, you just breaking like wind
You keep acting like losers how you ever gonna win?

TET:

Malloy's the one who needs to practice, I don't need any more.

MALLOY:

You're talking shit to Zac, you gonna settle that score?

TET:

I ain't worried about that cat. You must be scared of Zac.

MALLOY:

I know he got skills.

TET:

I ain't afraid of that.

MALLOY:

Well all right then, calm down, I'm working this out
I'd show you what it is but you're definitely not down.

TET:

Check this out, there's the door, what you waiting for?
You don't have to be here, you got shit to do I'm sure

beatbox

Acting like that book's your only responsibility
The R2-D Crew. What, you forgot your family?
Yo, I thought you was my boy, that we keep it tight—

(Tet stops the beat.)

Peace, get out, see you later tonight.
MALLOY: Man you are buggin'.

(Malloy exits.)

FINCH:

You know, little brother, I gotta make a point
There's more to do than kick back and smoke my joints.

TET:

Don't treat me like a fool, you know me better than that.

FINCH:

That's right, I know sometimes I have to pick up your slack
Soon there won't be time for that, so keep it together
Malloy, he's your friend, this family tie you can't sever
Even though we're not blood bro', we've been through a lot
I always called your mother "Mom" and you called my father:

TET:

"Pops."

FINCH:

So what does that make us? Where does that take us?
We stick together and they never can shake us
You and I can make things happen for real
Never have to hustle or dance for meals
Because we're rolling with skills and we got mass appeal
From the bottom of the heap to the top of the hill
They gonna know how we feel after we make meals
They can't make these cats stand still, too much will
Our parents never taught us to slip up or slow down
They taught us to work hard from sunup to sundown
They lived for positive and now they're dead in the ground
So tell me why we shouldn't be straight-up with our sound.

TET:

> Fuck this situation and this dark alleyway
> How you supposed to come up when we're living this way?

FINCH:

> That's the question I been questing to change
> Come on, I'll take you to a spot from back in the day.

(Finch and Tet climb onto the rooftop of the building.)

TET: Check out that view. That's downtown, right?
FINCH: Yeah, looks like stars but it's really city lights.
> But check this out:

(Finch makes some echoes, playing with the reverberation of sounds. The scene ends with them doing a beatbox freestyle as the echoes of snares and kicks bounce off the buildings of the city.)

scene 3

The DJ drops the needle on the record as the stage transforms into a club. Finch and Tet are onstage next to the DJ. Zac enters with his crew.

DJ: How you all feeling out there? You still with us? Don't forget to tip bartenders, they're keeping me drunk all night. I'm about to take a break. Right now we got two MCs who say they don't need no DJ; we'll see about that. Ya'll make some noise for the Beatbox Brothers.

> *(Finch and Tet do their beatbox routine. After they finish, Tet takes over with a beatbox solo. Finch sees Zac and calls him over to the stage.)*

FINCH: Damn man, you here already? I thought you were coming later. You wanna do something now?
ZAC: In a minute. Your boy is killing it.
FINCH: Yeah whatever, man, it's just beatbox, he gets to do it all the time. But this is special. *(To the crowd)* Hold on hold on let's get Zac to get up here. His crew wants to dance. Ya'll wanna see that?

(Tet continues beatboxing. Finch pulls Tet's mic from him in the middle of his solo.

*The DJ spins a beat while Zac and the Dancers launch into one of
their routines, stealing the spotlight from Tet. The crowd loves it. After
they are finished, Zac, Finch and the Dancers exit. Malloy watches Tet
from the shadows.*

Tet is alone.)

TET:

> My brother dissed me for Zac, that chump, that shit was bunk
> I'm sick of motherfuckers always faking the funk
> As soon as Zac gets back Finch plays the backstab
> There's nothing that he's got that I don't have
> It's super clear to me it's time to do my own thing
> The only peeps I trust are M and E
> We'll see who bends in the end and who comes out on top
> 'Cause if this don't quit, Tet won't stop.

scene 4

*Finch and Zac are freestyling back in the neighborhood. Malloy is watching
and writing in his composition book. A Man enters. Tet follows him in, starts
beatboxing, and gets the Man to stop and watch. Tet finishes.*

MAN: That was great.
TET: Can you help out?
MAN: I sure can!

(The Man hands Tet some change.)

TET: I know you got some real money.
MAN: I don't—
TET: Come on, come on, I work hard for my money.
MAN: I'm sorry.
TET: You understand what I'm saying? / Do you catch my drift? / Go
     reach for them dollar bills so this transaction can be swift.
FINCH: Hey.

*(Tet looks at Finch. The DJ drops the beat on the [1], on "sides," the second
half of "besides.")*

TET:

> See besides being hungry, addiction it feeds
> Needing five spots or whatever, I'll aim to please

I won't beg if you won't tease, like it dirty, you look clean
That makes it better 'cause I'll give more than your wallet a
Squeeze.

FINCH: Squash all that noise, boy.

TET:

Just write us a check
And leave it blank so you can bleed red blood from the neck.
I'm taking everything you got, don't have to go to your house to
Rob . . .

MAN: Why don't you just get a job!
TET: Motherfucker.

(Tet punches the Man in the stomach. He pulls out a knife.)

Next comes the slice
I'm gonna leave this body to be feasted by the mice
All I wanted was your money, now I want your life
You acting like a hero
It's time for the knife!

(Zac and Finch rush Tet and struggle to grab the knife [for eight counts]. The Man runs off.)

FINCH:

(1, 2) What is this, you can't just play with peoples' lives.

TET:

My pocket's empty so I lash against my strife.

FINCH:

Avoiding everything I taught you.

TET:

No, just doing what my big brother Mickey Finch tells me to do.

FINCH:

I don't tell or command, I just know a little more about the
Outs you can't seem to understand.

TET:

> I understand that if you sit and flesh it out
> Kick back and think about
> Then you're left with no grit in your hand.

FINCH:

> You think you're smoother using actions, not your mind
> Your mind's the strongest tool you have.

TET:

> Besides my knife.

ZAC:

> So you'd kill, leaving us, your boys, to deal?

FINCH:

> 'Cause you don't care, you're just out to get your fill
> Pull a knife, going in for the kill.

ZAC:

> And here we are trying to organize our skills.

FINCH:

> And while you kill, I'm on the streets making deals
> With this lifestyle we'll quickly disappear
> Straight out, I made a promise that I'd teach be true to you
> 'Cause we're about—no Moms, no Pops—just us two
> I go out, you question what I went through raising you?
> When I'm about day and night, getting clothes and feeding you
> You were out; you don't remember nights I didn't sleep at all
> 'Cause you're about the safety sleep brings, the world around
>   you stalled
> But for me I had no choice but to plan
> The best way to keep us alive, my man
> And you repay me by trying to kill, get yourself in jail
> Three square meals but there won't be any "outs" or "abouts"
> Just "should'ves" and "oughts"
> So go back to the spot, 'cause, yo man, here comes the cops.

(We hear a police siren. Finch pushes Zac out and comes back for Tet.)

TET:

> It's the beat, my beat
> Can't change the depths of the street.

FINCH:

But you'll get caught and left for bones without the meat.

TET:

I'm stuffed, shoved and struck by society
Nights I sleep in the alley's reality
While every greedy finger's getting stuck in the honey
I'll never decay in the system's insanity.

FINCH:

They'll be here any second, get off the pride tip
I'm trying to get you out of trouble but you sliding into it.

TET:

I'm the flash of life from the underside.

FINCH:

But just a pixel of light in this gallant blue tide.

TET:

You sent me out before, remember, from the days of old.

FINCH:

I never taught you to be cold, remember, just strong and
Bold
Your bones shook and roll
An egotistical stroll.

TET:

So watch the power of this youth in the world I control
(Beat) I'll take my part in . . .

FINCH:

Peace, fly like the bird.

TET:

Listen up, up, up!
My voice will be heard!

(The beat drops.)

FINCH: Not today.
Get the hell out of here.

(Finch pushes Tet out. Malloy and Zac follow. Finch turns around as the Cops enter.)

COP: Freeze!

scene 5

Ensemble 1–3 take on the form of a Greek chorus crossed with a stomp team. They create the sound track for the story with their bodies as well as speak the voice of the Cop. Finch is center stage in a pool of light. Malloy watches and writes in the composition book.

ENSEMBLE:

      What you gon' do? *(3, 4)*
      What you gon' do? Where you at?
      What you gon' do? *(3, 4)*
      What you gon' do? Where you at?
      What you gon' do? *(3, 4)*
      What you gon' do? Where you at?
      What you gon' do? *(3, 4)*
      What you gon' do? Where you at?
      What you gon' do?

FINCH:

      I just saw these people running.

ENSEMBLE:

      Where you at?

FINCH:

      I was just passing by.

ENSEMBLE:

      Where did you find this knife?

FINCH:

      Picked it up off the ground.

ENSEMBLE:

      Why'd you do that?

FINCH:

      I don't know why.

ENSEMBLE:

Where were you going?
Who were you with?

FINCH:

To my girl's house, just to kick it.

ENSEMBLE:

You're in a lot of trouble.

FINCH:

I don't know how.
It's evident you have no evidence, so now.

ENSEMBLE:

Your ghetto ass had something to do with this
All you do is stand here and lie
You're gonna tell the truth when we're through with this
Gonna hurt more than your pride.

FINCH:

I didn't do it. Why?
You know I never touched that guy.

(Finch tries to get away.)

ENSEMBLE:

We're not done with you yet.

(Finch is beaten down. Lights rise on Tet.)

Where you at? *(3, 4)*
Where you at? What you gonna do?
Where you at? What you gonna do?

TET:

(1, 2) I wish I knew what to do.

ENSEMBLE:

Where you at?

TET:

Another place where no one feels the same as I
Means I'm all alone.

ENSEMBLE:

> So what you gon' do?
> Where you at?

TET:

> Alley cat, live and die
> A low-down, dirty rat.

ENSEMBLE:

> Where you at?

TET:

> I'm out and about.

ENSEMBLE:

> What does that mean?

TET:

> It means there's nothing else for me to be *(3)*
> When everybody *(4)* looks at me as that
> What am I to do?
> So what's next?

MALLOY:

> Put this all back in check
> This home's a mess.

TET:

> Times are changing, time to get my respect.

MALLOY:

> Don't forget where you're at.

TET:

> It's about where we are.
> I can run this alley, fuck trying to be a star.

MALLOY:

> What about your brother?

TET:

> Let him sink and we'll glide
> I'll tell you why, 'cause I'll be "junior" till the day that I die.

MALLOY:

    You know what's at stake
    This story line you can't break.

TET:

    Don't come here bringing waves 'cause I'll cause the earthquake.

MALLOY:

    You're outta my head.

TET:

    Did I hear what he just said?

MALLOY:

    Let it go Tet, and bet you'll come out winning in the end.

TET:

    That's a friend.

MALLOY:

    I been loyal.

TET:

    I hold the royal hand
    (1) So kiss my ring if you're one of my fans
    Start off as a servant, soon you own land.

(Tet grabs Malloy's pencil out of his hand while he writes.)

    Pockets get phat, skills in demand—
MALLOY: Tet, stop!

(Malloy grabs for his pencil [on the (1)]. Tet pulls it away [on the (2)] and breaks it in half [on the (4)]. Malloy picks it up and begins to separate himself from Tet.
    Lights rise on Finch, who is in jail. Tet is alone.)

ENSEMBLE:

    What you gon' do? *(3, 4)*
    What you gon' do? Where you at?
    What you gon' do? *(3, 4)*
    What you gon' do? Where you at?

TET:

    What you gonna do?

FINCH:

    I wish I had something to do.

TET:

    Where you at?

FINCH:

    You don't feel the same as I?

TET:

    What you gonna do?

FINCH:

    Means I'm all alone.

TET:

    Where you at?

FINCH:

    It wouldn't matter if I die
    A low-down, dirty rat
    Where you at?

TET:

    Where you at?

ENSEMBLE:

    What you gonna do?

FINCH:

    Is there anything left for me to—

ENSEMBLE:

    Where you at?

FINCH:

    —be without that fact?
    What am I to do, 'cause this place is wack.

ENSEMBLE:

    Where you at?

FINCH:

> And we're doomed to stay.

ENSEMBLE:

> Out and about!

FINCH:

> Shifting in the shadows
> What you gonna do?

TET:

> That's exactly where I'll stay.

FINCH:

> Where you at?

TET:

> I'm all alone, no place to go
> Nothing to claim my own
> This home's a mess, yes
> That's what I said, this life is dead
> I've had it with you, Finch, I rule my own head
> This alley is my valley.

FINCH:

> That's what I said
> I stole my wad of sixpence, kept my pockets full of bread
> I did everything I could to put you where you're at today
> And here you are so quick to throw it all away.

TET:

> We're from the streets, that's the way I'm gonna stay.

FINCH:

> That's the words of a stray, you see a million every day
> Put you straight up to bat in the game and make you play.

TET:

> Instead of your game, I'll play my own way.

FINCH:

> You'll be on your own, nothing will ever change
> Still have the same aim, but not the same game

You can't just sit back, watching time go by
It lacks promise and heart, Tet, look me in the eyes
Loose your grip on this "streets" thing, that shit won't play
I'll wake up one day and find Tet here slain
So listen to reason, bro, hear what I say.

TET:

I hear what you're saying, but I'm not listening today
I *am* the streets.

FINCH:

I was dropped and left, you was sucking thumbs
From boy to man and then B-boy
I built this life, I beat the drum
This place ain't no joke, get that straight
So I'm relieving my mind, it's time to ease this weight
Before my time is up, whether I like it or not
This cell, it's always cold, whether I like it or not.

TET:

I can't help you with your pain, 'cause we reside on separate
    plains.

FINCH:

I can't condone your evil tone, that's it.

TET:

It's on.

*(Tet and Finch have a scratch battle, vocally scratching, trading four
counts back and forth.)*

ALL:

We're all alone, we've got to roam
And distance ourselves from this home
We know inside that the power's there.

TET:

I want my share.

ALL *(To Finch)*:
What you gon' do?

TET:

> I want my share.

FINCH *(To Malloy)*:

> What you gon' do?

TET:

> I want my share.

MALLOY *(To Tet)*:

> What you gon' do?

TET:

> I want my share.

ALL:

> What you gon' do?

TET:

> I want my share.

ALL:

> What you gon' do?

TET:

> I want my share.

ALL:

> What you gon' do?

TET:

> I want my share.

ALL:

> Where you at?

TET:

> I got my own back!

(Blackout.)

scene 6

Lights rise on Finch in his cell. The DJ makes a beat reminiscent of a heart-beat with kick and snare sounds.

FINCH:

       The street's not a word
       It's a code that we serve
       Now that honor's been lost
       What's the price, what's the cost?
       Because Tet broke the code
       Watch the plan, unfold
       This can't resolve by itself
       I gotta do something else.

(To DJ) Yo man, I got this.

(Finch beatboxes, doing the monologue at the same time.)

       I can beat this
       Fuck the bull
       The power to control is tangible
       And I felt this
       Against my will
       My spirit you can't break, my body you can kill.

       The street's not a word
       It's a code that we serve
       Now that honor's been lost
       What's the price, what's the cost?
       Because Tet broke the code
       Watch the plan unravel, unfold
       This can't resolve by itself
       I gotta find the answers, help myself.

       If I beat this
       I'll use my pull
       The power to control's attainable
       Then I'll do whatever
       To stay on track
       Grab the microphone and tell the DJ wheel it back.

(The DJ joins in with Finch by creating the same beat he did before, using kick and snare sounds.)

> I'll stop dealing
> I'll go to work
> Whatever to continue to function upon this earth
> I can beat this
> Yo I got this
> I can do this
> 'Cause it's my shit
> I can, if I
> I can, if I—

COP *(Approaching the cell)*: Finch, step out of your cell and follow the blue line.

(Lights fade on Finch and rise on Zac standing outside of the police station. Finch comes out of the station and sees Zac.)

FINCH: What are you doing here?

ZAC: I heard you got into some trouble.

FINCH: It's no trouble. It's nothing I can't handle.

ZAC: You would still be in there if it weren't for me.

FINCH: What, you bail me out?

ZAC: Yup.

FINCH: Well, I'll get you back. I don't need your cash.

ZAC:

> Proud Finch, too proud to take an inch
> Too proud to let your best friend help you in a pinch.

FINCH: This is nothing, I been here before now.
> I never needed nobody to bail me out.

ZAC:

> Yeah that's it, the doctor with the fix
> Got the crackheads on your side, 'cause you're dealing 'em shit
> All the kids we used to know wait in line for their hits
> When they used to run away 'cause we were coming to rip.

FINCH:

> Zac, you got it all wrong. See, it was a one-time pass, didn't
> plan to go long

But when my parents died I had to keep going strong
To move things along I had to keep flowing on.

ZAC:

We used to have dreams of me and you as a team
Take the world by storm, let 'em hear what we mean.

FINCH:

You took the storm by yourself, in a moment of need
You weren't here to see things fall apart at the seams
I kept baby stepping—life, it made me walk faster
I wouldn't be the cause of my own disaster.

ZAC:

I got a family to deal with, Moms, Pops and my sis
But you also gotta know that you're a part of it
Don't forget that, after all we been through
Amongst us, against them, not me against you.

FINCH:

Amongst us, against them?

ZAC:

'Cause of the clothes that we wear. Amongst us, against them
'Cause of the way we act.

FINCH:

Amongst us, against them.

ZAC:

The places we live.

FINCH:

How we're talked to and how we talk back.

ZAC:

Amongst us, against them
The crack house is not us.

FINCH:

The jail cell is not us.

ZAC:

The thickest mind outlives the bluff.

FINCH:

> Amongst them, against us
> The choice is ours to find the means.

FINCH AND ZAC:

> We're the only ones stopping us from touching our dreams.

ZAC:

> When I was on tour I was dancing, not rapping
> I always knew with you we could make things happen
> Let's put things together, get back on track
> Back onstage, in the studio, making it phat
> Back to the Dynamic Duo, we used to be one
> You finish my thoughts—

FINCH:

> —before you've hardly begun
> Ever since survival became my life
> Day after day it's been an uphill fight.

ZAC:

> I know what you're saying, but it's time to stop
> Time to start a crew, time to get our props
> Time is ticking away 'cause the time is right now
> We got the skills, got the power, got the strength, got the
>   know-how.

FINCH:

> Now I'm listening . . .

ZAC:

> We got it all we can't stall.

FINCH:

> And unlike the rest, these cats will never fall.

ZAC:

> Good to see you're on my side, let me tell you the deal
> When we're through with this mission, we'll be big time for real.

(Zac and Finch do their "Big Time for Real" dance. It is their fantasy of what their crew could become in the future. The Dancers create a stylized, fantasized version of a large concert. Dancing and rapping, Finch

beatbox

*and Zac are joined onstage by Tet and Malloy. In the end it all comes
back to Zac and Finch, and we realize that the whole production was in
their heads, just a daydream.)*

scene 7

Finch's apartment. Tet breaks in through the window.

TET:

> The loss of control, lost my home, now I'm ready
> To bring in the beat that will rock them steady
> If you're not on my side, if you're not on Tet's team
> You better get with me now before you get "smoke screened."

ALL:

> You ready for the streets?
> You ready for the real?

TET:

> I'm ready for whatever
> Borrow, beg or steal.

ALL:

> You got it like Finch?
> You ready little boy?

(Tet pulls out Finch's gun.)

TET:

> I'm better than Finch.
> I'm ready to destroy.
>
> Here is a power I've never had
> Cock back real fast and I'm ready to blast
> Been beaten down way too long and I'm finally out
> Converting past on pretense that my sight sees new routes.

ALL:

> Remember, Tet, you're nothing but a street kid.

FINCH:

> Think about that or you're gonna end up dead.

TET:

    Think about? What's there to think about?
    I'm 'bout to pillage and steal to get aggressions out
    The coin has been flipped; it'll be heads when it drops
    It's time to get out and bust some chops.

(Tet cocks the gun and climbs out the window.)

scene 8

The mouth of the alley. Malloy is carrying his composition book.

MALLOY:

    I still seek the people's story
    Where we fight for the truth to get free
    I thought these folks were family
    'Cause we walk the same ground and had the same needs.
    This world shows nothing but hate
    You spectate, judge others, while you think that you're great
    "It's all good," is what we say when we know that it ain't
    This line is so crooked, time to make it straight
    First I'm gonna finish this piece 'cause I'm a writer
    An MC, a B-boy, not a thug or street fighter
    Talk about the people that I know and reveal some
    Circumstance—no chance, cash advance, low income—
    Show them that I see them when I look in their eye
    That this is our chance to take this story worldwide
    I wanna show the love, the hate, the hope, in all its glory
    Show them that this is way bigger than Finch and Tet's story.

scene 9

Zac and Finch are onstage performing at the club. Tet enters, pushes his way through the crowd, pulls the needle off the record and grabs the DJ's mic.

TET: Yo, Finch!
FINCH: What are you doing here?
TET: You think you got the hot shit without me? Let's battle!
FINCH: Let's do this then.

(Finch and Tet beatbox battle. Tet repeatedly tells the sound man to turn his mic up louder. Eventually the sound man shuts Tet's mic off completely. The Ensemble and Finch clown around. Tet pulls out the gun. Everything gets silent.)

TET:

Well well, Mr. Finch, I say we battle again.

FINCH:

I don't know who you are, but Tet went off the deep end.

TET:

What do you know, Finch? I could be just like you
I'm a natural-born leader.

FINCH:

A leader to who?

TET:

It's what you started.

FINCH:

What I started?

TET:

Yeah, what you started
Now I'm the star kid.

FINCH:

Give me my gun!

TET:

Take it away, if you think you have the power.

FINCH:

Yo man, don't play.

TET:

There ain't no way that I will let this power, gripped in my hand
Fall into the clutches of another man.

ALL:

But it can.

FINCH:

> You only think of self, nothing else
> Nothing I can do, because of you
> Involves anything but our wealth
> Especially our wealth.

TET:

> But nothing can stop my stampede.

FINCH:

> For what?

TET:

> The need!

FINCH:

> Of what?

TET:

> The speed!

FINCH:

> For what?

TET:

> The greed!

FINCH:

> What?

TET:

> The greed!

FINCH:

> The seed that breeds the weeds.
> For greed?

TET:

> Brother, please!

FINCH:

> Take heed.

TET:

No need. Step back, I'll take the lead
I hold the reins, I move this steed.

FINCH:

So go on and shoot me, kid, if you're up to the challenge
'Cause that's the only way to bring in the true balance.

(Tet shoots the gun into the ceiling.)

ALL:

One!

FINCH:

Thought you were a smart one, but you're not.

ALL:

Two!

FINCH:

Had no plan, so you went and took a shot.

ALL:

Three!

FINCH:

Your cat hiss missed, and you think I'm
Pissed about this new twist, 'cause you insist on
Craving the control that takes you high as hell
You're so full of rage, your head's starting to swell
It's exactly what they want us to do under their spell
So every night they have the same story to tell.

ALL:

Escape!

TET:

Why?

ALL:

Success is rare.

TET:

Relax, I'm the leader, you're in my care.

ZAC:

> Who made you God to make nature's choice?

FINCH:

> With that piece of industry you speak a coward's voice.

ZAC:

> It's so easy to cock and pull that trigger.

FINCH:

> Find a word or thing to say would make you that much bigger.

ZAC:

> Don't just stay shut up, looking like a dumb punk.

FINCH:

> Waving that tool, hoping to find beginner's luck
> 'Cause you won't.

ZAC:

> You'll miss, your luck'll run out.

ZAC, MALLOY AND FINCH:
> Change that fate, that's what it's all about.

TET:

> Step back, or be a flash of the past
> This is my companion in the quest to blast
> My way to the top, and I'm displaying my pride
> Malloy, you fuck with my ride, we're gonna collide
> A kid from the block's got to do what's to be done
> Grab the light and run, toy with your soul, I've just begun
> So fear me.

FINCH:

> No hear me? I don't think you feel me.

TET:

> Drop it, Finch. I hear and feel you but you're starting to bug
> me.

(Malloy stands in between Finch and Tet, trying to stop the confronta-tion. Finch is hot and needs restraint.)

MALLOY:

> Be cool because it's my time to start
> It's really hard to realize that this is your arc
> I hope you see I didn't forget the times that have past
> I hope you see that this connection is built to last
> You talk, you talk back, it's outta control
> This terrorizing error is voiding your soul
> Now you're setting to blast, life is taking its toll
> The power of this unit is when we stand whole
> You're acting too blind, you can't heed the signs
> So I'll say this once, one last time:

FINCH, MALLOY AND ZAC:

> Loose yourself from the noose, find something divine.

TET:

> No, not this time!

(Tet shoots. Finch and Malloy react.)

MALLOY:

> It's the beat, this beat's controlling the heart's heat
> The difference between you and me is so concrete
> That's the aspect of life I never knew.

TET:

> You never could beat me.

MALLOY:

> I never tried to.

TET:

> Now here we are.

MALLOY:

> Yes, my blood bleeds red.

TET:

> A shot of reality, now you're dead!

(Malloy falls.)

MALLOY:

    Unluckily, you're someone who lives to kill the striving ones
    And use their pain and agony to fuel his attack
    You started this and you can't take it back.

(Malloy dies.)

TET: What? Did he say what I just thought he said? / I'm alive and you
    are dead?
      Malloy!!!!
FINCH: I don't think he understands.

(DJ drops the beat [on the (1)], the next "don't.")

TET:

    Man, if you don't know what you're saying then you should
      shut it
    'Cause if you had this gun, I would guarantee you'd love it.

FINCH:

    I know you love that feeling gripped in your hand
    'Cause it belonged to this man, understand
    What the hell is going on? All this shit's gone wrong
    You killed your boy, he ain't waking up, he's gone
    You just sealed your fate, all darkness no light
    You really fucked up 'cause you just ruined your life.

TET:

    I said, it's what you started.

FINCH:

    But what you finished
    You think you got trouble
    Now you're just in it
    You always had power.

TET:

    You always take it away.

FINCH:

    That's not power.

TET:

It is today.

(Tet points the gun at Finch. They struggle for the gun. We hear sirens.)

FINCH: You fucked up!

TET: You're not my mother, not my father . . .

FINCH: I treated you like a brother . . .

TET: Not a foe, not a friend . . .

FINCH: I treated you like *blood* brother. / I told you time and time that I'd be down till the end. / I went to jail for you once and I'm not going again.

(Finch gets the gun from Tet.)

So now what are you gonna do? You gonna run?

(Tet stays silent.)

You gonna shoot everybody so there's no witnesses now?

(Tet stays silent.)

What? What then?

TET: I didn't mean to kill him. You know I didn't mean it. It was self-defense, right?

(Tet is looking for sympathy, but no one is there for him. The sirens get louder.)

Come on Finch, let's get out of here.

FINCH: No, it's all on you. I have nothing to do with it.

TET: You have the gun.

FINCH: Deal with it.

(Finch puts the gun in Tet's hand and exits with Zac. The sirens get louder. Tet stands over Malloy's body.)

TET: I seek a new story / The battles and dreams of ancestry / Many paths to follow, this one was my choice / Should have silenced the gun, instead I silenced a voice / Did this path choose me, or did I choose it?

(Tet reaches down and grabs Malloy's composition book.)

Do I recite these lines or do I write a new script? / Folk, fairy and fake tale, the answer for me is / This is the story line I belong to.

(The Cop enters with his gun drawn as the lights fade.)

THE END

Tommy Shepherd is a father, husband, actor, playwright, B-boy, rapper, drummer and beatboxer. His wife, Anna Maria, had their baby boy in November 2007!

His most recent conquest was rewriting an incomplete script, formerly written by Duke Ellington, called *Queenie Pie*. The play was performed at the Oakland Opera in May 2008. In December 2008 Tommy created and performed his first one-act solo-performance piece *The MF in ME*, premiering at Intersection for the Arts in San Francisco for their *Grounded* festival of new works.

Shepherd has spent much of the last couple years acting in a children's cooking show *Doof* (food backwards), and performing and touring internationally with Marc Bamuthi Joseph in *Scourge*. His next project with Bamuthi Joseph will be participating as a musician/beatboxer in the *break/s*. Tommy is also co-founder of the live hip-hop band, Felonious: onelovehiphop, which plays throughout the world and also develops and creates theatrical productions. He also created the score for Donald Lacy's touring show *Color Struck*.

His next collaboration with Dan Wolf is *Stateless*, in which he'll be performing and creating the live musical soundscape.

Tommy was a long-time Hybrid Project resident artist at Intersection for the Arts, along with Erika Chong Shuch and Dan Wolf. He is a member of Intersection's resident theater company Campo Santo. Tommy has also been performing with Erika Chong Shuch's ESP Project, Intersection's resident dance-theater company. He was in the sold-out runs of the dance-theater piece *One Window* and *51802*. Most recently for Intersection, Tommy acted in and created the live score for *Hamlet: Blood in the Brain*, by Naomi Iizuka with Campo Santo, and he created the sound design and score with Howard Wiley for *A Place to Stand*. He also acted, beatboxed and composed a live score with Scheherazade Stone for *Domino* by Campo Santo with Sean San José, directed by Erika Chong Shuch, which premiered at Yerba Buena Center for the Arts in 2005. In 2004 he was an actor, the musical director and live vocal musician for the play *Fist of Roses* by Philip Kan Gotanda created with Campo Santo + Intersection.

Dan Wolf is an actor, rapper, playwright, producer and educator. As an actor, Wolf has worked with Word for Word, Crowded Fire, Intersection for the Arts, Shotgun Players and Porchlight Theatre Company. He is a founding member of the hip-hop band Felonious: onelovehiphop. His play *Beatbox: A Raparetta* (co-authored with Tommy Shepherd) has been produced in San Francisco, Oakland and Petaluma, CA; at the NYC Hip-Hop Theater Festival; and in Germany. He is currently creating *Stateless*, a hip-hop- and beatbox-infused theatrical collaboration with Tommy Shepherd, balancing German and Jewish history with the problems of racism and the Jewish/African American experience. He is also creating a piece based on the novel *Angry Black White Boy* by Adam Mansbach. As an educator he has worked with the Berkeley Repertory School of Theatre, Hybrid Project at Intersection for the Arts and Youth Speaks. Wolf is also Program Manager of The Hub at JCCSF (Jewish Community Center of San Francisco), which promotes the evolution of Jewish arts, culture and community.

For performance rights, contact: feloniousinfo@earthlink.net or visit www.myspace.com/feloniousonelove

death of a ho
a fairy scary whorey tale
or
the perils of following
the yellow bling road

by jake-ann jones

 Circa 1982 I was introduced into the hip-hop (then generally termed "rap") scene by my younger brother—who was busy filling our living room with turntables and beatboxes, cans of spray paint, and stacks of twelve inches by Spoonie G, The Funky Four Plus One More, Grand Master Flash and the SugarHill Gang, among others. The beat was infectious, the bravado hella sexy, and I was a fan, immediately and intensely. It was the days of fat laces, Lees with permanent creases, and graffitied hats, T-shirts, and anything else that stayed put long enough for my brother to attack.

There were no real rap videos to speak of. Yet.

For the next few years I hung out at the Roxy every week, listening to Afrika Bambaataa and Red Alert spin on the turntables, watching the Rock Steady Crew spin on the floors, and watching the likes of Run-DMC and the Zulu Nation blow up the stage in all their homeboy glory. To me, it felt like a revolution was being televised. Meanwhile, back in my Harlem hood, rap music emanated from boom boxes on the street corners and at the house parties. It was either fun and funky . . . or it was real and sobering—music as a witness to truth. As immortalized by Flash, "Don't push me 'cause I'm close to the edge / I'm tryin' not to lose my head / It's like a jungle sometimes, it makes me wonder / How I keep from goin' under . . ."

Somewhere along the way, the simple poetry and freshness of all that got sucked up and dragged under by the Reagan/Bush New World order. As a friend recently put it, "Bling was hip-hop's response to Dynasty and Reaganomics." In other words, hip-hop, like everything else in these United States of America, was quickly diluted and deluded by the ching-ching of Wu-Tang's poetic cream, "Cash rules everything around me . . . get the money . . . dollar, dollar bill y'all . . ."

Not to say there still wasn't, and still isn't, some great hip-hop music being made, 'cause, thank God, there is. But for an old-school head, now, more often than not, I'd rather ignore the nihilistic, self-hating, sex and bling-obsessed lyrics, and just settle for the beats. And meanwhile, youth culture across the board continues to be perverted by the American dream of getting more, more, more—by any means necessary.

Death of a Ho is the me in all of that. I remember the dawning of MTV. And because my own journey through adulthood has mirrored the journey of yesterday's to today's hip-hop/pop culture, my own spiritual and personal evolution hasn't escaped the bitter realities of what today's sell-out to buy-in culture has wrought upon my ideas of femininity, sexuality and race. My sometimes naive and self-pitying/often greedy and somewhat amoral/always calculating and therefore too-smart-for-her-own-good heroine is, unfortunately, a cipher of my own flat-out disturbed inner child.

Parents—watch out for music videos, is all I can say.

Now, as a mom, I'm already wondering about a list of counter-terrorism answers to my sons' questions about the lyrics and content of the hip-hop music they're probably destined to love. I have no idea how to reconcile, let alone explain, the contradictions and complexities of the music. Or the culture. Or, for that matter, being an American, at all. Or, feeling like a ho, since I'm inherently a capitalist/materialist in spite of myself, albeit one with strong convictions regarding our culture's lack of spirituality . . . the pimp/ho versus love/relationship economy . . . the sale of flesh . . . and the evils of bling.

Death of a Ho is, at the end of the day, my salute to all these unreconciled questions. It's a sample of images, beats, theory, pictures and poems; hopefully one can find some reason in its rhyme . . . and music in its madness.

'Cause, hey—it's like a jungle sometimes, y'all, and it all does *still* make me wonder.

production history

Death of a Ho: A Fairy Scary Whorey Tale or The Perils of Following the Yellow Bling Road received its first workshop presentation as part of the 1997 Brown University/Steinberg New Plays Festival. It received subsequent workshop productions at The Bay Area Playwrights Festival (1998; Rhodessa Jones, director; Kim Euell, dramaturg; Larry Andrews, visual artist), the Cleveland Public Theatre's New Plays Festival and New York Theatre Workshop. It received a workshop production by the Hourglass Group (Elyse Singer, Artistic Director) as part of its Next Stage Festival in New York City. Presented in association with New Georges, with support from the Jonathan Larson Performing Arts Foundation, performances were August 25–27, 2003. At the time, it was a musical called *Magic Kingdom: Tale of an American Girl*, with music composed by the author, Bruce Purse and "Prince Charles" Alexander. This published version of *Death of a Ho* reflects the most lucid interpretation of lessons learned through the development of both the play and the musical.

characters

CHOCOLATE, a suicide attemptee in a dream state, African American, thirties. Later the Woman with Wings.

GEECHEE FAIRY, Chocolate's transvestite/hermaphrodite fairy godmother; probably of African conjurings at her/his roots (although fairies don't have all that race stuff going on). Keep in mind the same actor plays Allen.

BRENDA, a photographer, European American, thirties or maybe forty.

GLORIA, wannabe actress, fair-skinned African American, early thirties.

SLAM, a super-macho rap star, African American, thirties. Later a dead ghoul.

CURT, Slam's A&R man, European American, thirties. Later a dead ghoul.

ALLEN, Brenda's investment banker husband, African American, forties. The same actor plays Geechee Fairy.

RONALD, Gloria's filmmaker boyfriend, European American. The same actor plays the Priest.

note on the play

It is important to consider that all the characters in this play are basically playing their scenes for Chocolate (she watches everything, even when she's not immediately involved). And since the scenes are all really manifestations of her comatose mind anyway, there isn't necessarily a "naturalistic" logic to their behavior . . . which can allow the horror part of the story to be really horrible, and the kooky stuff to be really kooky. So a really important thing is to link each character's motivation to Chocolate, and what's going on inside of her—'cause in the end, it's really all about Chocolate.

note on sound, music and rhyme

Music, sound and rhythm all bumped in my head and heart as I wrote this, so our drum/spirit must be a big part of the viscera of this play. Ideally some great beats accompany lots of moments, but rhymes don't have to be performed in any special way or thought of as "rapping." Whatever rhythm the performer brings to it can be enough.

note on video

"Chocolate the Zombie" can be that creepy, washed-out, slow-moving scary thing we hope we never become in this life or the next . . . or something less literal, but just as disturbing. The idea is to evoke Chocolate's worst nightmare of herself as she lies in a near-death state. It is important for us to remember she exists somewhere else, somehow else (likewise with the other zombie characters). Any other details mentioned regarding video are ideas to be considered, and reconsidered, at the discretion of the artists involved. When used, live-feed video has been both wonderful and distracting in past productions. For me, the use of video has something to do with revealing the fracturing of Chocolate's consciousness.

act one

In the dark, we hear an ethereal voice—the Woman with Wings:

WOMAN WITH WINGS: Are you watching?
  Are you watching?
  Turn it on.

(Video projection: "Death of a Ho . . . a Fairy Scary Whorey Tale."
  The video becomes a sea of faces, an audience, pointing and laughing at something before them.
  We hear the sound of unwholesome, breathy laughter.
  Chocolate appears, in front of her mirror.)

CHOCOLATE: All those years of being a good little colored girl . . . and where the hell did it get me? Well, that game's over. My soul is barren. No thing will live inside. No love, no life . . . There's a war going on, but the evening news isn't covering it.

(The laughter increases.)

What's so funny? What the hell do you know? All you want is fresh meat, your palate's acid and your entrails belch fire! If only my brain hadn't learned to forget my own name in exchange for your false fatted cow . . . if only I had the guts to barter with a better devil than you! I'd trade my sorry soul for a meaner magic than you ever did see, then you'd see how bad a girl I could be . . . GET OUT OF MY FACE! Dammit, I've had enough already . . . ENOUGH!

(Chocolate moves to break her mirror. We hear the sound of breaking glass. The laughter fades. Shards of broken glass rain down. The video goes out.)

(Lifting a shard of glass to her wrist) When I was a little girl, I thought if I could just smile like the women in the toothpaste ad, the world

wouldn't feel so damn hard all the time—like sandpaper rubbing against my skin. But even when I learned to smile . . . like this *(Gives a toothpaste ad smile)* . . . it still didn't work. Which is when I realized the problem was simply that I was invisible. So I prayed for my fairy godmother to show me how to become the biggest and brightest of all—'cause then, and only then, would world peace finally be attained: when everyone knew how special I really was. And if not world peace, at least my ass could get out of the ghetto. And hell, I woulda done anything, for that.

(Chocolate slits her wrist.
 We hear the sound of alarm bells; then a hospital heart monitor's beeping bleeds into the sound of a heartbeat, which melds into a beat-box rhythm.
 We see a video of Chocolate the Zombie. Chocolate, her face painted ashen pale with dark rings around her eyes, like the "walking dead," wears a hospital gown. Blood runs from her wrists and the corners of her mouth.
 Chocolate lies on the ground, her wrists bloody; she's having the nightmare.)

No . . . NO! THAT'S NOT ME!

(Geechee Fairy appears.
 The video goes out.)

GEECHEE FAIRY: Ya do anyting, eh? Girl, you a mess . . .

CHOCOLATE *(Sitting up, startled)*: Who are you?

GEECHEE FAIRY: What, don't ya recognize me? I'm ya fairy godmother!

CHOCOLATE: What? Fairy godmothers don't exist. And even if they did, you're not what I—

GEECHEE FAIRY: —expected? Well, dat might be . . . Carryin' the spirit of all things, male and female, hot and cold, good and bad . . . done messed wit' me looks. Den again . . . maybe de face of one's dark side never look too good, eh? *You* wished me up . . . Call me de Geechee Fairy . . . And what should I call you?

CHOCOLATE: Huh?

GEECHEE FAIRY: Ya name, girl, what's ya name?

CHOCOLATE: Oh . . . I . . . I . . . My mirror broke . . . and I can't remember . . . anything . . .

GEECHEE FAIRY: Uh-huh . . . Well, let's see . . . something appealin', I'd think . . . something sweet . . . and—tasty, huh? How about— Chocolate!

CHOCOLATE: Chocolate? What kind of name is that?

GEECHEE FAIRY: Lets people know you go down smooth. Important, if ya want to really get ahead in dis here world . . . Ya got a better idea?

(A beat.)

CHOCOLATE: Not at this moment, but—

GEECHEE FAIRY: I din't tink so. Fine, den. Chocolate it is.

CHOCOLATE: Well, if you're my fairy godmother, how are you gonna help me?

GEECHEE FAIRY: Depends. What is it you want?

CHOCOLATE: Well . . . to start over. With a better life . . . where I can get what I want.

GEECHEE FAIRY: Which is?

CHOCOLATE: Well . . . to be important. Desired. Recognized. You know—to be *somebody*.

GEECHEE FAIRY: Is dat it? What about de "world peace" part?

CHOCOLATE: Please. First, everyone has to know who I am. I have to be—rich, and powerful. Like, a star, basically. These days, the only way to get respect, is to be a star.

GEECHEE FAIRY: And how would you get to do that? Become a star? *(Points to blood on her wrists)* Ya better let me take care of dat . . . *(Wipes off the blood and bandages her wrists)*

CHOCOLATE: Well, you know, there are lots of ways. Maybe, be a famous actress . . . or a politician! Or a singer. I like to dance; I'd even be a dancer—who makes a lot of money. And . . . oh, I don't know.

GEECHEE FAIRY: Well, if ya don't know, I can't help ya. Ya gotta be specific, when ya bargaining wit' ya soul . . .

CHOCOLATE: Well, anything has to be better than the nothing I was. I mean . . . Am. The nothing I am.

GEECHEE FAIRY: Well, Chocolate, my sweet . . . maybe I got something for ya . . .

(A light comes up on a magic suitcase.)

CHOCOLATE: What the hell is that?

GEECHEE FAIRY: Well, sounds like ya tired of ya old bag—dis a new one. A magic bag. Good fa three wishes . . . plus one fa good luck. De antidote to your past . . . de key to ya future. Just open it up, and pick a beginnin'. Any beginnin'. Don't matter what it is . . . history up fa grabs in dis place anyway. 'Sides . . . it's all ya fantasy, right? But be careful . . . sometimes de bag, it like to play tricks . . .

CHOCOLATE: Tricks? What tricks?

(Chocolate opens the suitcase. We hear the sound of shimmery bells. We see shimmery lights.)

Oh wow . . . Is this for real? This is amazing! God, I wish someone could see this—

(Lights come up on the audience.)

What . . . who—

GEECHEE FAIRY: Ya wished for dem, didn't ya? Someone to see dis . . . and you, too? Ya captive audience . . . ya own private public. Well, dere dey are.

CHOCOLATE: But—I didn't mean that to be a wish!

(The lights on the audience fade.)

GEECHEE FAIRY: Like I say, be careful, girl! Dis what ya ask for—"meaner" magic, I tink ya call it?

> So watch what ya say
> and what ya thinkin', too
> 'cause dis bag can read
> ya mind fa you.
> Please beware, sweet Chocolate,
> what 'tis ya do
> 'cause when ya wishes up
> you may be, too.

Remember? Ya done sold ya soul, gal!

> So what ya wish fa—choose wit' care
> or ya dream come true as a true nightmare.
> Choose well, little daughta—choose very well
> or dis Geechee Fairy—gonna see you in hell!

(We hear the sound of the heartbeat, then a clap of thunder. Geechee Fairy disappears.)

CHOCOLATE: Yeah . . . great. Thanks for the hint. "Fairy godmother" my ass . . .

(Chocolate turns to the audience.)

OK. But if she's right, and this bag really works, now I have my chance—to pursue fame, fortune and happiness. And ain't that the American way? *(Closes suitcase)* Anything I want . . . there are so many possibilities. Hmm. I just want to try it out first, so let me pick something fun, to start. I know—maybe the music industry, that's exciting, glamorous—like in the videos! I always wanted to be one of those hot, sexy dancers—but a well-paid one. And maybe, one who gets to meet and marry a famous, loaded music personality . . . Yeah. What the hell, let's try it, see how it turns out. OK: I WISH TO BE A SUCCESSFUL, WELL-PAID VIDEO DANCER!

(Chocolate closes her eyes and opens the suitcase. We see shimmery lights. We hear the sound of a banging hip-hop beat.

Out of the suitcase she pulls a skimpy halter top, Daisy Duke shorts and a gun.)

Oh my God, is this real? Uugh! Why is there a gun in there? *(Throws the gun back in the suitcase)* Well, let's see . . . new clothes!

(As Chocolate puts on the clothes, Slam and Curt appear, each sitting on an end of a large couch, talking on cell phones.)

CURT: So he'll do it, he'll do it . . .
SLAM: I tole the muthafucka for twenty-five Gs, yeah, I'd do it . . .
CURT: He'll be there, growling at the cameras, selling your beer . . . *(To Slam)* We always wanted to do commercials, didn't we, guy?
SLAM *(Ignoring him)*: Shit man, these ofays got cash for days, but I'm the one making it for 'em, so they betta fork over that dime . . .
CURT: Yeah, things are great, we're doing something new with the act, gonna add some ass to the show . . .
SLAM: Yeah, man, the white boy finally came up with a good idea—thinks hos'll liven shit up onstage, so we tryin' some out . . .

(Chocolate steps forward in her new outfit; both men notice.)

CURT: In fact, here's some now . . .
SLAM: Aa-ight, peace, lemme know 'bout dat, word.

(They put their phones away, giving Chocolate lascivious looks.)

CURT: Well, hellooo . . .
CHOCOLATE: Hello! I was looking for the music-video people?

CURT: Uh-huh . . . well, maybe we can accommodate you, we, uh, do music videos; I'm sure you recognize the platinum-selling recording artist Slam the Mad Maxter? And I'm his highness's lowly A&R man . . .

SLAM: Man, shut the fuck up, you talk too damn much . . . So, ho, you dance, or what?

CHOCOLATE: Uh—'scuse me?

SLAM: Can you shake it?

CHOCOLATE: Shake what?

SLAM: That big-ass booty of yours, girl! We need some rump-shaking goin' on 'round here!

CHOCOLATE: Well, actually—

CURT: Yeah, that's right, we need to see you in action, honey . . . in fact, you're lucky—we're gonna arrange a little impromptu audition right here and now . . . and if you're good enough, we'll put you in the next video, you'll get to wear something hot, maybe some real sexy close-ups . . .

CHOCOLATE: Well, actually, I was looking for something a little more—

SLAM: Later for that, we ain't got all day . . . Shake that ass, bitch!

(Chocolate reluctantly dances a bit.)

CURT: That's right, you go, baby. Lots of girls would die to have a personal audition with the Mad Maxter . . . uh-huh . . . yeah . . .

SLAM: Uh-huh . . . nice . . . Awright . . . but if you really wanna be in this game, I got some further prerequisites for the job . . . *(Throws his cell phone to Curt)* Earn your share of my loot; hold my calls. *(Beckoning Chocolate to the couch)* Over here, sweet thing . . .

(Chocolate sits.)

Awright, now . . . And you a fine little chocolate thing, too . . . Can I get a bite?

(He makes a move on her.)

CHOCOLATE *(Pushing him away)*: What the hell are you doing?

SLAM: Whatchu think? Any ho working for me gotta be able to multi-task, baby . . .

(He moves on her again; she wriggles away. Curt grabs her.)

CHOCOLATE: Get off of me! Don't touch—

CURT: OK, OK, honey, calm down . . . Man, come on, that ain't right . . . *(Guiding her gently around the back of the couch)* You know you need to work on your finesse a little, maybe the females wouldn't play so hard to get . . .

(Slam approaches from the other side; Curt pushes her toward him.)

And you gotta remember to turn the music up, all the racket ain't good for business. And I want my piece when you're done this time, dude, we got a deal . . .

(Slam pushes her down to the floor behind the couch. As she screams, Curt grabs a remote control from the couch and aims it at an unseen stereo system. The music comes on very loud.
We see a video of Chocolate the Zombie observing images of nudity and exhibitionism in various music videos.
As muffled struggles are heard from behind the couch, Curt checks his cell phone messages. Eventually Slam calls from behind the couch:)

SLAM: So whatchu waitin' for, fool!

(Curt undoes his zipper and moves behind the couch as Slam stands and refastens his pants. Slam sits on the couch and checks his cell messages. After a moment, Curt stands, redoing his pants. Moments later Chocolate crawls from behind the couch, her clothes undone, crying.)

Whatchu cryin' for, girl, it's just getting a li'l piece, ain't no thing . . .
CHOCOLATE: You bastards . . . you want a piece, huh???

(She crawls to the suitcase, removes the gun and aims it at them.)

Then take this—AND GO TO HELL!
SLAM AND CURT: Oh shit!

(She fires. The sound of gunshots.
Blackout.
A video of Chocolate the Zombie watching various scenes of violence and gangsterism on TV, in videos and film.
The lights come up on Chocolate onstage, cradling the gun. She throws the gun into the suitcase and quickly slams it shut.)

CHOCOLATE: That's not—that's not me . . . that's not who I am . . . that's not who I am . . .

(The video of Chocolate the Zombie gives way to a video of Ronald.)

RONALD: OK, just, straight at me . . . right. Well. See, people have, like, this real, need to see themselves. See their—mirror, image, I guess, as powerful . . . desirable.

CHOCOLATE: Who the hell—

RONALD: So they construct images of themselves, and others. Fantasies. And sometimes they end up confusing themselves with their own—or somebody else's—fantasized constructions.

(The video quickly goes out.)

CHOCOLATE: What the—look, Miss Geechee Fairy, those men . . . I don't know what's going on here, or who those men were, or who that *(Pointing to screen)* is—but that . . . those men—that was really bad, they . . . Ms. Geechee Fairy, that wasn't supposed to happen, OK, so WHERE ARE YOU??? Shit . . .

(Frustrated, she slaps the suitcase on the side a couple of times, trying to make it work right. Finally she turns to the audience:)

OK. Fine. So, maybe this damn bag has some glitches. But I ain't about to get tricked out of getting mine by anybody. None of it really happened, gotta remind myself, I made it up. Well, not all of it, but . . . I'll take it as a lesson learned: like she said, I'd better be real careful, or I might get myself into something I can't get out of. *(Beat)* Shit, I never fired a gun, before . . . that was . . . *(Beat)* Yeah, this time, I'll go for something much more—contained, harmless. But, good money. And something that will still put me in the spotlight. OK . . . I know—a modeling assignment! That's it. A high-paying modeling job. OK. So . . . I'll think up an ad . . . and I'll answer it.

(Chocolate closes her eyes and opens the suitcase. We hear the sound of shimmery bells. We see shimmery lights. She pulls out a newspaper and opens it.)

Let's see: "Maids" . . . "Meatpackers" . . . here we go: "Model needed . . . generous fee; work with a well-respected professional photographer" . . . sounds good so far. "Wanted for photo study: female with experience in the sex-trade industry" . . . ? "All expenses, plus accommodations"? And—"a phone number" . . . sex trade—oh, Jesus—do they want a prosti—?! That's not what—MS. GEECHEE

FAIRY, WHAT IS WRONG WITH THIS BAG??? Great! So now I'm supposed to act like a friggin' hooker? God. *(Beat)* And I can't waste another wish, so what am I gonna do? That old witch thinks she's tryin' to teach me a lesson, but I'll show her ass. I'll call—since I have the number—and anyway, it's only a modeling job, I won't have to *do* anything. I'll milk it for what it's worth; and who knows, maybe I can turn it into something profitable. After all, as they say, sex sells; hell, even porn stars have their own TV shows these days . . .

(Chocolate lifts a phone out of the suitcase and dials. The sound of the phone dialing, then ringing. Gloria appears.)

GLORIA: In my opinion, it's a bad idea to begin with . . .

(Brenda appears behind a camera and tripod.)

BRENDA: No, Gloria, it's about art and politics, to begin with, for the gallery's subjectivity show . . . ?

CHOCOLATE: And Lord knows, there's one thing people are always willing to pay for: their wildest fantasies and darkest wet dreams displayed in living color—before their very eyes.

GLORIA: But—a whore?

BRENDA: Who better to represent the crimes committed upon the female body? And who to expose it, than me? Besides, *you* volunteered to do the text interview . . .

GLORIA: I didn't think you were serious . . .

CHOCOLATE: And if some freak is willing to give me the big bucks to stand in front of his camera and be his happy hooker, who's the fool? And what's he gonna do, ask for credentials? Besides, it's only temporary; I'll think of it as an acting job! I'll play the part, if it'll get me paid, but next time I better think of something foolproof— 'cause this damn bag is not to be trusted.

(Geechee Fairy appears in silhouette; her voice is augmented and strange. The phone continues to ring.)

GEECHEE FAIRY:

> Next time, ya say
> but each time you choose
> the poison inside ya
> gonna end up bad news.

CHOCOLATE: Oh, there you are. Look, this bag isn't working right—

GEECHEE FAIRY:
> Better recognize ya true fate
> or soon it be too late.
> The reaper, he won't wait
> and ya soul ya'll lose.

(Geechee Fairy disappears.)

CHOCOLATE: Hey wait a minute—come back here! What are you talking about?

(Ronald reappears on video.)

RONALD: See, the problem occurs when people get so desperate to find themselves in the picture, to see their image re-created in our mythic American unconscious, they forget they're consuming something that somebody made up. Which is why I'd rather be the one creating the stuff, y'know? At least, that way, I get to choose who's on top.

(The video goes out.)

CHOCOLATE: Who's on top??? —OK, WHO . . . THE HELL . . . WAS THAT?
BRENDA *(Referring to the ringing phone)*: WILL YOU ANSWER THAT?

(Gloria grabs the cell phone from her utility belt and answers it.)

GLORIA: Studio.
CHOCOLATE: Uh . . . yes . . . I'm, uh, calling about the ad?
GLORIA *(To Brenda)*: Oh my God . . . she's calling about the ad! *(Into the phone)* Uh, yes, I'm Brenda Ashley's assistant, how can I help you?
CHOCOLATE: Um . . . well. I'm—interested—in the job. If it's still available. Do I have the right number?
GLORIA: Uh, no, I mean, yes, you do, but no, it's not filled. I mean, yes, it's still available.
CHOCOLATE: OK. Well—I'm, uh . . .

(Chocolate spots something in the suitcase and pulls out a bus stop sign.)

. . . at the bus stop?
GLORIA: Uh, fine, stay put, we'll be right there.

(Brenda and Gloria exit.)

CHOCOLATE: Well—I hadn't figured on a girlie show. This is sho'nuff turnin' out to be one bizarre ride to the freak side; final destination: dolla' bill, y'all . . . Americaville.

(We hear the sound of a cash register ringing, giving way to jungle cries and animal shrieks. Brenda and Gloria reenter. Brenda has a camera and binoculars; Gloria wears dark glasses and an overcoat.)

BRENDA: That must be her.

GLORIA: How can you be sure? She doesn't look like a hooker.

BRENDA: No, but, she looks, kind of lost. Doesn't she?

GLORIA: Lost as in, wanton?

BRENDA: No, lost as in . . . missing a home. A place. That's it. She looks home . . . less.

GLORIA: And are hookers usually home . . . less?

BRENDA: Well . . . unless they stay with their pimps, or in some fleabag room with a hundred other whores.

GLORIA: Uh-huh. And how do you know that.

BRENDA: Gloria . . . haven't you ever watched TV? Oh, let's just ask.

(Brenda approaches Chocolate; Gloria doesn't budge.)

Hi. I'm Brenda Ashley. Did you . . . by any chance call about the ad?

CHOCOLATE: Uh, yeah . . .

BRENDA: I thought so. I'm so glad to meet you, uh—???

CHOCOLATE: Uh . . . Chocolate.

(Chocolate notices Gloria, who is pretending not to stare over her shades.)

Oh . . . Well, Chocolate, this is my assistant, Gloria.

GLORIA: Ross.

BRENDA *(Joking, referencing Diana Ross)*: But you don't have to call her "Miss"! *(Awkward pause; she laughs)* I can't tell you how excited I am. I was starting to think we'd never find—you know.

CHOCOLATE: A ho? Why . . . we're practically everywhere, don't you think?

(A beat.)

BRENDA: Um . . . Well! Are you hungry? Why don't we eat, food's always a good place to start. Where should we go? There's Cobb's Cajun . . . great gumbo . . . or—

GLORIA: Seitan Place, I'm off meat this month . . .

BRENDA *(To Chocolate)*: Cajun or seitan?

CHOCOLATE: I don't want to eat at any place called "Satan."

GLORIA: Sei-tan . . . is a meat substitute. Wheat gluten?

BRENDA: Let's do Cobb's. Taxi!

(As Chocolate grabs her suitcase, we hear the sound of a taxi honking. Traffic noise. The three women move to a table. Chocolate sits in the center.)

So. How about a nice rosé, to celebrate our—journey?

GLORIA: I'm not drinking till after dusk this week; I'll have soda with a twist.

BRENDA: Fine. Chocolate and I will, though, won't we? I'll get a bottle. Now, you must be starving! Don't worry, this is on me, get whatever you want. Let's see . . . I've had the sizzled lamb chops with basil and apple pancakes, that's really good; the shrimp bisque and scalloped potatoes is nice. Oh, and I love the super-chunky gumbo over peas and dirty rice. Cornbread's good with that.

CHOCOLATE: That's fine.

BRENDA: Which?

CHOCOLATE: All of them. If that's OK.

(A beat.)

GLORIA: That's a lot. One entrée here is really . . . a lot.

BRENDA: And they make the best dessert. You've gotta save room for dessert.

CHOCOLATE: If it's a problem—

BRENDA: No! No. If you can eat all of that, you just go right ahead, honey, and more power to you! I wish I could eat like that . . . Only in my dreams, right?

CHOCOLATE: Exactly . . .

GLORIA: I'll just have the vegetable soup.

BRENDA: I'll have the gumbo, too. Waiter!

(We hear the sound of a beatbox. Curt and Slam appear—they are now dead ghouls. Slam's face is gray-black. His right eye is now a mass of blood and exploded flesh. He wears a waiter's white apron around his waist. Curt's face is ashen white. His heart is marked by a red stain with a bullet hole in the center of his shirt. He wears a white chef's hat and apron. They swoop toward the table holding three white plates, upon which sit three bloody hearts, which they place in front of the women. Brenda and Gloria eat their hearts, unaware of the ghouls. Only Chocolate sees them.)

SLAM:

> Nahnahnahnahnah
> ain't no way li'l bitch
> gonna have to pay
> to scratch your itch
> to get rich.
> Think you played the Max?
> Shit, I'm hot on your tracks
> from the other side
> gonna tear up that there hide.

And here she is—dinin' in fancy restaurants, like a queen—and where are we?

CURT: We're history, deceased, out of here . . . DEAD . . .

(Chocolate begins to eat her heart, gagging as blood drips down her chin.)

SLAM: . . . thanks to her. And your punk-ass idea to add hos to the act . . .

CURT: Ass is cash, bro, we were talking "show" business!

SLAM: Don't call me bro, hear? If you listened to me, we wouldn't be here now.

CHOCOLATE: YOU'RE NOT HERE NOW, YOU CAN'T FOLLOW ME INTO MY NEXT WISH! IT'S NOT SUPPOSED TO WORK LIKE THIS!!

BRENDA: Chocolate? Did you say something?

SLAM: Well, now—looks like that little magic bag got the joke on you . . .

CHOCOLATE *(To Brenda)*: Uh . . . No . . .

(A video shows Chocolate the Zombie pulling out her hair. We hear the sound of a beatbox melding into the beeping of a heart monitor.)

CURT: Enjoy your meal . . . 'cause you ain't got too many left.

(Slam and Curt disappear.
Chocolate looks up from her frenzied eating, blood covering her face.)

CHOCOLATE: I . . . I think I'm gonna be . . .

(Chocolate grabs her suitcase and runs from the table, retching. She sinks to her knees, violently shaking the suitcase.)

This is some bullshit, man—what the fuck is happening here?!!

(We hear the sound of a heartbeat. The video of Chocolate the Zombie is replaced by one of Geechee Fairy.)

GEECHEE FAIRY: What was it ya said—ya'd do anything?

(We hear the sound of a mirror breaking. The video goes out.)

BRENDA *(Beckoning)*: Chocolate?

(Chocolate rejoins the women. They all move to Brenda's studio. Chocolate holds her suitcase, staring off, as Brenda speaks.
Gloria is on the phone, talking in an intense whisper we can't hear.)

Chocolate? Oh. OK. Um . . . And this series, I took these in Europe, a year or two after the wall came down, you know, in Germany? But what I did was contrast the event of that wall coming down against all the other walls still existing—between us, as humans . . . Like, here are the graffiti writings of the skinheads, the, anti-Semitic stuff, the, racist stuff . . . And this was in Amsterdam, one of those districts where women were just there, basically hanging out on their walls . . . for sale. Really disturbing. That's kind of what stimulated me to, y'know, do what you are . . . I are going to . . . y'know. Do. And then, these: just shots of the natives and their reactions to me, the "Ugly American," I guess . . . that wall, you know—between the, uh, gazer, me—and the objects of my gaze, or the gaze of the camera—them—and that dynamic, ya know?

GLORIA *(Into the phone)*: Sure, hold on. Brenda—

BRENDA: Oh. *(To Chocolate)* I'll be right back . . . Put your stuff down, relax.

(Brenda takes the phone. Gloria acts busy, occasionally glancing at Chocolate's back.)

Hello, honey. What? Oh. Well, yes. Well . . . honey, actually, I wanted to tell you myself, but—can we talk about this later? She's right here, and I've got to get back. Thanks. *(Hangs up)* Gloria . . . couldn't you have let me tell my own husband about . . . ?? *(Waves vaguely toward Chocolate; to Chocolate)* God. So. Let's talk! I guess you must have lots of questions . . . Lemme see. I just feel like I should explain. I mean, I want you to feel comfortable about this. Because—my job is to *take* . . . moments. You see what I'm saying? In a way, I *take* moments from people's lives . . . and some people feel that's—exploitive. And, well, yes—it is. But *whyyy* do I do, what I do? In order to create a mirror to, an expression of, the human condition. And pictures don't lie. You can't deny a picture. At least, not the kind I take. *(Beat)* Well, I mean, once in a while, I do take other kinds, too. Like, magazine stuff . . . fashion, makeup, you know. For money. How vapid. But, then—that's why I do this.

CHOCOLATE: Is there some place I could change?

BRENDA: Oh. Uh—of course. That, that, over there, over there, that way.

(Chocolate crosses with her suitcase to a rolling curtain. She goes behind it and begins to change. Although her head is visible, Brenda and Gloria seem to be oblivious that she hears them.)

Well, obviously this wasn't going to be a breeze. She's probably used to being taken advantage of, I mean, think of what she's been through, Gloria, what she's seen!

GLORIA: Brenda, this is ridiculous. I mean, it's one thing to go outside, and take pictures . . . but it's totally another thing to invite this woman you do not even know into your place! I mean, who is she? Streetwalkers are just that, STREET-WALKERS—

BRENDA: Gloria, do I detect some kind of animosity, towards Chocolate? Because I don't know why you're reacting—

GLORIA: Because, Brenda, I'm just about sick of all your phony liberal bullshit . . . I mean, you're so busy empathizing with everybody, you can't even—

BRENDA: Oh, Jesus, I swear, Gloria, you are such a fucking prig, you'd think *you* were the white person here! Anyway, where's your spirit of adventure? I mean, look, this is the real world, right here, in our studio—

GLORIA: In *your* studio. I just work here.

(Chocolate reenters, transformed, wearing upscale ho gear the likes of which one now sees regularly on the runways in Paris, Milan and in Victoria's Secret shows and, perhaps, with a stunning new wig.)

BRENDA: Wow.

(A beat.)

CHOCOLATE: So—what's the fee?

(Brenda and Gloria exit. Chocolate strips.)

Well. At least that little bag seems to come equipped with everything one needs to play out whatever little fantasy they have in mind. But, as for this little—diversion . . . Obviously Miss Brenda's the one signing the checks, and Gloria's just the house girl, so as long as li'l Miss Anne's happy, I'll be cool. So, if I can just—

(Slam appears from behind and grabs Chocolate around the throat.)

SLAM: And this kind of attitude is exactly why you're about to kiss these nice people good-bye. 'Cause you done sold your soul—that's why all your little dreams gonna turn out all F-ed up no matter what you do. Your fantasy? Well, look how your damn fantasy turned out this time—LOOK!

(They turn to view Gloria and Allen in Allen's office. Allen, a successful investment banker, is dressed in a suit and tie and wears expensive glasses.)

GLORIA: You know, it's—I'm completely offended, Allen, I mean, how can she bring this hooker into the place where we work together, this black woman who's a hooker, and not realize how insulting that is to me? I mean, even if I am half Portuguese/Dutch on my mother's side and Louisiana Creole on my father's, I *am* a woman of color—

ALLEN: I know you have a difficult time admitting that, congratulations . . .

GLORIA: And, I mean, it's hard enough putting up with her "all of us suffering women" bullshit, but it's a whole other thing when she starts bringing colored hookers in off the street! I couldn't take another minute of it! I'm sorry, but your wife has lost her mind; whatever drug she's on, it's not working. I mean, is she not constantly trying to find the meaning of her life—the meaning of her existence—in someone else, someplace else—the more exotic, outlandish and ridiculous the better? I'm sure that's why she married you.

ALLEN: OK, that's—

GLORIA: Besides, I'm tired of answering her phones, what is it doing for my career, nothing! I'm supposed to be studying my craft, and acting!

ALLEN: So, then, act! What happened to that movie-making friend of yours? Thought he was gonna put you in a video or something.

GLORIA: Ronald's fine, but I'm not going to become a star doing industrials for Kmart.

(We hear Allen's cell phone ring. He picks up.)

ALLEN: Yes? OK, OK, calm down! Then we'll need to check those offshore accounts again, it's got to be somewhere, and I'm not taking the fall for it this time . . . . *(Ends call, pulls out a wad of bills)* Look, I wanted to get you something nice, but . . . take this. Buy yourself something sexy to wear for me, next time I see you.

(Video of Allen and Gloria appears. As the rest of the scene plays out onstage, it's also captured on video.
Gloria takes the money.)

GLORIA: Do you think I'm beautiful?

ALLEN: Aw, sugar, you know I do.

GLORIA: As beautiful as Miss Snow White?

ALLEN: Brown sugar, baby. Brown sugar's the sweetest of all.

GLORIA: Then how come you married Brenda?

ALLEN: Diabetes runs in my family. Now let me get a taste of you . . .

(They kiss.)

GLORIA: That whore is trouble. Maybe if you put your foot down . . . Brenda will get rid of her. *(Beat)* Allen?

ALLEN: I'll see what I can do.

GLORIA: Yeah, well . . . I hope you're not taken in by her.

(He squeezes her ass.)

ALLEN: You don't have to worry about that. Besides—ain't a ho on God's green earth could hold a candle to you, baby.

(Gloria's expression is one of suspicion as Allen's words sink in.
The video shows Chocolate the Zombie intently watching the previous scene on a monitor. She smiles in pleasure, revealing rotting, blood-covered teeth.
The video goes out.)

SLAM: Was that part of your fantasy, too?

CHOCOLATE: OK, I'm sorry, for killing you, or whatever . . . but, we have to work this out, make a deal, or something . . . because obviously hell, or the afterlife, or wherever you keep coming from, isn't working out for you. But you don't seem to understand the rules of this—

(Curt appears.)

CURT: No, *you* don't understand, honey . . . the "rules" changed once you offed us . . . and now the name of this game is "Death of a Ho" . . . And guess who the ho is?

SLAM: Next time we see you, you got a choice: we seen how you used that little bag to make up whatever little scenario you want, and we want a chance to make up somethin' too—our lives. So think about it, 'cause if you don't hand your li'l magic suitcase over, your fantasies gonna start turnin' into nightmares.

CHOCOLATE: Well, you can forget it, 'cause you're not getting it! We're gonna have to figure something else out . . . if you just give me a chance to at least, make some cash. *(They disappear)* Hello? HELLO??? Shit.

(Brenda appears with her camera. During the following Chocolate picks up her suitcase and moves behind a rolling curtain to change. Only her head is visible.)

BRENDA *(Regarding the camera)*: With this, I create a moment I can be sure of. You see, I have very little in my life to hold on to. Though some would say because my husband is successful and I can "indulge" myself, my art, I have it all. Ha! is my answer. It's strange, but . . . it's almost as if, I know you, from somewhere . . . but, that's not possible, is it? When I first saw you, I thought how lost you looked. But, then, who am I to talk? I've often felt that I've misplaced a large part of my own life—my own self—somewhere, along this way. After all, how many of us can truly say we've lived out our dreams, our ideals, of what we wanted? Or, for that matter, even figured out what those dreams and ideals are in the first place? Maybe that's what draws me so strongly to you . . . As for my life— I know my husband has affairs like he changes ties. Gloria insists he married me because the color of my skin went so well with his corporate uniform—and that may be true! But my photographs are the only thing in this world I can call my own. And since he's allowed me this, I call it a very even exchange. Marriage may be the only truly civilized way to whore. *(Beat)* I've always been attracted to darkness. We're all walking a dark path in this universe. Whenever we close our eyes, everything fades to black. Just like death. And most of the time, we can't even tell our insides from our outsides . . . until we see someone else's blood.

(Beat.)

Dance for me. Please? I'd like to take your picture . . . while you dance.

(Chocolate comes out from behind the curtain wearing a bustier, heels and a nun's habit.)

CHOCOLATE: Yeah, I'll dance. But this bad-girl crap stinks, too. Then again, don't it all? Only, I know I wasn't always like this . . . so twisted up and confused. I had my days of innocence, belief. Things were so much simpler; I knew my name. I knew what my parents hoped for me. I didn't know much else, but it didn't seem to matter. Nobody asked me what I thought, so I kept my fantasies and dreams to myself. But I was a sweet kid, back then. Such a good girl. In fact, when I was little, my first wish and only aspiration was to be a little brown version of the perfect Holy Virgin herself . . .

(We hear the sound of a Catholic hymn mixed with a beatbox bass and drums.
The Priest appears in silhouette.)

PRIEST: Mother Mary never had sex. Mother Mary was a holy virgin. Mother Mary was a perfect woman, which is why she was the mother of our Lord Jesus Christ.
CHOCOLATE: . . . 'cause my parents sent me to Catholic school, thinkin' it would protect me from the dirty realities of the world around me. And of course, in Catholic school, Miss Mary was "it" . . . no woman could compare to her. And I thought, Wow, imagine being that adored and honored. And just because I was clean . . . and pure . . . and white.
PRIEST: Mother Mary never had sex; Mother Mary was a holy virgin . . .
CHOCOLATE: It wasn't till I was almost twelve and got my period that I realized I was never gonna be clean and white and pure like that, no matter how hard I tried . . .
PRIEST: Mother Mary was a perfect woman . . .
CHOCOLATE: And, after the initial disappointment, part of me was relieved. 'Cause I figured, if she got used like that, without being asked, not even knowing who really knocked her up, it sounded to me like being the perfect woman was one step removed from being a doormat.
PRIEST: Which is why she was the mother of our Lord Jesus Christ.
CHOCOLATE: But on the other hand, if she was the perfect woman, and she was being treated like that—hell, then I *knew* nobody was gonna give a shit about me . . .

(The Priest slips on a pair of dark glasses. Chocolate begins a seductive dance in front of him.)

Then, at around fifteen, one afternoon after school, this junior priest stopped me when I was leaving and asked me to come by one of the anterooms where the priests would having little meetings. He was nice, and kinda cute. So I went by, and he led me to a back office, and gave me this speech, about being so tortured by the temptation of lust. Then he held out his hand, and asked me to pray with him. And as I knelt down, he called me Mary. And as I prayed, holding his one hand, I knew that with the other one, he was jerking off right there next to me. And although I was scared, it kind of made me feel powerful . . . and I thought, hey, maybe I didn't have to be completely and totally pure and white, to still be as wonderful . . . as the Holy Virgin. He never asked me to go to the back office again. But all these years later, whenever I think about Catholic school, and all the lessons we got about being good, obedient little angels of God . . . it's that moment, I remember.

(The Priest suddenly grabs her roughly.)

PRIEST: Too bad, honey . . . you played the fool again. 'Cause we keep her that pure, so that whores like you can remember to get down—

(He pushes her down to her knees in front of him.)

—on your knees—

(He jerks her head toward his crotch.)

—and pray!
CHOCOLATE: NOOOO!!!

(Blackout.
The scene prior to the memory of the Priest resumes. Chocolate and Brenda are alone.)

BRENDA: Chocolate? Is everything all right?

(A beat. Chocolate begins to strip off her outfit.)

CHOCOLATE: Look, I need to—
BRENDA: Rest. Of course. Let's break for the day, we got some great stuff—powerful, paradoxical, poignant . . . You'll stay here, of course. I don't know why I feel like I can trust you, but I do. There's a bed, a tub . . . and I'll leave all my numbers on the fridge, call me if you need anything. How about we start tomorrow at about ten?
CHOCOLATE: How about noon . . .

(Chocolate steps behind the rolling curtain.)

BRENDA: Well . . . uh. Noon is fine . . . I'll just clean up in here, then I'll be gone.

(Brenda, unaware that Chocolate watches her from behind the curtain, crosses to the nun's habit left on the floor, and brings it close to her face, inhaling deeply. Finally she opens her eyes and meets Chocolate's. Brenda is caught, habit in mouth, inhaling voraciously.
We hear the sound of a mirror breaking.
Brenda disappears.
We hear the sound of a heartbeat, the heart monitor beeping. Slam appears on a gurney, covered in a bloody sheet, rolled in by Curt, wearing a bloody surgical costume and holding a bloody scalpel/razor.)

CURT: The suggestion is to whether the body in detention should be questioned, sequestered or arrested, especially since said body is a dead body, a shot-in-the-head body, useless, now without any particular retail, wholesale or even fire-sale value, unless we speak of the fiery flames wherein the departed currently bastes, burns and blackens, blacker and blacker and black-black-blacker—but, this is an autopsy, so let's autop, *si?* OK. So. The bullet entered the victim's head—BOOM!—.38 eyeball out the CORNER SOCKET!!! Blowing his right brain out his ass . . . Well. Not exactly, but since being shot in the head could undoubtedly be a real pain in the ass. Hey, hey, hey, what do we have here? *(Wrenching a gold tooth from Slam's mouth)* Look, Mom, there's gold in this here nigger!

(Slam's mouth locks shut on Curt's finger. Curt screams in pain, pulling away his hand and displaying a stump where his finger used to be.)

My fucking finger!
SLAM: You rottin' muthafucka, you better stop messin' with my caps, 'fore I cap you one—

(Chocolate, dressed in a robe, bolts from behind the curtain. Slam and Curt grab her.)

CHOCOLATE: Look . . . That bag is all I have. And you can't have it. I don't even think you could use it if I gave it to you, because—you're . . . imaginary!
SLAM: Imaginary?

CHOCOLATE: Look, you were just part of a wish I made. You weren't supposed to—*do what you did to me*, though! Maybe, I shouldn't
have—killed you. I made a mistake, but—
SLAM: You damn straight you made a mistake, bitch, and I don't give a
fuck about your stupid wishes. It's time you see who's running this
here show. *(To Curt, regarding her wrist)* Cut it.
CHOCOLATE: What?
SLAM: I said, CUT IT!!! Confused? Lemme show you . . .

*(Slam shoves Chocolate's arm toward Curt who raises the razor and
brings it down on her wrist. Chocolate screams.*
Blackout.
We hear the sound of loud knocking.)

ALLEN *(Off)*: Brenda! Brenda!

(Allen enters.)

Brenda?

*(Chocolate rises from the floor. Blood is spattered on her robe and a
bloody towel is wrapped around her wrist.)*

What—Good GOD!
CHOCOLATE: Oh no—not you . . .
ALLEN: Are you all right?
CHOCOLATE: Fine, I'm fine—
ALLEN: You're bleeding—
CHOCOLATE: I said, I'm all right!
ALLEN: Well . . . who—you—where's Brenda?
CHOCOLATE: Who knows, gone, wherever you people go when I can't see
you—
ALLEN: She left you here? So you must be the . . . And you're slitting your
wrists—with my razor . . . I'm taking you to the hospital.
CHOCOLATE: No!

*(Chocolate is about to faint. Allen seats her in a chair, then sticks the
razor and the towel in his pocket.)*

ALLEN: What a mess. You know, normally I wouldn't meddle in my wife's
affairs, but this wasn't a good idea. Brenda doesn't like to listen to
me, but sometimes I do know what's best . . .

CHOCOLATE: Yeah, and I guess your "best" includes fucking her assistant's brains out, huh? Somehow I think she'd disagree . . .

ALLEN: Excuse me?

CHOCOLATE: But this is turning out to be such a wack scene, maybe I should just cut my losses and—

(Weakened even more, she starts to fall. Allen catches her, carries her to the couch, then goes to the kitchen off. He brings back a wet cloth and a glass of water, and places the cloth around her neck.)

ALLEN: Here. Drink this. *(Beat)* Look, I don't know what you think you know about me and Gloria, but . . . *(Beat)* You know, somehow you seem very familiar to me. Have we met, before?

CHOCOLATE: Oh, please . . .

(A beat.)

ALLEN: You know, you may have fooled Brenda, but for some reason, I don't think you are.

CHOCOLATE: Are what?

ALLEN: A . . . a—

CHOCOLATE: prostitute? And why is that?

ALLEN: I don't know. Just a feeling. Or maybe, wishful thinking. But if you were, a—

CHOCOLATE: —prostitute.

ALLEN: . . . I think it would be quite unfortunate. I mean, a good-looking woman like you, who obviously has a mind—deceitful as it might be . . .

CHOCOLATE: Uh-huh. And what's the most unfortunate part? That I'm "good-looking"? Or that I have "a mind, deceitful though it might be"? You know, you have nerve!

ALLEN: Please—I didn't mean to offend you. I'm just . . . interested, is all.

CHOCOLATE: Why?

ALLEN: Like I said . . . a woman like you . . . deserves to be doing something *better* with your life. *(Holding out his hand)* Look, I don't even know your name. I'm Allen.

(A beat. She slowly takes his hand.)

CHOCOLATE: Yeah, I know. Chocolate.

ALLEN: Chocolate. That's different. *(Still holding her hand, regarding her wrist)* So, why would you do something like that, anyway?

CHOCOLATE *(Pulling away)*: Look, I just want to go to bed, OK?

ALLEN: OK. You obviously don't want to talk about it, because you don't trust me, right?

CHOCOLATE: I don't want to talk about it, 'cause you don't exist, you weren't even here before I made this whole thing up, OK?

ALLEN: Aha! So I thought. You made it all up, it's all a hoax. Who was it then, someone at the bank, who hired you?

(A beat.)

CHOCOLATE: Oh, that's right. You work at a bank. Well, then, look. Maybe you *can* help me. I need to get out of here, I really do. And see . . . I can disappear. Poof. Be gone. So that Brenda will never have to know about Gloria, and this will all go away. But . . . I need some money.

ALLEN: Oh. First you pretend to sell your body, then you blackmail me?

CHOCOLATE: You wanted to help, this is how you can help, OK? Shit, you're the one who brought up blackmail, black male. Besides, it ain't even your money. And you don't think you're sellin' your body to get that fat paycheck? You just doin' it behind a desk. Or, does only a woman sellin' pussy count as real hoin'?

ALLEN: How on earth did you get to be so hard?

(A beat.)

CHOCOLATE: Look. If you can't help me out, then why don't you just go.

ALLEN: Because I think under that tough act you're scared shitless. Maybe even running from someone . . . or something. And I can't help wondering what, or who, made you do that *(Nodding to her wrist)* to yourself . . . and wondering if you might try it again. And even if you do make it through till morning . . . tomorrow'll just be one more day of playin' whatever game it is you're playin'. Somehow none of that makes me want to leave you here alone . . . in all good conscience.

(A beat.)

CHOCOLATE: This whole damn thing has gone crazy, outta control. She gave me this bag, promised everything would get better, and instead everything's gotten worse . . .

ALLEN: Well, Chocolate . . . they say even in your worst nightmare you can turn things around—if you want to.

CHOCOLATE: Yeah, well whoever said some stupid shit like that ain't ever been in this situation . . .

ALLEN: Maybe you're barking up the wrong tree . . . maybe whatever you're looking for—whatever you think you need—isn't on the outside . . . it's on the inside.

(He gently touches her face; she recoils.)

You still don't recognize me, huh? But I know I've seen you.

CHOCOLATE: Look, you've got your wife, and you got her assistant, so I'm sure your hands are full—

ALLEN: It's like . . . I've seen your face—

CHOCOLATE: —so why don't you just go, 'cause I really don't need any more drama tonight—

ALLEN: —almost like I've seen it in my own mirror . . .

(He reaches out to stroke her skin again; this time she doesn't shrink back as much.)

. . . the texture, of your skin . . . a shade almost overwhelming in its density—as though, it might swallow me whole, like home, and the unknown, at once. Do you believe me? That I know you? *(Beat)* Y'know, I bet all you want, all you've ever wanted, is to be loved . . . just the way you are . . .

(Something strange begins to happen with the lights. We hear the sound of a heartbeat.)

CHOCOLATE: Please . . . no. This isn't happening . . .

(He grabs her hand and puts it to his heart.)

ALLEN: Don't be afraid, Chocolate. Maybe, if you can just stop being afraid, you can stop feeling all that greed and desperation—and maybe you'll never have to feel like a dead, nameless whore again . . .

(He pulls her to him and kisses her intensely, passionately. She struggles against him for a moment, then gives in. Their embrace becomes desperate. The sound of the heartbeat becomes louder.)

CHOCOLATE: I can't!

(The sound of a mirror breaking. We hear Geechee Fairy's laughter and a mix of horror-movie and beatbox music.
Slam and Curt appear dressed as Dracula and Renfield.)

CURT (*In bad Transylvanian accent*): Vell. Az zey say, za chickens come home to vroost. And vee know how you people like zat gveazy vried chicken. Eezn't zat vight, Venfield?

SLAM: Yo mama, massa. *(Holding up a water bug, swallowing it)* Damn! Never knew roaches tasted so good. Coulda saved me a fortune in Combat traps in the projects . . .

CHOCOLATE: Look—

(Slam grabs Allen from behind and takes the razor from his pocket.)

SLAM: Think you gonna push up on anotha nigga right in front of my face, bitch? Watch this . . .

(Slam slits Allen's throat.
Chocolate grabs at her chest and screams in pain.
We see a video of Chocolate the Zombie in a hospital bed, hooked up to a heart monitor and convulsing. We hear the beeping of the heart monitor—the heartbeat becomes irregular.)

CURT: Rub-a-dub-dub—time for the grub!!!

(Curt catches Allen's sagging body and begins to suck his bloody throat. Chocolate, in pain, holds her chest and struggles to speak.)

CHOCOLATE: Oh . . . Oh . . . God—what's happening . . .

SLAM: The good times is up, ho.

(Curt throws down Allen's limp body.)

CURT: Ve vant za bag, beetch.

SLAM: And until we get it, every time we stop by to say hello, one of these fool's gonna get iced.

CURT: And each time vone of zem expires . . . back in zee vreal vorld, you are vone step clozah to de-e-a-a-t-t-h-h . . .

CHOCOLATE: No . . . stop—

SLAM: And three strikes, you out. He was one.

CURT: Zee bag—or your life. Sink about it. Or soon, dinner vill be on *you*.

(Curt and Slam disappear.
Chocolate staggers toward Allen's body and touches it with her toe. He's dead.
In the video, Chocolate the Zombie staggers to a mirror and breaks it.)

CHOCOLATE: Oh shit. Oh fuckin' shit.

(She struggles to retrieve the suitcase.)

I gotta get outta here. Somewhere they can't come, someplace—
OK. Someplace where no dead, half dead, whatever, *men* are
allowed! Um. OK. I WISH TO BE AT A—a—a . . . AN ALL-FEMALE
RESORT, far away . . . in like, ACAPULCO. And the first thing that
happens when I get there is—I find a pile of money . . . yeah. This
time I'm startin' off with some of my own—fuck this workin' for
it shit. AND, DEFINITELY, SLAM AND CURT CAN'T FOLLOW ME.
(Regarding Allen's body) OR . . . HIM, NEITHER.

(She opens the suitcase. No light or sound. Nothing happens.)

What? Somethin's wrong. Um. OK. Maybe—maybe it's 'cause,
Slam and Curt—'cause—'cause I can remember them! That's right,
I can remember them, so, they can follow me . . . OK. OK. I wish
to be at an ALL-FEMALE RESORT, IN ACAPULCO. And, I, bring a
pile of money, in, in this suitcase, of course! What was I thinking,
I bring the money, a lot of money, tons and tons of money, enough
to last me at least, I don't know, a hundred years (factoring in infla-
tion) . . . BUT WHEN I GET THERE, I HAVE AMNESIA, SO I CAN'T
REMEMBER SLAM OR CURT OR ANYBODY HERE. I don't remember a damn thing—except how to use the suitcase. Gotta remember that. OK.

(She opens the suitcase again. Nothing.)

Oh shit. Ohshitohshitohshitohshit. Oh God. Please, don't tell me
this damn thing's run outta—oh shit. What did that fairy say?
Three wishes, plus one for good luck. OK. Slam and Curt were one
. . . and the ad was two . . . and— *(Looking at the audience)* Oh my
God . . . you were three . . . but I should have one more! GEECHEEE
FAIRY! GEECHEE FAIRY, where are you?! I wish . . . I wish . . . Oh
God . . .

*(In the video, Chocolate the Zombie convulses. Then the video sputters
out. The sound of the beeping heart monitor fades.*

Chocolate turns to the audience.)

I . . .

(But there is nothing to say as she stands there, surveying her mess.)

act two

Chocolate is covered with blood and earth; she considers the bandages around her wrist.

CHOCOLATE: I gave up on being the Virgin Mary right after I saw blood in my underwear for the first time. To this day, whenever I forget who I am . . . only the sight of my own blood reminds me. *(Beat)* What am I supposed to do now, huh? HOW AM I SUPPOSED TO GET OUT OF HERE?

(Chocolate crosses to the rolling curtain, begins to change clothes and wash off the blood and mud. Brenda and Gloria appear in the studio. Brenda inspects negatives. Although Chocolate watches them from behind the curtain as she changes, neither of them sees her.)

BRENDA: Look at these . . . she is unbelievably photogenic. And it's not just good looks, it's . . . her pain. Her completely, unabashed, naked—

GLORIA: OK, Brenda, I get it.

BRENDA: It's like she knew exactly what I was looking for and gave it to me—

GLORIA: Uh-huh. And where is Miss Super Tart, anyway?

BRENDA: I don't know . . . out, apparently . . .

GLORIA: You better check your valuables.

BRENDA: I already did. I was here early, had the house to myself last night; Allen never came home, never even called.

GLORIA: Oh?

BRENDA: Anyway, when I got back this morning she was already out. But everything's fine, and her stuff's still here. Look at this one . . . Jeezus, it's like she's been doing it her whole life!

GLORIA *(Breaking down)*: Oh God, Brenda, would you just shut up!

BRENDA: Gloria! What's wrong??

GLORIA: Oh, Brenda, you don't care.

BRENDA: Of course I care, Gloria, what is it?

GLORIA: I hate my life, I hate everything about my life!

BRENDA: Gloria! Why?

GLORIA: Uuugh!! I went on an audition this morning—my third this week—and, along with a hundred other desperate women, waited for two hours to stand in front a table for two minutes, to be told "thank you." For a no-line walk-on role: a receptionist, in an outside office, who enters a boardroom and drops an envelope filled with suspicious documents on the president's desk. No lines, but supposedly "high visibility" because that envelope, is like, where the whole plot turns . . .

BRENDA: Oh, Jesus. Gloria, you're crying over a walk-on?

GLORIA: It's Harrison Ford's desk! And the other board members include Gene Hackman, Vin Diesel and Tommy Lee Jones . . .

BRENDA: Really? Wow. *(Beat)* Oh, Gloria, who cares?

GLORIA: *I* care, Brenda! I practiced walking last night, for an hour. Spent days, deciding what to wear: which heels, how short a skirt, hair, up or down . . . And I probably don't have a snowflake's chance in hell, because, I'm not tall enough or short enough, or white enough or black enough, or pretty enough or plain enough, and—

(She breaks down again.)

BRENDA: Gloria . . . I don't think you hate your life. I think, because all you've ever been acknowledged for is being beautiful, you've come to value your looks above your other qualities . . . and now you realize being pretty isn't all it's cracked up to be! Right now you might feel cheated, and powerless, but who knows? Maybe, this will be the beginning of a new road. To . . . a new self-discovery. And recovery!

(A beat.)

GLORIA: Fuck you, Brenda. You think you are so superior. So . . . intellectual. So "in touch" with "life's priorities." You don't know the half of it.

(Ronald enters.)

RONALD: I got your message, came as quickly as I could . . . .

GLORIA: Oh, Ronald . . . I can't take it anymore!

RONALD: Shh, shh. Ya know, fuck those jerks, honey, what do they know about talent—or anything? And meanwhile, guys like me have to shoot training videos. I don't know. If things don't change in this country's film industry soon, I'm going to have to go abroad . . . or start shooting rap videos . . .

(Chocolate passes by them and begins to sort through her belongings, collecting all the cash and change she can find.)

GLORIA: Oh, and Ronald, look! Brenda's photographing a hooker and calling it a theoretical study. Never mind there's not a shred of proof she isn't some straight-up con woman off the street who knew Brenda would believe she's a whore anyway, since she's black *and* answered the ad . . .

BRENDA: Now, Gloria, that's . . .

GLORIA: But then, we all know how much Brenda loves her "coloreds"—'cause then there's me, her lowly photo assistant, whom she steadily patronizes with her beginner's course in feminism—I may not be as dark as Aunt Jemima over there, but I'm tinted—or should I say, tainted—enough . . .

RONALD: Uh, wow, maybe I should take you home—

GLORIA: Oh, no, Ronald, you're going to hear this, because if you plan to spend the rest of your life with me, you need to know what you're getting into, marrying into negritude!

RONALD: Uh—

GLORIA: Finally, let's discuss her marriage to a prized, if aging, Mandingo stud, whom she alternately coddles, despises or ignores, while spending every dime he makes traveling to faraway places, to take pictures of foreigners, whose company she prefers to her black buck, no pun intended!

RONALD: Uh—m-marry? I-I-into—into negri-what?

BRENDA: All right, Gloria, enough! Chocolate—I'm sorry, about this. It seems like Gloria had a bad audition, and now she's acting out . . .

GLORIA: Acting out? I'll show you acting out—

RONALD: I mean, I—I love you, but . . . we never said anything about marriage! I mean—well—we didn't! And besides, look at me, what, I'm a broke, starving nobody!

BRENDA: Ronald is a filmmaker, Chocolate.

RONALD: Well. Actually, I'm still trying to figure out what kind of stories I want to tell. So I'm shooting industrials, commercials, stuff like that. But not for long. I'm really into cinéma vérité, but, uh—well, actually, I'm looking forward to the day I can make a big-budget action flick and call myself a studio whore, know what I mean? Although . . . I really want to be remembered for making art. Anyway. That's me.

GLORIA: Well. I have a very bad headache. I'm going to lunch.

BRENDA: Fine. Chocolate and I need to get started, anyway.

RONALD: Um . . . Miss—

(Chocolate stares at him in dawning recognition.)

CHOCOLATE: You!! . . .

RONALD: Miss Yew? Well—are you really a prostitute? 'Cause if so, I'd love to, maybe get some of your—experiences—on film. I mean, I bet that would make for some really provocative footage.

GLORIA: Ronald! . . .

RONALD: What? Would that be . . . what? Did I say something wrong? I mean, I'd pay you, of course. I mean, this could lead to something—big!

(Gloria disappears in a huff.)

Boy. That audition really got to her. Well. I better . . . *(Passing his card to Chocolate)* Call me. Please. I have a really good feeling about this . . . .

(Ronald disappears.)

BRENDA: Chocolate? Why, you look like you've seen a ghost!

CHOCOLATE: I cannot believe this shit, when will it end?

BRENDA: Well, the contacts are amazing, they just send chills down my spine! I know this sounds silly, but . . . I just can't tell you how much your being here means to me. It's like you answer some sort of question, for me. As though our meeting was . . . destiny. I don't think I've ever shot so well before.

(A beat. She crosses and kneels before her.)

It's almost as if . . . there's a part of you in me—or, vice versa . . . like, you're on the inside and I'm on the outside. Is that crazy? You make me want to feel what you feel. What do you feel, Chocolate? I know you feel . . . something.

(Brenda touches her gently, then takes her hands, slowly kissing one, then the other. Chocolate jerks away.)

CHOCOLATE: You wanna know what I feel? Like I'm losing my mind. Like, I woke up in a bad horror flick that won't end. I mean, for once, I thought I had it all, right here, success, within my grasp, y'know? I don't know what that feels like . . . but I thought, with that stupid bag, for once I was gonna get to. And instead, now I'm stuck here . . . with you. *(Beat)* Your husband is dead, Brenda. I dragged him out—into a yard I didn't know would be there. And I dug a hole—with a shovel I'd never seen before—a hole big enough to put your dead husband in. Your dead husband, who came in the package with you, who I didn't expect either. I didn't expect any of this, and now that damn bag doesn't even work . . .

BRENDA: Chocolate, I'm sure your life is very . . . complex. But . . . I do know that, sometimes, if we try to go back to the beginning— truthfully—then, sometimes we can start over . . .

CHOCOLATE: Didn't you hear what I said? YOUR HUSBAND IS DEAD!

(Brenda looks at her strangely.)

BRENDA: Dead? Allen? *(Beat)* You know, that's funny. I—I had a dream, once . . . about death . . . and it's almost as if you were in it . . .

(Brenda moves to where Chocolate's mirror was at the start of the play. She becomes more and more possessed throughout the following.

We see video of Chocolate the Zombie, interspersed with an equally ashen pale and dead-looking version of Allen creeping down a spooky hall.

The sound of the heartbeat.)

Or maybe it wasn't a dream at all . . . maybe it was just a fairy tale. There was a woman, standing before her mirror, except, she couldn't even see her own reflection, because her mirror was filled with other people, staring back, where her face should have been . . . people, who, it seemed, were somehow better than her, happier than her, had more than her. And they blotted out all vision of who she was, or had been . . . and soon, in fact, she forgot what she looked like at all, or what her name even was, because she got so used to seeing them, instead. And after a while, she started to want to please them . . . so that they might learn to love her . . . and maybe, give her all the things they had. But instead, their contempt for her only grew, and grew . . . until now it became hatred she saw in their eyes . . . and she began to cry . . . and her tears were so large and fell so heavy, and formed puddles so quickly around her she knew she would drown . . . and then . . . they started to laugh . . .

CHOCOLATE: Stop it . . .

BRENDA: And then she knew she would die because their laughter was so loud and so long that she had to break her mirror to stop their laughter from burning her ears and liquefying her heart . . . But it was all because she'd wanted so much more, so much more than anything she'd ever seen, anything they could ever give her! She wanted something she couldn't even name—and I know that feeling, I do! Because we all want so much more than we even know, than we understand, that it becomes a hole, a gap inside of us, until there doesn't seem to be an end to our search to try and fill that want, until we can't stand to think that maybe there's so much we'll never get it—

CHOCOLATE: WHAT DO YOU WANT FROM ME?!?!

BRENDA: —until we want so much, we forget, what all the wanting was supposed to make us feel in the first place, we forget what we're supposed to do now, why we're alive in the first place—I know this, and I, too, have tried to die, tried, like she did, like you—

CHOCOLATE: NO! NO! I'M NOT . . . I'M NOT—

(Brenda, crazed, almost maniacal, grabs Chocolate's hands.)

BRENDA: Oh, Chocolate . . . don't you see, that's why you did it, that's why you did everything you've done, so that this moment, something new can happen, something different . . . like you dreamed it, let's imagine, that we're free, you and me, really, FREE—and we *can* be, because it doesn't matter now, don't you see, it's all just a dream, anyway, and we can end it—

CHOCOLATE: GO AWAY! You're fuckin' mad! Just—get away!

(The sound of the heartbeat stops.
Brenda resumes her former self and begins to reload her camera.)

BRENDA: Chocolate, did you know, in many native and aboriginal cultures, to allow one to take your picture is to allow them to steal your soul?

CHOCOLATE: I'll tell you what I know—my name is not Chocolate; it never was! And I know you're all trying to take me down with you—and I know that DAMN FAIRY GAVE ME THIS TRICK-ASS BAG, AND NOW IT'S NOT WORKING ANYMORE, AND IF I DON'T GET THE FUCK OUTTA HERE, I'M GONNA DIE! *(Beat)* And I don't want to die . . .

(Brenda holds her camera out to Chocolate.)

BRENDA: Well, then . . . maybe it's time Mama got a brand-new bag.

CHOCOLATE: And what am I supposed to do with that? What is it, a "magic" camera? I don't need any more presents from you freaks.

(The video image shows the camera as it moves into a close-up on Allen, revealing himself as Geechee Fairy.)

GEECHEE FAIRY: Take de camera, gal. If ya want to get out of dis alive . . . take it. It may help ya . . .

CHOCOLATE: Oh my God . . . what happened to you??? Why are you wearing—Allen's dea—wait, *you* were Allen?

(The video goes out. Geechee Fairy appears onstage.)

GEECHEE FAIRY: It was an experiment . . . didn't turn out like I plan. 'Cause dose ghouls getting more powerful, gal. I din't realize dey could inflic' such harm . . . when dey try and kill Allen, dey wreck me up, too . . . But lucky fa you, I'm still here, so we no count in dem tree strikes.

CHOCOLATE: But what about my last wish? The one for good luck?

GEECHEE FAIRY: Girl, I tole ya, da bag play tricks! Ya betta tink of sometin' else to get yaself outta dis situation . . . and fast. If dey get to de photographer, de black girl and de white boy, ya ass is toast. 'Cause in case ya ain't notice . . . ya damn fantasy is killin' us all; an' de camera may be de only chance ya got to save ya soul . . . and ya life.

(Geechee Fairy disappears.)

CHOCOLATE: But how? How do I make it work?

BRENDA: So many things to consider in one's quest for the gold; but maybe if you turn the lens around, at least all the glitter won't seem so real.

(A beat. Chocolate takes the camera grudgingly.)

CHOCOLATE: Why not. Everything's so fucked-up already . . . maybe I'll get lucky.

BRENDA: Well, if nothing else—at least, now, you get to be on top.

(We hear the sound of game-show music with a hip-hop beat. Video shows a studio audience laughing, nodding and clapping throughout the scene. A giant wheel appears onstage. Slam and Curt appear. Curt is the game-show host; Slam is Contestant #1.)

CURT: And welcome to "Death of a Ho: Wheel of Ho-Dom!" . . . the game show where the most desperate to succeed lose their way, their mind and their life, on their way to fame and fortune!

(Slam and Curt reveal a giant roll of cellophane. After quickly wrapping a piece of cellophane over Brenda's mouth, they begin to wrap her body.)

Look, honey, keeps it tasting fresher, longer!

CHOCOLATE: OK, OK . . . Look, you've got the wrong idea. See, that bag doesn't even work anymore, and even when it did, it didn't do what it was supposed to. So you guys are after something that—

SLAM: Stop the bullshit. This ho ain't got it yet. Time to let her in on the rules of this game . . .

CURT: Right-o! Contestants will spin the wheel to decide who answers our trick question correctly. And whoever wins gets to decide the fate of our special guest, Brenda the Photographer! So first, let's take a look at what our choices are for Brenda the Photographer on our Spinning Wheel of Ho-Dom!

(The wheel spins, landing on a triangle that reads:)

Choice #1 is "The Burning Stake"! Our Joan of Arc model is perfect for harlots, crazy women, women suspected of being witches—or fairy godmothers; of being in concert with witches—or fairy godmothers; claiming to have visions and/or speak to God, or suspected of writing, reading or speaking in public.

(The wheel spins again:)

Choice #2 is "The Iron Maiden"! Perfect for young virgins, old virgins, harlots, wives, mothers, sisters, grandma or any gal thinking about, talking about, or thinking about talking, or thinking about sexual needs, desires or fantasies of any kind.

(The wheel spins again:)

Choice #3 is "The Cross"! Perfect alternative for harlots . . . or, the female martyr type . . . like our plasticated babe Brenda . . .

(The wheel spins again:)

Choice #4 is "Freedom"! Hmmm. In this context, I don't quite know what that means, or how it might be attained . . . but it certainly sounds less painful than our other selections, wouldn't you agree, audience?!?! And now, for our trick question: "Who Are You . . . and What Is Your Name?" Let's start with Contestant Numero Uno. Can you answer the trick question: "Who Are You and What Is Your Name?"

(We hear a hip-hop beat. The song "Solid Gold Spade" plays:)

SLAM:

> S: for Show them how
> L: for Leave them wondering
> A: for American survivor
> M: for Made for plundering.
>
> Slam!
> I'm the man who got juice
> And a plan to get paid
> Like the Gottis done did.
>
> Slam!
> Didn't make up the rules
> But I'm taking the game
> You just watch me kid.
>
> Slam!
> Getting paid nice, son
> In the land of the free
> And the home of the brave.
>
> Slam!
> Till the bling been blung
> Want a solid gold spade
> To be diggin' my grave.

(The beat fades.)

CURT: Uh-huh . . . Well, that's very uninteresting, but tonight we'll see if your answer wins the prize on "Death of a Ho: Wheel of Ho-Dom!" *(To Chocolate)* And now, Contestant Number Two, "Who Are You and What Is Your Name?"

CHOCOLATE: I . . . I . . . My name is . . . Look, this—it's bullshit!

CURT: All right, audience, you heard it: Contestant Number Two's answer to the question "Who Are You and What Is Your Name?" was: "It's bullshit." Contestant Number Two, is that your final answer?

CHOCOLATE: No! You know that's not what I meant! I mean, this game . . . you! THE BAG IS OVER, DONE, FINISHED, so all this, is bullshit! You want to do her? Fine. Why should I care? She isn't real, any more than you are, so GO AHEAD!

(Beat.)

SLAM: Man, disqualify that ho! I won this shit!

CURT: I would agree. Audience?

(The video shows an enthusiastic audience clapping and cheering: "Slam, Slam, Slam!")

I think the answer is clear: Slam the Mad Maxter is our new winner! So Slam, my rottin' ghoul, you get to decide the fate of Brenda the Photographer! What will it be: "The Burning Stake" . . . "The Iron Maiden" . . . "The Cross" . . . or . . . "Freedom"? And just for the record . . . my vote would be "The Cross." Although watching the plastic melt all over her in the flames of "The Burning Stake" might be fun.

SLAM: Fuck dat. Turn her to cheese . . . so our girl can taste what's waitin' for her. "Iron Maiden" the bitch.

(An iron maiden's door appears. Curt and Slam grab Brenda and toss her behind it. We hear a horrible noise as Brenda is destroyed. We hear the sound of a fast, irregular heartbeat and the heart monitor going haywire.
Chocolate grabs her chest in pain.
On video, Chocolate the Zombie and Brenda the Zombie examine rotting body parts.)

CHOCOLATE: Oh, God . . . help!

(Geechee Fairy appears.)

GEECHEE FAIRY: Use de camera, girl!!! Use it! Steal they soul, it's all they got left, evil or not! Go on! Shoot 'em! SHOOT 'EM!

(Chocolate grabs the camera and starts shooting madly.)

SLAM: YO, SHE GOT A CAMERA!

CURT: Oh, shit—I'm outta here!

(Curt disappears, but Slam is caught in the line of fire. He screams and is suddenly half frozen in space in a strange, contorted way.)

SLAM: Yo, Curt! Don't leave me here, man! *(To Chocolate)* Yo, yo, stop shooting that camera. I'm dead, bitch, I'm pure soul—whatchu tryin' to do, freeze my shit into nothingness?? You take my picture that's it, I'm history! QUIT IT!

(Chocolate is seized by another stab of pain.)

CHOCOLATE: What's happening to me?

GEECHEE FAIRY: Ya dying girl! Ya need his soul to give you strength—capture it in dat camera, you might live longer!

SLAM: Man, shut up!—or woman—whatever you are . . . Didn't I already kill you? *(To Chocolate)* Come on, girl, have a heart!

CHOCOLATE: Why the hell couldn't you have just left me alone to pretend, for once, I could have what I wanted??

SLAM: Come on, girl—your ass might be desperate, but you ain't dumb. I showed up 'cause your "pretend" world ain't filled with nothin' but the players you imagined . . . and you imagined me. The thing you need to be askin' is why your head is so messed-up . . .

CHOCOLATE: Oh, like, I was neglected as a child? Or permanently fucked-up by an unfortunate sexual experience? Or that I'm a product of my environment or—???

SLAM: Who you lookin' at? We all got our sob stories—but that don't mean we just give up and hand our shit over to the highest bidder. But because you did, now you gonna live up to the name of this little show . . . and die, ho. Curt's already after the filmmaker and the light-skinned ho as we speak. Now, maybe you let me go, I can convince him to leave them alone . . . You want to get out of this alive, you gonna have to cooperate . . . and give up that bag.

(A beat. Chocolate considers the suitcase, then the camera.)

CHOCOLATE: You want the bag, huh? Well . . . maybe that won't be a problem.

(She aims the camera toward him and shoots.)

SLAM: NOOO!!

(We hear the sound of a soul being frozen. The heartbeat sound normalizes, the flatlining ends. Slam disappears.)

CHOCOLATE: Damn. And to think all I ever wanted was for someone to take my picture and make me a star . . .

GEECHEE FAIRY: Ya don't have much time . . . get to de other two fast—before dat white ghoul—or ya finished fa sure!

(Geechee Fairy disappears.)

CHOCOLATE: Maybe that film guy knows how this whole camera thing works . . .

(Chocolate removes a phone from the suitcase. She takes out Ronald's card from her bra and dials. We hear the phone dialing, then ringing.
Ronald appears on video. Gloria sits near him, wearing a Marilyn Monroe outfit, holding a snake and an apple.)

RONALD: Capturing souls on film? Well, uh . . . filmic images might be said to capture our souls, because they seem real . . . but they're completely dead; since the image or subject of whatever it is we see doesn't really exist . . . it has no real identity.

(Ronald and Gloria enter. They sit in front of a video camera and a tri-pod.)

Only the person creating it really has any "say" in what's being presented. The fastest way to destroy the "real" identity of something, is to "represent" it. So if you wanna destroy the idea of something—a martyr, a holy man, a movie icon, a politician?—make a made-for-TV movie about 'em! And poof—death of the *real* martyr, death of the *actual* holy man, death of the *living* politician. The real is replaced—by the unreal. Like, take what I'm doing with Gloria, here. Gloria has disappeared—reconstructed, as Marilyn, who, with an apple, and a snake, immediately becomes Eve—but not! Original sin, get it, fall from grace, get it, imposed on a suicidal bottle blond—all imposed on Gloria, a biracial female! I mean, wow! I mean . . .

(Ronald is becoming extremely aroused. As he speaks, one hand unconsciously moves to his crotch.)

. . . that's political . . . that's a statement, that's . . . whew! I created something, better than Marilyn, more resonant than Eve, more vulnerable than Gloria, she's . . . oh . . . she's—bigger—better, than all of them. She's . . . oooh ohaaaaaaaaaah-AHHH! *(He comes)*

CHOCOLATE: OK. Right. So. All I really want to know is—where does the soul go, after you take the picture?

(We hear the sound of circus music, somehow distorted. The stage takes on a spooky carnival atmosphere. Curt appears in a scary clown outfit, carrying party balloons.)

CURT: All right, let's get this party started right! But be warned: these babies are filled with enough poison gas to do in a three-ring circus, so hands up and nobody move! *(To Gloria and Ronald)* You two, over there . . . *(To Chocolate)* You, this way. Come on, move it. Now, take the camera off your neck, real slow . . . SLOW! Or these two will be turning into some real party poopers!

(Chocolate slowly removes the camera from around her neck.)

Drop it on the floor!

(Chocolate drops the camera. Curt grabs it.)

And soon as you hand over that bag, I'm makin' a few wishes of my own—and I don't think you're gonna like what I dream up. Your problem is, you're too shortsighted. You're not capable of thinking big! You wanna know what I would have done with those wishes? I would have created my own world power! Fame? Fortune? Stardom? Try land, arms, oil, uranium—millions of citizens depending on me to guide and protect them—now that's power! Instead, I end up a slaughtered A&R man in your miserable little suicidal fantasy world . . . left cryin' the tears of a clown . . . while you tried to skip town. But, back to you:

(The video shows Chocolate the Zombie and Brenda the Zombie.)

You've been living it up on life support while we've all had to hang around, trapped like so many moths around a dying flame—OH, THAT WAS POETIC!!
GLORIA: Oh my God, Ronald, I knew this woman would bring nothing but trouble to our lives!
RONALD: Shh, don't worry, honey, this is grit, this is raw, this is . . .
CURT *(Shaking a balloon at him menacingly)*: SHUT THE FUCK UP!
RONALD: . . . not good.
CHOCOLATE *(To Curt)*: Look . . . You can have the bag. It's right there, go 'head, take it!

(Curt grabs the suitcase.)

CURT: Smart move!! OK, now, let's see: I want to be alive again. Now! *(Beat)* SHIT! I said I want to be alive again! NOW!! *(Beat)* Aww, man—you bitch! What did you do to it?
CHOCOLATE: Nothing!

CURT: STOP LYING!

CHOCOLATE: I told you before, it stopped working a long time ago! Look . . .

CURT: No, *you* look!

(Enraged, he pulls out a giant needle and pops a balloon near Gloria and Ronald. We hear a giant pop, then the hissing of gas, then a distorted version of the kiddie song "Pop Goes the Weasel." The stage begins to fill with a weird emission.)

GLORIA: Oh my God, what is that? It smells like something died when that balloon popped—

CURT *(Laughing hysterically)*: It was THE WEASEL! Uh-huh, real weasel skin, and insides, uh-huh! DID YA THINK HE COULD LIVE PAST THAT GIANT NEEDLE?!?! Phew, what a stench!

RONALD: Uh, 'scuse me—speaking of dreams, let's not underestimate the power of images, in uh, creating the great American "dream." And, uh, I just want to add, as a pacifist, humanitarian and artist, committed to bringing the stories of all human beings to light, that I'd rather have a heart than a poison-filled gas balloon—

(He drops dead; Gloria screams.)

GLORIA: Ronald! What about my video reel!?

(Gloria drops dead.)

CURT *(Exploding with laughter)*: DELAYED REACTION!

(We hear the heartbeat and the beeping of the heart monitor. Chocolate is struck by a violent pain in her chest.)

CHOCOLATE: Oh, God—

CURT: Well . . . that means . . . you should be just about dead.

(We hear the heart monitor flatline. Chocolate collapses, grabbing her heart.)

CHOCOLATE: I DON'T WANT TO DIE!

CURT: Ya shoulda thought about that before! Bet you're sorry you ever tried to mess with this clown! But on that note—death scenes bring me down—so I'll be seeing you in hell, ho!

(Curt disappears.

During the following, the video shows Chocolate the Zombie and Brenda, Ronald and Gloria Zombies, spliced with images of the real-life characters.)

SLAM: . . . *I* showed up 'cause your "pretend" world ain't filled with nothing but the players you imagined . . . and you imagined me. The thing you need to be askin' is why your head is so messed-up . . .

PRIEST: . . . Mother Mary never had sex, Mother Mary was a holy virgin. Mother Mary was a perfect woman, which is why she was the mother of our Lord Jesus Christ . . .

BRENDA: . . . And then she knew she would die because their laughter was so loud and so long that she had to break her mirror to stop their laughter . . .

RONALD: . . . they construct images of themselves, and others. Fantasies. And sometimes they end up confusing themselves with their own—or somebody else's—fantasized constructions . . .

GLORIA: . . . never mind there's not a shred of proof she isn't some straight-up con woman off the street.

GEECHEE FAIRY: . . . choose well, little daughta—choose very well . . . or dis Geechee Fairy—gonna see you in hell . . .

CHOCOLATE: Just get out of my head, damn you—GET OUT! This wasn't supposed to end up like this . . . I made a mistake, I MADE A MISTAKE! I wanted to feel something, besides emptiness, failure . . . Maybe the American dream was never my dream, but this country is everything I am, my milk *and* my honey, I learned my lessons well! But if, in the end, this is what I have, then what is my dream? AND WHOSE DREAM ARE WE ALL DREAMING, 'cause it's killing me, the whole land is poisoned—IF I'M A HO, I'M AN INNOCENT ONE! 'Cause trying to kill yourself for forgetting your own name isn't a crime . . . it's a punishment . . .

(The video voices fade to a low murmur. The heart rate stabilizes.

The lights rise on the place where Chocolate's mirror was at the start of the play. Chocolate staggers toward it.

Geechee Fairy appears.)

Please . . . help me . . .

GEECHEE FAIRY: Sorry, darlin' . . . dis time, I just come for de bag.

(Geechee Fairy takes the suitcase.)

Too bad. Freedom got a high price . . . some folks gotta work harder den others to pay it. But de trick is not to sell ya soul—just tryin' to break even.

(Geechee Fairy disappears.)

CHOCOLATE: Freedom? Was that what all this was about? Freedom . . . Yeah . . . maybe that's what I was lookin' for. Maybe I just thought I wanted all that other stuff . . . I wish . . . I wish . . . I wish it wasn't . . . too late.

(We hear the heart monitor flatline, then die out. Chocolate slumps to the floor.
After a moment Geechee Fairy returns, holding the suitcase. She rolls the curtain in front of Chocolate's body.)

GEECHEE FAIRY: Well. I might as well leave this . . . won't de me no good, anyway.

(She places the suitcase on the floor.)

Anyway, damn ting still owe a wish fa good luck. Maybe . . . just maybe . . . I make dat wish fa bot' of us.

(Geechee Fairy closes her eyes and silently wishes. She opens the suitcase. Nothing happens.)

Oh well. Betta luck next time.

(Geechee Fairy exits.
A few seconds pass, then a light begins to glow. The stage turns ethereal. We hear the sound of a new beat.
The woman who was Chocolate steps from behind the rolling curtain. She wears a hospital gown and multicolored wings. When she speaks her voice is resonant and other-worldly.)

WOMAN WITH WINGS:
> I died inside my mind
> and dreamt
> a world of vivid love.
> My tears of sorrow
> drenched my soul.

A garden grew
from up above.
Without
the need for more I leapt
toward
a light
that called my name.
The name it called was Peace.
The name it called was Trust.
The name it called was Truth.
The name it called was Flower.
Those names I took
and lived again
to love myself.
Death had no power.

(The Woman with Wings takes off the wings and the hospital gown.

The stage changes again. Video shows the Woman with Wings tenderly covering the Zombies in flowing cloth.

The new beat continues.

The Woman with Wings sets up Ronald's video camera downstage and aims it directly at the audience. She pulls a stool nearby and sits, watching the video of herself and the Zombies.)

WOMAN WITH WINGS: So, *Death of a Ho*, my first piece, was inspired by the idea of a near-death experience. *(Holding up her taped wrists)* I wear these to remind me to be careful what I wish for. Being the red-white-and-blue-blooded gal I am, I figured somebody needed to give a ho a break, for once. 'Cause as they say, all God's chillun got wings. And by the way, I do believe in fairy godmothers.

(She turns on the video camera. A live-feed video is projected of the audience.)

This, is the beginning of an idea for a new piece . . . using a live audience to examine how much of any group soul can be captured as its members engage in a shared dream. I have no idea what to call it.

(Her cell phone goes off.)

WOMAN WITH WINGS *(Answering cell phone)*: Hello? What? *(To audience)* Oh my God—it's Hollywood calling! *(To phone)* Yes? Oh, you have?

Oh, you are? Well . . . Sure. I can do that . . . I mean, why not? For that kind of money, I could do just about anything!

(We hear the sound of a mirror breaking.
Blackout.)

THE END

Jake-ann Jones's plays include *Portrait of the Artist as a Soul Man Dead*, which received its world-premiere production at St. Paul's Penumbra Theatre Company; *Under Frank Observation*, presented at The Public Theater's New Work Now Festival, New York Theatre Workshop's Just Add Water Festival and Crossroads Theatre Company's Genesis Festival; *Juno, the Universal Power Child*, produced and presented as part of NPR's New American Radio series; *Black Bitches Brew*, produced by Aaron Davis Hall and Hartford's Company One; *Eclipse in Bottomsville*, presented at Nuyorican Poets Café in New York; *Firedance at the Palace*, produced as part of New York's MCC Theatre's Mortality Project and *Monsters, Mirrors, and White Magic*, presented at BACA Downtown in Brooklyn.

In 2002, a musical adaptation of Jones's play *Magic Kingdom, an American Girl's Tale* was presented by New Georges and the Hourglass Group; the musical later received a 2003 Jonathan Larson Performing Arts Foundation Grant to fund a further development workshop. She was a 2000 Penumbra Theatre Company Cornerstone Artist awardee, and co-author of the 1998 Urban World Film Festival's Grand Prize winning screenplay *Spook City*. She has received a Brown University Weston Playwriting Award, a Jerome/NYSCA Franklin Furnace Performance Art Grant, a Seymour Peck Award for Creative Excellence, and artist fellowships with New York Theatre Workshop, Mabou Mines Development Foundation, Inc. and the Bay Area Playwrights Festival.

Her plays, essays, articles and fiction have been published in St. Louis's *Eyeball*, *The Portable Lower East Sider*, *New Word*, *Shade Magazine*, *The Mac Wellman Journal* and Brown University's *NuMuse*. She was featured in the book *Women Who Write Plays*. She has taught playwriting and solo performance at City College, Queens College, Brown University, The Writer's Voice and the Frederick Douglass Creative Arts Center.

transformationals

word becomes flesh

performed letters from father to unborn son

by marc bamuthi joseph

author's statement

I am incredibly excited about the timely nature of a piece which is specific to fatherhood from the perspective of a black man in his mid-twenties. Within the African American community, the absent father has become a stock type in our modern mythical canon. Joining sambos, bucks and pickaninnies, it is the post-post modern caricatured experience of African American paternity, commonly referred to as the "baby daddy." Scholars and social critics have deconstructed the environment that would allow such a social phenomenon to exist, while preachers and demagogues berate absent fathers for their behavior, but an essential missing element of this discourse is the voice of the father himself. *Word Becomes Flesh* fills this critical void in our musings about the trajectory of black manhood in America.

My artistic intention is to deepen the relationship between spoken language, body language and the body politic. Further, I am personally invested in the opportunity to create a living document for my own son, who recently celebrated his third birthday, and is the purest inspiration for this piece. These performed letters incorporate elements of ritual, archetypes and symbolic sites within more secular constructs of hip-hop culture. This work aims to reach a distinct standard in theater by displaying a commitment to using dance and movement to enhance the poetic experience, a commitment to literacy and education within and beyond the staged performance of our work, and a fierce penchant for the political—all in an effort to provide a voice, and access to a historically silenced community.

production history

Word Becomes Flesh: Performed Letters from Father to Unborn Son was written and performed by Marc Bamuthi Joseph. It was directed by Gloria Bigelow with technical direction and design by Sean Riley; the music was composed by BRAVO, the musical direction was by Paris King, the musicians were Ajayi Jackson (trap drums) and Sekou Gibson (Haitian-skin drums), the dramaturg was Roberta Uno and the choreographer was Adia Whitaker.

Word Becomes Flesh received its world premiere at the NYC Hip-Hop Theater Festival at Performance Space 122 in June 2003. It has since received productions at more than twenty-five venues throughout the United States, including the Dance Theater Workshop in New York City, the New WORLD Theater at the University of Massachusetts in Amherst, the Yerba Buena Center for the Arts in San Francisco, the University Musical Society at the University of Michigan in Ann Arbor, the Museum of Contemporary Art in Chicago, Miami Dade College and the King Arts Complex in Columbus.

invocation

Hype music begins. The lights come up on Marc.

MARC:
> Welcome to the spoken world
> The living word
> A dream deferred
> Reverse returned back to the original path.
> For whites
> For browns
> For blacks
> For greens
> Feel me?
>
> Welcome to the spoken world
> Unspoken heard
> Unfocused blurred
> A bird of youth
> A sooth
> A truth
> A muse of mind
> You are divine
> Feel me? . . .

(Blackout and simultaneous crashing sound. We hear the sound of a heartbeat begin. A light comes up on Marc. Marc dances to the heartbeat, a physical express of shock, his knees buckling.

The lights fade to a spot on Marc's face once he is standing behind a chair. Blackout. The chair is removed. The "son" light comes up, an amber-toned special light to be used when Marc speaks directly to his son.)

> *Today* I heard your heart beat and it hit me
> Right at my knees and
> Buckled me

I lost my legs
I'm trying to find them again
Looking in familiar places
I begin with language
My blood.

Birthing you is my process, too
You have an intrinsically intimate relationship with your mother
But your dad didn't check out when you were in the womb
And you probably feel the stress I put your mother through
But heartbeat
Please realize a brother be feelin' stressed, too
And blessed, too
Heart beating down the door of mortality
Talking 'bout
Guess who?
Got to so some *walkin'* 'bout here
All the squawkin' will no longer do
Heartbeat, these are my tools
Verbal music and movement
In twelve movements.

seen 1

for pop

The sound of the heartbeat stops. Lighting tells us we are in a classroom. The son light remains.

MARC:

In 1984 every young black man in New York City had a pair of
Adidas shell-toes or Puma suedes
Except me
In 1984 I got my first pair of tap shoes
Black and patent leather like the Nicholas brothers used to rock
My pop wasn't cool with me tap dancing
It reeked of America to him
Coming from Haiti my dad desired American wealth but he
shunned American culture
He didn't understand that the two are really one
Nor did he realize that tap dance is African drum
The percussive *(Tap-dances a little)*

Mirrored sharp pound of sharks shanked against exterior of slave
     ships decaying vomit rocked counter-rhythmic to Atlantic
     waves
Picture the men entrusted to speak stories through song
Shocked mute by the trauma
For them *(Taps)*
Was born
Rhythm be verse when blood bleeds back to lines black like Nile
     riverbeds
There was no outlet to reconfigure communicative way of djem-
     be lullabies
So Africans new to the New World
Devised other means of making the fading Gorée Island seashore
     real
To those who had never seen
"Well, son, it kinda sounded like . . ." *(Taps)*

Understand the innovation
Syncopation constructed to reflect dancing celebration of birth
     and love and harvest
An entire social order divested of its principal means of
     announcing its own being
That was the African in the European colonized state
The colonies made it an offense
Punishable by death for folks of color to be in possession of any
Noisemaking instrument
However they had enough business sense not to devalue their
     property by chopping off our feet
Leaving just enough space
To bring back the beat. *(Taps)*

Tap dance
Adhoc repository of rhythm reflecting the organizing principle
     of improvisation
The nations built jazz
Chitlins
Behind the back, look aways
We stay transcendent through the transformative art
Conjuring conjecture
The extra mile is where we start
Yet, despite this start, tap dance has become an oft-used
Understated metaphor for the sycophantic antics of the buffalo
     soldier

Turned buffalo shuffling
With a quick Republican vote
Aww, that nigga just tap-dancing for the man
Hands framin' a face featurin' a grin so sick it masks the emascu-
     lated in a false sense of peace
Grinding teeth despite the pain.

In 1984 I would tourjete through the raindrops *(Taps)*
Imagining the wind was my pops
Propelling my flight
Pop's pride lifting me beyond crack-
Cocaine
Ronald Reagan around the corner
1984 sauna-hot
Carl Lewis blazin' and I'm blazin' . . .
Pop, will you listen to me?
It's what I wanna ask but I keep tap-dancing around the questions
Projectin' all the security my nine-year-old body can muster
Wilting in the cool hot of my father's disconnection.

Fuck it
My dad was in the home
He didn't beat my mom
Me and my sister are both healthy and college-educated
Almost Cosby kids
We blow afro-bombs through ego, superego, id
Cuz Freud's paradigms of the mind
Didn't have colored folk in mind
So I'd dissect mine for self
For sure.

(Marc executes a manjani* lick on manjani text.)

1984 I learned to tap dance
Not Clarence Thomas
Or Bamuthi
Song and dance
That is a misnomered
Misappropriation of the art form
Derived from rhythmic regeneration of Gambian *manjani*
Reconstructed for Virginia shores.

* A West African rite-of-passage dance.

(Marc does an Ellington lick on Ellingtonian text:)

1984 I learned to perform
Slide through space
Face to face with *Ellingtonian* jazz
I learned my movement was jazz
Improvised truths out of false structures
1984, father-son relationship ruptured.

Pop wasn't listening to me
so I'd play call-and-response between my feet and the floor.

Pop . . .
Pop . . .
Pop . . .

(Stops.)

I don't feel like tap-dancing no more.

(Heartbeat sound rises.)

Son,
This is to sever the cycle
Our *story*
Remade in your flesh
Living words
A spoken world so you will never have to guess
About why I might choose to be absent.

seen 2

late

We hear a guitar lick, "Late" music begins, a melancholy jazz tune. A special light comes up center stage. A slide of "Wise Man, Clever Boy," a painting by Eesuu, is projected.

MARC:
Nothing
Will disrupt my principles
Like the scent of potential sex

Striding through the summer heat
Beneath my window.

(Marc arrives at center stage. A scarlet light comes up on him.)

A black widow
Wisdom grown ripe in my Eden orchard
Sweet torture.

(A turquoise light comes up on another part of the stage.)

Now I was committed to this other woman
An Ailey dancer in perpetual flight
My night come to life
My light
Told her my stars and foundation were in order
But I lied
Didn't even sense the shift
Abandoned the present for what seemed to be a pre-sent gift
And
Nothing
Will fuck up a man's principles like
The scent of potential sex striding through the summer heat
Unless of course his principles are arranged in such a way that it
wouldn't even occur to him to creep
But I ain't met that nigga yet.

And her crescent-moon eyes flipped my Earth
Made me rise with dusk and dusty rose of sunset
Syncopated in six
I'd like to think it was more than the scent of sex; I sought the
sis on the side like Similac to simulate real live love
Without the strings . . . without all the little shit that complicates
things . . . like commitment
And, hey, we two adults both wit it
Knew trouble when I saw it and entered it . . .

And it mighta been the red wine or the sienna lights
But for a minute I thought I saw God that night
Not the old white dude with the gray beard sittin'
On some throne in the clouds
I'm talking about God

She
First flap of blood-red butterfly wing
Still cocoon damp
Flight in first warm spring wind.

God . . .

For a minute I imagined that there was no will
Just an openness to what will be
Acquiescence our only choice is degree of consciousness by
    which we consummate
What God has already seen.
Like a fated love and tender recurring dream
Dreamt three nights in every lifetime
Your lifeline's most peaceful sleep and
I believed she
Left her will behind and
I had no choice in this
In the beginning there was light
And our ships had been crossing in the dark night ever since
Spirits elliptic in orbit
An axis
A season whose time has come again.
Like autumn following summer you could feel our embrace in
    the evening wind . . .

But
In truth
It was just the two of us
Black and blue
Indulgent in summer heat
Tempted by what lay beneath
And taboo
In reaching out to be held close by someone new
Arriving through the summer heat into one another's lives *just* in
    time . . .

(The turquoise and scarlet lights go out.)

But niggaz can't never be *on* time.

So no surprise when she tells me she's late.

(The lights go down, then the slide goes out.

We hear a drum lick, which leads into the "Brown Boy" music theme, joyful, expectant jazz, in the spirit of Grant Green or Cal Tjader. The lights come up and the slide "Fear of a Black Planet" by Eesuu is projected.)

seen 3

ode to a brown boy

MARC:

Five months into her pregnancy
She emails me a scanned image of her sonogram
Sonic waves fashioned in the shape of our son
What I'm seeing is sound
My senses transformed by this image of a boy
Floating
Buoyantly drifting
Like my hold on immaturity slipping away
A son
It is now *he* and I . . .
Am scared shitless.

I am nearly twenty-eight
The cosmic age of Saturn's return
Karmic retribution awaits like economic reparations my ancestors
    have earned
The universe on the verge of payin' me back
I feel like everything starts over again
Beginning with this image of blue sound
Heartbeat profound
I've printed the email out and it's sitting now, peacefully on my
    lap
A son . . .

I've never been a woman
Y'know that's a story unto itself
But *this* being
I've spent my whole life seeing a brown boy's days to come
And before they reach eighteen so many brown boys' lives
    already done
Brown boy
Feared

Brown boy
Step aside, we don't want you here
Brown boy
Only respect those who respect you
Brown boy
Live your life knowing the mainstream world only respects a few
Brown boys
And this will never be tolerated as an excuse
Brown boy
Guilty until proven innocent
Demonized
You stand accused but you stand firm
Like sacred ground brown . . .

Boy, am I supposed to teach you these things?
How many brown boys left to be taught by the wilderness
Destiny hung
Hinged
A doorway to death
Your life is great white fetished hyped and hexed
Do I tell you these things right away brown boy
Only five months in the womb we've been hunted for so long,
    my son
My son, are you going to be hunted, too?
Brown boys randomly meet two of they patnas
Take a minute to hang
The law quick to label 'em a gang of brown boys
And I don't know if we chasin' dreams or runnin' from police.

All this runnin' can't just be about a race of brown boys . . .

Though there is no finish line
Consumed by the condition of race in
Land of the free by the blood of the slave
Young
Black
Men.

(We hear a flurry of drums. A special light comes up on Marc.)

Son,
I am racing through the streets of Mostar
Most of the time art feeds you Ramen noodles

But sometimes your art lands you in Europe
South of Bosnia
1999
At the end of the twentieth century, there is still a segment of
    humanity
That finds reason to practice genocide
Rwandan blood on the fields captures fleeting global attention,
    but here there is an alliance of international troops gathered
    to keep the peace
They do so with menacing tanks that they drive through the
    streets
Foot soldiers carrying M16s
And *somehow*, there are kids listening to me and a crew four-deep
Bust poetry:

Represent
Re present
Reap re-sent
We pre-sent
We present up in here
Presented to the moment blown in on God's breath
Young black men.

During my two weeks there I rarely met a man my own age
Most social occasions were inclusive of the very young and
A host of elders
But men in their mid-twenties and thirties
Represented the generation of young boys who went to war a
    few years earlier and had never come back
And sometimes downtown Oakland looks the same way to me
You can't fight a war on crime
Without casualties, brown boy
Your mere presence creates conflict
They'll fire ten thousand teachers but
Have plenty of money to build more jails and
They wonder how you end up a convict
It wouldn't be called a system unless it worked . . .
And you are the one it often works against
Brown boy
Native son
Invisible man
There's a war goin' on outside
I guess this is when your training begins.

(We hear dance music that leads into "Pro-Choice" music, a blues song. Marc executes approximately four minutes of modern-based movement inspired by images of military training, indecision and resistance to change.)

seen 4

pro-choice

MARC:

    I was raised Catholic in New York during the Reagan-Bush era
    In conservative times
    Liberalism takes on a cool cachet for preteens
    Just beginning to see the world in politics and polarities
    New York Post delivered on our family's doorstep
    Every summer
    Bumpers
    Bensonhurst
    Howard Beach
    Dummied down to black and white for any fool to see
    And I naturally saw my way to the left.

    On my way there I picked up slogans
    Read some books
    Learned to look a woman in the eye
    Learned it was okay to bring a man close to your chest and cry
    Sweet Honey in the Rock, poetry, dance . . .
    A sensitive guy
    Which by definition means that I'm pro-choice.

(Marc gets a chair and sits center stage. The music stops. A female voice-over says:)

VOICE:

    A *woman's* right to choose
    What she does with the contents of her womb . . .

(The word "Choice" is projected on screen.)

MARC:

    When I was fifteen I sat in a waiting room
    Sitting with the obvious choice weighing heavily on my heart

Trying to look at ease
Like my dumb young male ass
Had any other reason to be at a gynecologist's office other than
    to . . .

She was honest enough to tell her family
They totally supported her decision
I decided not to tell anybody
I still haven't told my own mom . . .
I told myself I was too young for it to really count
Fifteen . . .

A baby was *not* an alternative, son
And if the mother feels like she has only one real feasible option . . .
(And it doesn't involve a lifetime commitment on your part . . .)
It's not as difficult
To be pro-choice.

(The female voice-over of the mother says:)

VOICE (SFX):
    Black
    I keep tryin' this herbal thing I heard about
    But I don't think it's working
    I just feel sick all the time
    I think we should make an appointment.

MARC:
    A life inside my love
    We drove to the clinic assuming
    A pill
    A chemical detour to make the decision a little easier to swallow
    They called her name and we entered
    She lay back
    The nurse applies a clear jelly across her flat brown stomach and
        slowly runs an instrument across her midsection
    "You're too far along to take the pill," the nurse says, and gestures
        to the screen by the bed
    We turn to see the baby.

    A pulse of light
    Which might have been a heart
    Glistening faintly

Was once an idea
Safe as concept
Swimming inside her
Effortless struggle
Hauntingly real
I should be overjoyed
Instead my knees break in fear.

The decision made before the baby has eyes to cry
Or lids to blink its tears away.

(The female voice-over of the mother says:)

VOICE (SFX):

Black, I'm pregnant
I'm having the baby
You can decide if you want to be in its life or not.

MARC:

And why should any man have the right to tell a woman what to
do with her body?
Sounds *great* at the peace rally, but when you've really fathered a
child you don't think you're ready for . . .

(The female voice-over of the mother says:)

VOICE (SFX):

RIGHT TO LIFE!
RIGHT TO CHOOSE!

MARC:

And, son, sometimes we just hope we choose right
Cuz we choose to sacrifice
We choose to believe that we've been thusly chosen to produce
life
We choose to ignore the voices vehemently clinging to the past
with all their might and we might choose to run
Bussin' sprints like track stars in this rat race
Runnin' it with blackface is hard enough without a daughter or a
son
Ask a roomful of young black men about their fathers
You'll see of the choice to stay or leave
Most are confronted by their own demons and emenies

And the choice to go
Seems to be a popular one.

(Marc takes the chair offstage. The lights shift into a "boogeyman" effect: a mix of sickly green and red light. Marc reenters and transforms into the character of the "Nigga Mentality," personifying him as a gnarled, trollish, pained figure with a low, raspy voice.)

seen 5

self-portrait: the nigga mentality

MARC:

    Your first enemy is me, the
    Nigga mentality
    Living in a box at the center of the sun
    It's the final lap of lux and I cannot see the leader
    Trapped in the crosshairs of thirteen heaters with a singular aim
    Like distant thunder a voice rains
    Boy, what is your name?
    My impulse is to obediently respond but knowledge absconds
    I've forgotten
    Command of the fact displaced in memory's space by images of
        pickin' cotton
    Justified in the name of his only begotten son
    Apparently he was born up the block from where my carrier
        comes from
    Ill conundrum but paradox is not new
    They call me confused . . .
    Uh-uh
    I'm very well trained
    I just can't find my name in the bone-white glare of this box
    Only unlocked by a key lurking somewhere out there in the dark
    Belly of the beast marked "Do Not Touch" and
    Without fail I listen
    It's not in my disposition to question what I'm told
    I'm goin' on six centuries old
    My lineage unfolds with
    Hate
    Hate was my great-great-grand
    Had several kids dispersed across several lands
    Man co-opted then made manifest

Parties like Division
Greed
Murder
Excess.

Greed had incestuous sex with his cousin Neglect from the West
Genetic defect produced an unfortunate deformity
They had a baby named Ignorance, who just couldn't see
Ignorance fell in love with Hate
Who by now had turned in on herself
Burned within self
It would make your heart melt
There was a heartfelt connection between Self-Hate and
    Ignorance
Came thence my racist parent
I mean
My parent Racist . . .

Traces of the seed originated with Greed
So Racist's primary need was to feed a hunger for eternity
Universal props
So he dropped the "t"
Substituted with an "m"
He said forget the racist individual
I'll be Racism
An institution.

God-complex delusions started coolin' with my dad
Gave him dap
Told him you alla dat
And Racism got phat off his own PR
Said, I'm the star of this show . . .

Now here he go
He embedded himself in the cornerstone of all the new nations
Made himself chair of the house of appropriations
Nothing was safe . . .

Until chaste Capitalism slipped in the frame
"Hey baby, what's your name?"
Racism spittin' game cuz Capitalism was a looker
But she flipped it on him like he was a two-bit hooker.

He took her
And shook her
(Cuz Dad's way was violent)
But she looked him dead in the eye
And he fell steady silent
Compliant.

She said, "Look, Racism . . . we gonna do it like this:
First of all we're gonna pretend that you don't exist.
Then we'll tell the world to serve me,
A much more attractive interest,
But we'll shape everything so we both benefit."
She leaned over slowly
Kissed him on the lips
Pops nodded his head
It's been that way ever since . . .

Shortly thereafter, they had my brother
Slavery
A few years later
Along came me . . .

I'm actually glad I don't possess all these family traits
I don't hate anyone except my carrier and his crew
But I do love my master
And I worship his truth
I must admit
I'm whipped weak by Greed's fleet genes running through my core
I got mounds of self-hate behind the closet door of skeletons and
    secrets
Wearing sins and Friedrich Nietzsche's brilliant theories
But I grow weary drawing defenses against self-constructed attacks
I try to relax
Contemplate my link to ignorance
Which makes no sense
Cuz I *gots* knowledge
I know:
Timbo
Polo
Nike
Moschino
Nautica

Hilfiger sean john vuitton dolce and gabbana prada kani levi's bk
   ck dkny anne klein fubu
Guess rolex lex beamers benz . . .
I know them all
And I know the ends don't justify the means
I know God is rectangular and grayish green
I novus ordo seclorum, don't include me
I know how to serve my dignity up on a platter
I know how to serve my master
I know how to run in place
Faster and smoother than panthers and cougars and coons, Oh my!
I know, suh . . .
But I don'ts know why otha minds inclined to design systems
   which confine my carrier
And bind them to themselves with political ties for the sole
   purpose of promotin' their own economic advantage
I don't understand it
We share the same planet but these walls are like granite and
   I cannot escape
All this light got me twisted
Consumed with a fable written in invisible ink that
My master swears is my fate
My master eliminates all fiction
I will deviate never
I'd rather beat my head against the walls of a cell
Tryin' to remember my name forever
Three rows of 222 bird's eye–sized holes
Callin' gently
Subtly
Suggesting in the dark
Might be a key which gives my name back to me
But I don't want to be in the dark
I don't want to be in the dark
I don't want to be dark
I don't want to be dark
I don't want to be dark
I don't want to be
I don't even want to be . . .
The almighty
Nigga mentality.

incarnation illustration
shadow work

The stage is dark.
> *The lights slowly rise as Marc pops into a pose of a man in handcuffs.*
> *Blackout.*
> *The lights slowly rise as Marc pops into a pose of a man knotting his tie.*
> *Blackout.*
> *The lights slowly rise as Marc pops into a pose of a man being hung from*
a tree.
> *Blackout.*
> *The lights slowly rise as Marc pops into a pose of a man clutching his*
gold chain.
> *Blackout.*
> *The son light comes up.*

MARC:
> Son,
> Mine is the last generation to have known life without hip-hop
> Who watched it descend like the falling break a dawn
> Breakdown at daybreak in a basement in *Brooklyn*
>
> *("Memory" music, part ska/part funk, fades up.)*
>
> And all over the map from Dakar to Mostar to Au Cap to Oaktown
> > to Osaka.

seen 6
oh where oh where . . .

Flashing colored lights come up—the inside of a nightclub.

MARC:
> It's Friday night.
>
> Dance floor's packed
> Been in the club for twenty minutes
> Heard four songs by MCs who've been indicted or convicted of
> > sexual abuse
> The dance floor's packed.

Sprung off concubines and Courvoisier
The DJ plays something beckonin' all his hos
To push that ass back and forth
Descriptions of acts of force blarin' through the speaker
Plastered in platinum.

It's Friday night
The social antonym and opposite of Sunday morning.
Don't need to hear a sermon
But my discernin' ear makes it hard to dance past
These commercially constructed demographically
Projected and contrived rap hits
Wit the half-wit hooks
MCs clearly payin' less attention to lyrics
Cuz they focused on how good the girls in the lead video look
And look . . .

I ain't mad at makin' profits
Or doin' business
I'm mad cuz I'm at the club and I can't float through the culture
     I love
Without swimming through an endless stream
Of bling and bitches
Creatin' cookie-cut batches of hip-hop progeny
Paradin' to barely melodic
Danceable misogyny.

Nigga I'm at the spot
Ain't really tryin' to think my way through this hip-hop
But I'm telling you the dance floor's packed
And diddy's like thirty
And them kiddies is like nine
And they on the same track
Serializing a simulated game of "hit it from the back"
It's on some R. Kelly math
No one wants to add or subtract
And I'm apt to think
That because this music is synonymous with youth culture
There's this crazy generational divide between the majority of
     folks the music is made for
And the rest of us
Which is like anyone over the age of twenty-five
And I'm buggin'

Didn't know twenty-seven was gonna qualify me to be an O.G.
I don't wanna be one of those folks who thinks you set trippin'
Cuz you listen to Funk Flex
Or watch videos on BET
It's what happens when a culture evolves and becomes an industry
But I wanna reflect the potential
Like a hip-hop memory.

Fadin' me back to dance floors packed all over the map
From Dakar to Mostar to Au Cap to Oaktown to Osaka
Kids throwin' 'em up
Speak no English
Rhyming right along with Tupac
Hip-hop got global cities, states and nations payin' attention to
    what young black men are sayin'
And the opportunity at hand spans more than surface entertainment
Keep waitin' for Rocawear to make bullets
So the escalatin' murder rate will also be a fashion statement
MC . . . the world is hangin' on your every word, MC
Might be hung by your very word, MC . . .

*(A microphone comes up. Marc and the drummer freestyle. The music
ends.*

    The son light comes up. We hear the sound of a heartbeat.)

seen 7

silence

The female voice-over of the mother says:

VOICE (SFX):
> Black . . . I'm havin' the baby. You can decide if you want to be in
> its life or not.

MARC:
> ONE, I am not married and am not going to marry your mother.
> You were CLEARLY meant to be and WE were not.
>
> I cannot raise you under a roof of "I have regrets" of "We
> didn't START this as a commitment" of "Sssshhh, don't wake the
> baby" of "I'm having an affair" of "Don't you DARE use our son
> like a fuckin' PAWN" of "I'm tired of this" of "I NEVER WANTED
> this" ravaging your sleeping subconscious what kind of environ-

ment is this and growing up so much of what I ever saw or read
says you gotta be married first to have a kid and you can't grow up
black and male and not know about the cycle of bleak statistics we
in . . .

You might be my sole truth
In the midst of a self-composed creation myth
And the fact is I can't live no more fictives.

My raised right foot is anvil-heavy, hovering
Above the fateful step I cannot seem to take
Silence.

Wind blowing harmony to the rhythm of insect night song
A tree holds the weight of a young man hung in her muscle
    memory
Weeps forty-one leaves like libation
The city can't support its tired nodding head.

Silence.

Son,
When I can't handle the truth about myself
I either avoid it or rewrite it
Decorate the ugly in metaphor
Bathe it in blue ink
Dress it up like a young boy at a summer birthday party.

I lie.

Three months in the womb
I am wishing you away
Inside your mother
You are an emblem of infinite possibilities
Inside my mind you are a symbol of disappointment
A gap between what I've spoken
And the truth
Or really what I've neglected to speak
Cloaked myself in quiet
No one has ever accused the mute of lying
And I am wishing you away, son
So I won't have to run
So I won't have to look in your eyes some day

And only think of damage done
I am in love
And it is not with your mother
And I have neither courage nor faith to say anything
To anyone.

Silence.

(The turquoise light comes up.)

I am nearly twenty-three
We meet
It's perfect
She moves across the continent
We struggle through
Together
Our love a castle built for revelation
She is my Ailey dancer in perpetual flight
My night come to life
My light
It is hard but the best things often are
And it's worth it
This is forever
It's perfect
And we journey around the sun twice
We manage to endure through the frustration of absence
Strangers tease us
Call us chocolate angels
Swear we only take our wings out at night
To fly
Too high
Can't see solid ground.

Too far
To touch
Too used to the sound without sight or skin
And nothing
Will disrupt a man's principles
Like the scent of potential sex . . .

Three months in the womb
Man plans
God laughs

I know this is no accident
The world is slowly finding out about you
But I haven't told *her* yet
In the deepest darkest heart of me
I'm praying for absolution in tragedy
You an anonymous casualty
There are future muscle memories that I'm already trying to forget.

Silence.

Son,
You are becoming more than a sum of cells
And I am losing my ability to articulate my world
Exiling myself to hell
And it has no fury
Like what I think might be her wrath
And we've been partners for years
I can't afford her the decency of exposing myself to her honestly
So *she* can decide and act
And the fact is
I *know* that children are God's greatest gift
It's hard but prior pain gives me some perspective
I know that right now I'm embarrassed and ashamed and confused
And fearful, but in time I will get over all of this
But how do you tell the real thing
That you've been living a myth?
Exactly *when*?
What is the timing that's most appropriate?
And if you could just
GO AWAY . . .
I WISH
And it's
All these waves of emotion
All these levels of destruction at a time of creation
I'm being swept in by the undertow
On top of a peak
Pacific ocean miles and miles beneath . . .

Anvil-heavy hovering
Deep breath
My feet
My fault
Is everything I'm gaining worth the love I've lost?

What kind of asshole am I?
Silently wishing for something to go wrong
Silently been lying to myself all along.

Silence.

I am no martyr
If all of us conceived and had children only when we were good
    and ready
There'd be about three people on the whole planet.

Somewhere in my soul I know there is no road where the silence
    ends and the lying begins
Understand this
Comprehension does not atone for the bond I've disrespected
    and abandoned
I'm damaged, son
Am more and less than a man
Am not defined by these hefty words I might speak.
Three months in the womb you are so fragile
And I feel so weak
Barely held together by a growing truth
That settles beneath my feet in the glaring
Glowing heat
Of my
Silence.

seen 8

letter 9/11

Music begins. The following is a choreographed piece of modern dance. A pre-recorded version of the following poem is played via voice-over with the movement. The movement spells out some of the text, literally inscribing letters, words and phrases onto the stage space. The lights dim with the footwork and go up full on the moves.

MARC:

    Son,
    You are seven months in the womb when the Earth stops spinning
    Out of still and silence emerges a drum
    I think the sound might be you

Early morning stretching and knockin'
But your auntie's in the next room
Screaming, "TERRORISTS!"
And I soon know that I've been hearing the sound of
Thousands of hearts dropping
You can smell the stank of sulfur smoldering in a war room in
the East.

Son,
I tell you these things because
I don't know how this moment will appear in your history books
Your texts will come with DVDs where you will see
The images as we did
Over and over again
They will show you
Bodies hurtling from burning towers
Like Africans escaping slave ships
They will show you
Anger
Sadness
And patriotism
But won't peer into the hearts of suspicious men who
Know there are no accidents or coincidences under the sun.

Son,
Every TV set in America is on right now but
It's all white noise
The clearest sounds are heartbeats and war drums
Within hours the face of evil is everywhere
A brown man from the Middle East
A former operative of the CIA
I wonder if your history books will mention this
Will it even be one of those sidebar trivialities
What will they edit out on your supplemental DVD
Will they include things most of us never got to hear or see?

The image of Dick Cheney lighting a cigar off a burning
Oil-soaked Franklin
While getting a lap dance in the jacuzzi at his undisclosed location . . .

(Which I keep thinking is a house in the Caymans
Which he bought with a slice of the fifty-six million that
Haliburton gave him as a parachute when he retired . . .

[Not that this screamed Vice President For Hire
Not that he would feel entitled to get his peoples back
By, let's say . . .
Capitalizing on this rising hysteria to justify war against Saudi
    Arabia
And later Iraq
Creating a need to rebuild the national infrastructure
And then say
Shepherding those contracts to his original crew . . .

(Which is something he did do when he was secretary of defense
When Bush's father was president . . .)])

Son,
The political past became irrelevant on September 10 . . .
I wonder
In your history books will you ever hear the voices of dissent
Will the future act like Ground Zero ash
Palpable misery silencing them . . .
Or will you get to hear the sounds as we did:

(Marc puts on gloves, a long jacket and a top hat during the last lines.)

The fetal kicks
The hearts dropping
The war drums pounding
The ire rising in the minds and hearts of
Suspicious men . . .

(Music comes up.

   Slides are projected of Kara Walker–like imagery: abstracted antebellum-era iconography.

   As the music changes, the dancing shifts dramatically, from modern-based movement, to a hip-hop version of a minstrel's buck and shuffle. The dance goes through thirty-two bars of the shuffle and then abruptly ends on the word "vagabond.")

seen 9

of coon-mammies and baby-daddies

MARC:

   Vagabond
   Grandmère looks like she wants to submerge

My entire body in a *vat* of holy water
Instead
She pulls me close to her chest and says
Pou-pouch
For the good of the baby
You must marry his mother.

I close my eyes and a long lineage of minstrels, coons and mammies
Open their arms to welcome me to their family
I am their heir for the twenty-first century:

The *Baby Daddy.*

(The slide projector turns off.)

seen 10

conditions, options and africa as fantasy island

MARC:
What if all you were able to see
Was all you had ever seen?
What if your subconscious put bars over the doors to your own
    dreams
Jailed them in a cell next to your possibilities?
Would you be able to break every one out?
Would you be able to set all a y'all free?
I pose this question to young Steve
A sophomore at Berkeley High
About sixteen
But, son, I'm really talking back to me.

Your mom is acting like at any second I'mo up and leave
I feel reluctantly accountable
Her comfort means your safety
She got me safely situated
And it seems like in all my classes
I'm asking my students to write about breaking free
I know there's a blueprint for a better way encoded inside the
    similes when the youth speak
So here comes Steve.

(Marc takes on the persona of a stereotypical high school sophomore.)

STEVE:

> Yo, B
> In Africa we were all kings and queens
> Pyramids, astronomy . . . we Africans
> We can do anything.

MARC:

> Steve
> Africa is genocide
> Post-colonialism
> Is not one way of life
> Is *black*
> Is in the midst of an AIDS epidemic
> Is *not Fantasy Island*
> There are no pygmies bringing you
> Fresh goat milk or piña coladas in coconut shells when you land
>   at the airport
> Is cutty, is fast-paced
> Long days
> A woman raped sliced into and engorged like Belgian chocolate
>   cake
> Is spinning like all of us toward an unforeseen fate
> Engage in our traditions and culture
> But romanticizing is a fuckin' mistake
> We are a people
> You want freedom
> You gotta be ready to give what freedom takes
> And do it with love from
> Heaven above to Ginen
> Utopic delusions confuse the fact that freedom is a *practice.*

> Grandmère,
> Could it be
> That we don't all have to defer our dreams?
> Could it be that the world is ready to see
> Something new? . . .

seen 11

dare to dream

Marc executes a movement phase five different times while speaking the following stanza, with a deep concentration on exaggerated breathing, almost wheezing.

MARC:

> Somewhere between Mother Nature and Father Time
> There's a spiraling myth about
> A father
> Forever chasing the rising son
> A modern Sisyphus stuck behind a boulder of sol
> The father is mythic and misfit
> A mystic
> A self-destructing missile
> Amiss amidst a monolithic image of what he's supposed to be
> A father
> Chasing the rising son
> Like the horizon rushing to the seam of sky and sea.

(Marc breaks out of the movement sequence.
> *The classroom lights rise.)*

> She would give birth in water if she could
> Our conservative insurance and threadbare wallets say she can't
> So we compromise
> Natural birthing class
> Easy to come by in the Bay Area
> Land of hemp, granola and all things alternative
> It's almost our turn to share how we're
> *Feeling* with the rest of the group
> Sitting in a circle
> Generation X
> Our coach is at the chalkboard:
> "Drug Free Vaginal Birth."

> (Personally
> Knock me the fuck out
> But maybe that's why I was born this sex
> I don't possess a woman's strength
> Her body's all stretched

Our baby's body's growing in length
Arms, legs, chest, head . . .)

You wanna do this drug-free, go right ahead, be my guest
Now I'm about to be a guest on the hot seat.

INSTRUCTOR:

Black
By this time next week
You'll be a *father*
How are you *feeling*?

MARC:

Maybe I should be paying attention to this white lady's question
But man I'm reelin' back in a daydream of
Mother Nature and Father Time
Crackin' riddles about a cat undulating his spine as he strides
    towards
The son in the east
Thinks he recognizes self in the rising
But he just cannot see
He is blinded by light
His life like time in a dream
The place where relativity ends so long as we sleep.

And somewhere
There are eight pairs of future parental eyes
All on me
Waiting to see if I'm *FEELING*
Anything—but what I'm feeling is the struggle of the pursuant
    father in my daydream
I'm *FEELING* the visions of mythic men we see in solar mirrors
    when we sleep
I'm *feeling* damn good
I'mo be a father next week and then all of a sudden I'm
Feeling like I can't . . .

*(Marc conducts a repeat of the movement phrase with exaggerated
breathing, near wheezing.)*

sfx: interview with paris

For approximately three to five minutes a red-light wash alternates with individual pools of red light as Marc dances to trap and Haitian-skin drumming. A recorded interview between Marc and musical director Paris King is played in concert with the live percussion. When the trap drums are played, there is a spotlight on the trap drummer, while the rest of the stage is in black. When he finishes, the lights switch to the red wash across the stage, a clip from the interview is played as voice-over, and Haitian percussion plays underneath. Marc's dancing is in reaction to what is being said in the interview.

seen 12

the birth

MARC:

> Push and breathe
> And push and breathe
> And
> Push and breathe . . .
>
> On TV her water breaks at a restaurant
> And Sherman Helmsley delivers the kid in the back seat of a cab
> It's all over in five minutes
> Cut to the Jiffy commercial
> Good night.
>
> *(The son light comes up.)*
>
> In real life
> The end is just the beginning
> Birth rights
> You arrive like Mandela released
> Like the judgment
> Color after the rain
> Blackouts
> Black holes
> Cursed nights
> Black-and-white fictions
> Welcome to the world
> The end is just the beginning
> Birth rites

Mother Nature and Father Time
Making matter a fact
An act of deliverance
An alleluia . . .

On TV
The mother grabs the father by the neck:
"You did this to me you goddamned . . ."

In real life
There isn't much humor in the pain
I am holding her hand
Reminding her to breathe
And I notice that death is on the other side of her
Whispering seductively in her left ear
She wonders out loud if it's not too late to change her mind
If she still has to go through with this:
"What are my other options?!"

She is Jesus on the cross
Elegua among the waters
Veve on the ground
A warrior's sojourn in sands.

And it's been drama but we are still here
Friends
Committed like the horizon to raising a son
We are family for life
The end is just the beginning
Even when *forced* to breed
Somehow the human impulse impels us to bleed
And sweat
Serenade fuck-yous to death
We are still here
Ever stillborn
A Yurugu twin
Doubly conscious
Glory unto the Lord and the levitating morn'
Don't ya mourn, Martha, this is all it took for us to get this far.

Birth rights
Blackouts
Black holes

Whole earths
Hold on
And push and breathe
And push and breathe
And yet you have *always* been
As young as the universe is old
Welcome back.

Birth rights
Blackouts
Black holes
Whole earths
Hold on
And push and breathe
And push and breathe and . . .

epilogue

move

The son light comes up. Marc improvises modern and West African movement throughout the epilogue.

MARC:
You gotta move, M'kai
You got mountains to climb
Skies to fly, seas to seize
Meet new ancestors swinging in the breeze, clinging to the
    thought that trees really be hangin' onto do-re-mi
The melody of the melancholy mired in mud
Then risen like moons like mau-mau
Like maroons must *move*
M'kai, mountains to climb, skies to fly, seas to seize
Seeds to roots to branches to leaves
The deepest part of God's imagined possibilities
Billowing like a willowing wind
Are one
Are men
Must move . . .

My son M'kai is almost two years old now
Three months before he was born my grandfather died.

Three times in one night
Flatlined and revived
Slipped into a coma twice
The last time he came back bragging about this man-child
He'd just met in the after-death
After which his word became flesh
Became sacred text
The next testament
My first breath
My firstborn
A boy
And man . . .

He looks just like my granddad
They recently met inside of a revelation while Granddad was
    doing orbital revolutions around his life
The last time he was confronted at a crossroads by my son M'kai
Of blood and bone and sacrifice
Sanctified
Granddad said, "I can't wait for you to meet your son . . ."

For the first time I really understood where the old man was
    coming from.

I believe in him and I must
There's this race to be run and my folks is losin'
Past is prologue
Our epicenter is an ancestor's epilogue
An epithet if we ain't eased that ancestor's burden yet
He used his great-grandfather's death as a scroll to scribe a scripture
Whisked the man back to life with unborn whisper
Son, do you know who you are?
An ascendant descendant deciphered from stars.

Intone the indescribable like a shadow, my son
We are men
Bury nothing but bones
Cry rivers of tears
Deeply we run
A race to be won
Guided like Harriet with visions of sugarplum skinned
Hung thin strange fruit our roots reach deep
We men are men

marc bamuthi joseph

Amen
Amin
Your din your duty
Your destiny to move
Like the way you move me
Your destiny to move like the way
You
Move
Me . . .

(The lights come slowly down.)

THE END

Marc Bamuthi Joseph, originally from New York City, is an arts activist currently living in Oakland, CA. In fall 2007, Bamuthi was named one of America's Top Young Innovators in the Arts and Sciences, and was featured on the cover of *Smithsonian* magazine. He is a National Poetry Slam champion, Broadway veteran, Goldie award winner, featured artist on *Russell Simmons Presents Def Poetry* on HBO and the inaugural recipient of the United States Artists Rockefeller Fellowship. In recent years he has toured through Tokyo, where he performed at the first International Spoken-Word Festival, and in Santiago de Cuba, where he joined the legendary Katherine Dunham as a part of the CubaNola Collective. He has entered the world of literary performance after crossing the sands of "traditional" theater, most notably on Broadway in the Tony Award–winning *The Tap Dance Kid* and *Stand-Up Tragedy*. His works, presented throughout the United States and Europe, include *Word Becomes Flesh, Scourge, De/Cipher* and *No Man's Land*. Bamuthi's latest project, *the break/s*, is an international travel diary across planet hip-hop based on *Can't Stop Won't Stop* by Jeff Chang, and premiered at the Humana Festival of New American Plays in spring 2008. He developed this piece while completing the Arts Institute Fellowship at the University of Wisconsin–Madison. His critical writing is currently featured in Jeff Chang's *Total Chaos* and his first nonfiction book, *Line Breaks: A Source Guide to Hip-Hop Theater*, was published by The University of Wisconsin Press in spring 2008. A resident of ODC Theater and Intersection for the Arts in San Francisco, Bamuthi's proudest work has been with Youth Speaks where he mentors 13–19-year-old writers and curates the Living Word Festival for Literary Arts.

thieves in the temple
the reclaiming of hip-hop

a spoken-word, hip-hop theater performance piece

by aya de león

author's statement

At heart, I am a novelist. I am fascinated by the long story, plot, the opportunity to develop a relationship with a protagonist, the journey. Hip-hop theater is the prose of hip-hop, the long story, the novel equivalent of the form. Hip-hop theater stories, by virtue of their length, are able to encompass complexity and contradiction, as well as to facilitate character transformations that are beyond the scope of rap music.

My venture into hip-hop theater, into spoken word in general, is the result of a long detour from a novel I've been working on since 1996. When I brought a short version of *Thieves in the Temple* to the NYC Hip-Hop Theater Festival in 2002, I was just excited to do my show in New York. The message of *Thieves*, however, struck a chord with audiences and the hip-hop theater community. It became evident to many that:

- Women belong at the center of hip-hop
- The rap industry is corrupt, and women's sexuality as portrayed in rap music is not authentic
- Women need to take up the call to be creators, not just consumers, of hip-hop.

Thieves is a battle cry for grassroots consumers and creators of hip-hop, particularly women, to snatch back our generation's culture. There was a strong demand to see the work developed into a full-length show, and the community of artists present expressed an eagerness for me to fill in the gaps in a show that was partly about hip-hop, and partly about my journey within it.

I fell in love with hip-hop in college, listening to a radio show in Boston called *The Thunderstorm*. It only came on during the summer on the radio station WILD which had a dawn-to-dusk license, and added a few extra hours of programming during the longer summer days. I was so hungry for the music in those days that I taped the programs. I still have the recordings.

I wrote rhymes as a teenager, but never performed them—where would I have done so? High school, early eighties, West Coast, not from the 'hood? I wrote rhymes as a young adult, knowing I ought to perform them, but what right did I have to be a rapper? Post-college, late eighties, East Coast, living in the 'hood but not *of* it. I settled. I settled for being a fan, a consumer, and hoped that one of the brothers would say what I thought needed to be said.

The testing ground for the MC is the cipher. Can you grab the mic and just flow? Are you so filled with rhyme that, given an opportunity, it will just spill out? I was terrified to rhyme off the top of my head in front of anyone. I was more terrified of having to grab the mic and forcefully insert myself into a crowd of young men. My female conditioning taught me to wait my turn; my college-bound conditioning taught me to prepare myself ahead of time. My mother wasn't black; she was Puerto Rican, and not from New York. I didn't even know how to play the dozens (the African American art of the insult or "trash talking"). Nothing in my experience had equipped me for the cipher, a highly competitive, braggadocious, male environment. Even as an outspoken teenage feminist, the cipher was too threatening to all my personal defenses. I stayed by the radio.

It is no surprise, therefore, that freestyling, the litmus test of the true MC, is the central crucible of the final version of *Thieves*. At the universal level, the protagonist must face her fear and her demons, in order to claim her rightful place in her community. On the personal level, the solo female must face a crowd of hostile men and believe in herself enough in order to reclaim hip-hop for herself and all women. It is her internalized sexism she must stare down. Although the specter of male violence, particularly sexual violence, looms in *Thieves*, it is an empty threat. A young woman, however, who has even grown up in a world filled with real violence against women becomes so terrified that the mere threat is sufficient to shut her up. The climax of this play is a moment of discernment for the protagonist. She discerns that the strong spoken threat of sexual violence will not be carried out, and she has no real obstacles but her own fears of male disapproval and failure.

The four elements of hip-hop—MCing, DJing, graffiti art and breaking (B-*boy*ing)—are all nontraditional fields for women. As in all nontraditional fields in a sexist society, women face many barriers, both internal and external, to participating. The field of theater, however, is a more traditional field for women. Hip-hop theater provides opportunities to insert women's stories into a tradition where we are notoriously missing, misguided and misrepresented. A large reason behind the demand for *Thieves* is that I was able to express truths *about* hip-hop in a theater piece that could not be fully expressed *in* hip-hop:

> Mos Def said hip-hop is going where we go
> I'm going somewhere positive . . .
> I will take hip-hop with me.
> —*Thieves* (2002 version)

My intention as a hip-hop artist is threefold: I seek to help us reclaim hope; I seek to unmask the authentic pain beneath hip-hop's braggadocio, and I seek to create healing. The hip-hop community in general, and the African American community in particular, is suffering from an epidemic of hopelessness. I want to create art that encourages people to find their own power and to use it. It is easy to get discouraged by the brutal-yet-glamorous images we see in media. But as Public Enemy said, "Don't believe the hype." My rap-industry characters are written to give audiences a glimpse into the nervous breakdown hiding just beneath the surface of the bling-bling mask. And then comes the healing. Beyond standing on a stage and preaching to the audience *about* healing, I create my work by healing myself, and then bringing those personal lessons back into my work. Healing begins in the body. As a black/Puerto Rican woman in her thirties, I have fought hard to love my plus-size body. Whether I'm talking gleefully about cellulite or using my own body to play Lady Triple X-Rated and shaking my scantily clad ampleness, the audience sees me fully connected to my body. You can't fake that onstage.

I co-facilitated a breakout session on gender and hip-hop at a Ford Foundation forum. One male participant suggested that contemporary sex-kitten MCs were celebrating their bodies. In an uncharacteristic moment of outrage, I broke out of my role and asked him, "How can you say she's celebrating her body? That's not her hair; those aren't her eyes; those aren't her breasts; that's not her stomach; those aren't her thighs. How can we say she's celebrating her body if she had to mutilate it before she could show it to us?"

I am committed to embodying the healing and modeling it as part of performance. "Cellulite" uses the authority of the stage to contradict all the self-hatred that we have been taught. "Fat women are wonderful—I thought you knew. All bodies are naturally beautiful. Where have *you* been?" Then the poem uses participatory learning techniques, by having the audience model the behavior of affirming the fat body:

AYA: It's jiggling baby
AUDIENCE: Go 'head baby

It doesn't matter whether everyone in the room agrees with me or not. It matters that for the space of the poem, I have turned the theater into a body-acceptance zone. The room is generally changed for the duration of the show.

"Do you feel me?" ("Have we communicated here?") is a question many hip-hoppers have asked. The question I want answered is, *"Has this changed you?"* If the answer is yes, then my art has been successful.

The following questions may arise for you in your reading of *Thieves*. Here are my initial responses:

Is this what I saw onstage/in the video?

The version of *Thieves* anthologized here is a hybrid, halfway between the forty-minute version of 2001–2002 and the final, full-length version of 2004.

The short version, originally directed by slam poet Roger Bonair-Agard in 2001, debuted at the Hip-Hop Nation Festival at San Francisco's Yerba Buena Center for the Arts, and a revised version was part of San Francisco's Afro-Solo Theater Festival that same year. The show went on to the NYC Hip-Hop Theater Festival, received a guest residency at New York Theatre Workshop, and toured with the hip-hop theater All Stars in 2002.

The final, full-length version, directed by Ellen Sebastian-Chang, was workshopped at the Latino Theater Initiative of the Mark Taper Forum in L.A. in 2003, and premiered at Yerba Buena in 2004, followed by a run at the Oakland Box Theater and two performances at D.C.'s Hip-Hop Theater Festival that same year. A video of the performance at the Oakland Box Theater was released in 2007.

Why a hybrid version?

Ellen Sebastian-Chang is a powerfully visual director who focuses a great deal on the audience's sensory experience in the theater. She designed the lighting for the show, and under her direction we developed the soundscape in collaboration with hip-hop Renaissance man Carlos Mena of Casa Mena records. That soundscape was the heartbeat of the final version.

Text is not sufficient to communicate the richness of the final story, which was told as much through sound, light and movement as through words. Therefore, we have decided to anthologize a hybrid version, which retains the text-driven story structure from the original version, and also includes sensory elements, characters and nuances from the final version. Copies of the complete script and information on the video of the final production can be obtained from www.ayadeleon.com.

Thanks to all the fabulous folks who helped realize this vision.
Peace.

production history

Thieves in the Temple: The Reclaiming of Hip-Hop (A Spoken-Word, Hip-Hop Theater Performance Piece) was performed by Aya de León with choreography by Amara Tabor-Smith.

Thieves received workshop and excerpt productions in 2001 at the Yerba Buena Center for the Arts—Hip-Hop Nation (San Francisco), the AfroSolo Theatre Arts Festival (San Francisco), Lincoln Center (New York); in 2002 at the UC Berkeley Bridge Conference—20th Anniversary of *This Bridge Called My Back*, the 3rd Annual NYC Hip-Hop Theater Festival at Performance Space 122, Arizona State University's Double Helix Theatre Company with the Hip-Hop Theater All Stars, Planet Hip-Hop (NJ), UC Riverside Hip-Hop Theater Festival (CA) and New York Theatre Workshop; in 2003 at the Mark Taper Forum (Los Angeles) and the National Black Theater Festival (Winston-Salem); in 2004 at the D.C. Hip-Hop Theater Festival; and in 2005 at the Bay Area Hip-Hop Theater Festival.

Thieves received its world premiere at Yerba Buena Center for the Arts in 2004 and a full production at the Oakland Box Theater in March 2004.

In spring 2007, *Thieves in the Temple: The Reclaiming of Hip-Hop—The Movie*, premiered at various Bay Area venues. The production that was filmed was a full-length version from the 2004 Oakland Box Theater performance.

prologue

dream sequence

The audience is seated as pre-show music plays (something like Lauryn Hill's "Doo Wop [That Thing]"). The house lights are fully up. Suddenly the music grinds to a halt and the lights go out, as if there has been a power outage.

    After several seconds of darkness and silence, the sound of a rising wind, accompanied by chimes, bells and a haunting, subtle melody, begin to swell.

    Lights come half up on Aya. She is difficult to see clearly. The dim lighting is meant to reflect a dream or a premonition.

AYA *(Singing)*:

> Way back in the '80s
> when hip-hop was live
> male MCs respected the ladies
> we wanted black people to thrive.
>
> Then somehow we lost the love
> somewhere along the way—
> it's the time for the reclaiming of hip-hop . . .

(Music starts with the sample: "Who you callin' a bitch?" [a lyric from Queen Latifah's "U.N.I.T.Y"] followed by a breathy, spare beatbox track, as Aya begins to rap:)

> When I was young, I thought I couldn't be an MC
> cuz I was a girl
> and so nobody encouraged me
> all those years I held back, what a shame
> hip-hop slipping down the drain
> I sat on sidelines and complained
> waiting in vain
> instead of using my brain
> I had nothing to lose

and everything to gain
but female conditioning conditioned me to wait
I checked my calendar, my watch
that shit was ten years late
cuz it was my voice
that I was longing to hear
I got a lot to say
come near and open your ears:

(On the edge of the stage, looking into the audience members' faces:)

I'm not a pimp
I'm not a ho
I'm not a slanger or a noc
I probably won't get any respect if I roll up on your block
but I respect myself
enough to tell the truth
not play some gangster role
just to impress the youth
it's uncouth and unethical
instead I practice breath control
work with young people and I try to make them skeptical
don't believe all that you see on TV
every gold-tooth MC ain't got a ghetto pedigree
stop fronting, start hunting for your true identity
cuz the hip-hop community gots mad diversity
bring authenticity that people can feel
I don't conceal I will reveal and this is how I keep it real
real hair real nails real tits real ass
real smart real age and I'm built to last . . . built to last . . .
    built to last!
Yeah!

(The music fades.
  Singing:)

'Cause it's the time for the reclaiming of hip-hop . . .

(Pre-show lights and music grind back on. The song fades out and the
house lights dim as they would for the beginning of a show.)

UNDERGROUND ANNOUNCER *(Voice-over)*: Are y'all ready for tonight's featured performer? *(The audience responds)* Y'all ain't ready. This sista

has been blowing up poetry spots all over the country. She was featured on HBO's *Def Poetry*, she was a member of Team San Francisco 2000 in the National Poetry Slam, and she even taught spoken word at Stanford University. Give it up for our featured poet Aya de León!

(Lights up on a single microphone on a stand, center stage.

Aya, an African American/Puerto Rican spoken-word performer, in her thirties, enters. Her hair is in cornrows and she is dressed in a black hoodie track suit with white stripes. She also wears classic Adidas shell-toe sneakers. Aya bounds excitedly to the mic.)

AYA *(Into mic)*: Wassup y'all? Make some noise if you love old-school hip-hop! *(The audience claps and cheers)* All right. This is for the old-school hip-hop heads. Now, this first piece that I wanna do has an old-school hip-hop sample in it. And since I don't work with a DJ, I need you all to be the sample, is that all right? *(Roar of agreement)* All right. Now this sample is taken from a conversation between a man and a woman:

> And the man says, "Let me hear your earrings jingle."
> And the woman says, "They're jingling, baby."
> And the man says?

(Some members of the audience respond: "Go 'head, baby.")

(Delighted) That's my people. We do have some true old-school heads up in here tonight! So that's your line. When I say, "They're jingling, baby," you say, "Go 'head, baby." Let's practice. They're jingling, baby—

AUDIENCE: Go 'head, baby!

AYA: They're jingling, baby—

AUDIENCE: Go 'head, baby!

AYA: You guys are great! Now remember to come in on cue. This poem is called . . . *(Poses with her hip thrust out)* "Cellulite."

cellulite monologue

AYA:

> Sell-you-light, that's right
> they try to sell you lite beer, lite cake, lite cookies
> Pepsi lite, 99% fat free

but who's trying to be fat free?
certainly not me.

(Aya drums on her thighs so that they shake.)

Let me see your thighs jiggle
they're jiggling, baby—

AUDIENCE: Go 'head, baby!

AYA:

This is a poem for the fat girls like me
don't tell me I'm not fat
that's like saying I'm not black
yes *technically* my skin is brown
but I say I'm black because I'm
down with the blackness
like I'm down with the fatness
because fat is health is life is vitality is fertility is womanly.

(Aya pokes her abdomen so that it shakes.)

Let me see your belly jiggle
it's jiggling, baby—

AUDIENCE: Go 'head, baby!

AYA:

It's the way women's bodies are built—we jiggle
even really thin women jiggle a little
unless they work out to have a body of steel
but who wants to look like that? Get real!
This poem is a thank you
to the big bodacious mujeres de Cuba
who taught me by example to
know no shame, show no shame
to the big-body women of the West Indies
who know how to wind-wind-wind at
Carnival time-time-time
let me see your hips jiggle.

(Shakes hips.)

They're jiggling, baby—

AUDIENCE: Go 'head, baby!

AYA:

> A sick society
> turns women's bodies into problems to be solved
> cuz anorexia ain't sexier
> and bulimia ain't dreamier
> therefore next time you count calories
> don't forget to count the thousands of years that women's suit-
>   ors have thought
> that cellulite
> was quite all right
> and were ready to embrace abundance.
>
> So—
> next time you're working out on your Nordic Track
> don't forget to savor the sensual feeling of sweat
> sliding down the rolls in your back
> and next time you're working out in step-aerobics class
> don't forget to enjoy the bounce of your ass.

(Shakes rear end.)

It's jiggling, baby—

AUDIENCE: Go 'head, baby!

AYA: Special thanks to LL Cool J for the sample. "Cellulite" has been an off-the-scale production.

old-school reminiscing

AYA *(Quietly)*: It's jiggling, baby . . . Go 'head, baby . . .

> *(Aya removes the microphone from the stand and begins to dance around the stage, singing a medley of old-school hip-hop songs from the late-1980s. The song samples in the medley reflect the wide range of hip-hop styles from that era. The style of her movement and vocal tone changes, as she transitions from party songs to militant songs to sexy songs to battle rhymes. Aya finishes the medley in a classic B-boy pose: arms wrapped across her chest, legs apart and firmly planted.)*

That's what I'm talking about—
Old-school hip-hop
That was my music
That was my music
That was my music
That was my music!

(Aya comes out of her reverie and addresses the audience:)

Now, I hate contemporary rap, but back in the day, I was such a hip-hop head. In the 1988 presidential election, I made my own T-shirt with a Sharpie marker. The front said "Chuck D for President." *(Turns her back to the audience)* And the back said "And Flavor Flav for Vice, boyeeeeeeeeeeeeee!"

And I loved hip-hop back in those days 'cause it was all about— Revolution! Hip-hop was all about—Power to the people! But then the nineties came along, and it was all about—The Benjamins? The money? What? Hip-hop, you betrayed me . . . sold our revolution out for a gold chain, three rocks of crack, a girlie magazine, and a record deal. And you know what? It was the record deal that really killed it.

(Aya storms angrily across the stage and exits.)

set style

DJ *(Voice-over with music)*: Next up on the mic, we have that fresh rap artist, just signed on the Mighty Ignant label, and I hear he's gonna freestyle for us. Yo, make some noise for Set Style!

(Aya enters from backstage, dressed as Set Style, a gangsta-rap-styled young African American man in his early twenties. He wears a brightly colored shirt, covered with comic strips, and a matching baseball hat turned to the side. He has on a platinum chain with a "$$" pendant. He often stutters and his movements are agitated and frantic. He's panicked after hearing the word "freestyle." He heads back and looks offstage.)

SET STYLE *(Speaking to his manager offstage)*: Yo-yo-yo, Leon! Yo, Leon! They want me to freestyle? You know I don't freestyle. That's why my name is Set Style. No doubt. My style is set. I-I-I-I have to? Nigga, what did I just say? . . . In my—in my contract? I-I-I didn't see nothing about freestyling in my contract . . . *(Takes a deep breath and sounds the next words out awkwardly)* Extemporaneous performance antics? . . . Naw—naw naw, Leon, I can't. No, look, fool, I got a freestyle disability. For real. No, no, no, I got Tourette's syndrome. Yeah. But as a gangsta rapper, that shit hits differently. Instead, in-in-instead of making me twitch and cuss—I-I-I cuss all the time, anyway—it makes me twitch and *(Looks over his shoulder out toward the audience to make sure they can't hear this part)* —makes me twitch and be sensitive. Yeah, and freestyling almost always brings on an attack. I've—I've—I've worked hard to overcome this disability. Cuz that type of shit will fuck up my image . . . What do you mean I-I-I-I gotta do it or they yank my contract? *(In a plaintive, adolescent voice)* Leon—nigga! Damn! *(Resigned)* How how— how long do I gotta fucking freestyle. Two minutes. Aight. I-I-I-I might not get an attack in two minutes. *(Nervously straightening his shirt)* I can't believe this bullshit.

DJ *(Voice-over without music)*: Ahem, I said the next artist coming to the mic *right now* is Set Style!

(Lights up as Set Style assumes a thuggish attitude and strides up to grab the microphone. He struts across the front of the stage. He has a completely hardened gangsta-rapper persona. He doesn't stutter or whine.)

SET STYLE: That's right! Thank you. I know you mufuckahs love me.

(Raps:)

> Set Style, in the place to be
> Set Style, you can't fuck with me
> Set Style . . .

(He turns to look back at Leon.)

Yo, Leon, start the clock!

(His movements have a frenetic quality: he moves back and forth across the front of the stage in a hostile crouch, a paranoid, agitated moving target. His rap style is typical in both form and content. Rapping:)

> He started the clock
> I'm grabbing my jock
> I'm slanging that rock
> And packing my glock.

Set Style, I got to get paid—

(Suddenly, he begins to stutter and twitch. The fit is brief, but it leaves his body slack. Unlike his gangsta-rapper persona, he is unexpectedly wide-eyed, and his body position is open and vulnerable. He stays rooted to one spot and doesn't speak into the microphone, which dangles from one hand.

In a high, boyish voice, as if his "inner child" is speaking:)

I lay awake in my bed and I feel afraid
My heart has a big owie and I need a Band-Aid.

Gunshots I been hearing since the age of three
And I would worry, yikes! Is somebody gonna shoot me?
(Pouting) Other kids used to pick on me
Mama act like she sick of me
Grandma be hella strict wit' me
I retreat into fantasy
A future where no one mess with me
Women want to have sex with me
Everyone is impressed with me
But nobody can get next to me—me—me—

(Another fit returns him to the gangsta-rapper persona. With each fit he twitches, stutters and staggers around the stage until the transformation is complete. Rapping:)

I mean, I like to shoot niggas and fuck hella bitches—

(Suddenly he's back to his inner child.)

Ooooooh! My grandmamma said she'd whup me if I ever said
    that word.

(He looks around the audience anxiously.)

Is my grandmamma here? I hope she ain't heard—heard—
    heard—

(Another fit returns him to the gangsta-rapper.)

I said, I like to shoot niggas and fuck hella bitches
I wear Versace britches

I'll fuck up your whole crew
Send you to the hospital to get hella stitches
I'm vicious—icious—icious—

(Another fit returns him to his inner child.)

But what would I wish for if I had three wishes?
Well, first I'd wish that my daddy didn't die
And second off, I'd wish that my mama wasn't always high
Cuz we was hella po'
In the ghetto
Not enuf time or love, and not enough dough
That typa situation makes you grow up fast
You act tough on the outside, but inside you made of glass
(Mournfully) And if I had a third wish I might wish I may
Would be to get out of the 'hood and make the pain go
    away—way—way—

(Transforming to the gangsta-rapper.)

Naw, I wish for the world's biggest gun and I'd say
All y'all mothafuckas can make my day—day—d-d-d-day—

(Transforming to the inner child.)

No, I'd wished I lived on Sesame Street
Spend the day with Cookie Monster and have cookies to eat
And Ernie and Big Bird would kick it with me
And my day would be brought to you by the letter E and the
    number three. Three three—thra—thra—three—

(Transforming for a final time to the gangsta-rapper.)

Cuz I'm Set Style, in the place to be
This freestyle, got a little to free
Cuz I'm hardcore, you can't fuck with me
And I'll beat down any punk-ass mothafuckas I see
(With offended dignity) And I regret
That my Tourette's
Revealed the truth in this freestyle set
But I'm in debt
And I need to get
This money . . .

(To Leon offstage) Is my fucking two minutes up yet?

(He is obviously relieved, but acts as if nothing has happened.)

Yeah! Set Style, what? What?
Yeah nigga! Y'all can't fuck with this. Set Style!

(He jams the mic back into the stand and struts back toward Leon.)

Now give me my fucking money. Shit.

(Set Style exits.)

lady triple x-rated

DJ *(Voice-over)*: Moving right along. Next up is one of the most controversial artists of our day. Also on the Mighty Ignant label, she's been called one of the ten most negative women in the U.S. by *Ms.* magazine, and her world tour was picketed by angry women in Europe and Japan. Please give it up y'all for Lady Triple X-Rated.

> *(Sound of prolonged loud applause. Aya steps onstage as Lady Triple X-Rated. She is an African American rap artist in her late twenties. She wears a black outfit that is little more than a one-piece swimsuit, with a neckline that shows lots of cleavage, and short-short bottoms. She wears a blond wig and very high-heeled black boots. She holds a "40," a forty-ounce bottle of malt liquor, in one hand. She poses with the liquor bottle near her crotch and sneers. Crossing downstage, she poses with the bottle resting on one of her buttocks, which she thrusts toward the audience. She growls. Finally, she struts across the stage and poses, open-mouthed, with the liquor bottle pressed between her breasts. The applause continues as she steps out of the pose and turns on her heel, swinging the 40 in a wide arc. She poses, arms outstretched, then leans forward from the waist, with a naive expression on her face.)*

LADY TRIPLE X-RATED *(In a high, mock-innocent voice)*: Bitches wanna picket me? *(Takes a generous swig of her 40 and assumes her own voice)* Shit, *(Angrily)* you don't like the concert bee-yotch, then stay ya ugly ass at home. *(Looking around the audience in disgust)* These intellectual hoes talking about some bullshit that don't have nothing to do with reality. *(Disdainful)* These feminists is really just a bunch of fat ugly bitches playa hatin', cuz they don't look half as good as me.

(She grins and runs her hands down across the side of her breast and hips, then takes another swig of her 40. Throughout her monologue she maintains the sense of posing, as if she expects a camera may record her at any time. She is playing more to the imagined photo op than the audience.)

And they seem to have a lot of fucking free time on they hands if they spend it worrying about me and wanna fucking *(Assumes nasal, prissy, Standard English voice)* "critique the image I'm portraying." *(Resumes her own voice, enraged)* Yeah, a bitch can read. *(An angry challenge to the audience)* Surprised?

(She takes a long swig of her 40 and poses like the Statue of Liberty, with the bottle in the air, her other hand on her heart.)

So this is for all y'all *(Sneering)* "image-critic bitches." When y'all are ready to pay my bills, I'll wear whatever the fuck you want me to wear, and I'll say whatever you bitches want me to say. But until you trying to get up off some cash, shut the fuck up and stay yo stank ass in the ivory tower, cuz you can't do shit for me. *(Seductive)* Niggas got the money, and I got something niggas want.

(Again, she caresses her body provocatively, and takes a long swig of her 40. Mocking:)

So before you write your next dissertation saying what bitches like me are about, *(Suddenly angry, confrontational)* let me tell you *exactly* what I'm all about.

(Slowly, she steps off the stage into the audience. She growls, part temptress, part predator. She moves slowly, confidently, surveying the audience members. She takes a final swig of the 40, emptying the bottle, then hands it to an audience member.)

(Seductively, to an audience member) Here, baby, will you take care of this for me? Thank you, baby.

(She turns and struts deliberately back onstage, swinging her rear end with every step. Rap music begins. The beat is hard, industrial and grating. She strides across the stage and grabs the microphone. Rapping:)

I be shaking my ass
do you think I'm hot?
I be shaking my ass
like what? Nigga what?

(Throughout the rap, she dances, poses and struts, gyrating her hips and chest. With each "Do you think I'm hot?" she makes eye contact with a different member of the audience, daring them to deny her sex appeal. With every "What? Nigga what?" she thrusts her pelvis at the audience. Although the verses chronicle a life of hard times, she speaks these words with a hardened, disdainful apathy.)

My mama started early and my daddy left quick

(Kneels.)

I was twelve years old when I sucked my first dick
it made me sick *(Coughs)*
but I learned fast

(Rising from her knees.)

I could climb out of the ghetto on my tits and ass.

And I be shaking my ass
do you think I'm hot?
I be shaking my ass
like what? Nigga what?

I don't always use a condom or birth control
I had my first abortion at thirteen years old
I'm not sure who's the daddy of my daughter Ashley

(Pantomimes stroking a young child's hair. She smiles.)

all I know is she wants to be just like me.

And I be shaking my ass
do you think I'm hot?
I be shaking my ass
like what? Nigga what?
I be shaking my ass
I get paid a lot.

I'm the gangsta bitch
the video ho

(Her movements become even more risqué.)

the freaky-deaky chick who's always ready to go
I'm the centerfold
I'm the porno star
and twenty years from now I might be wasted in the bar.

But I be shaking my ass
do you think I'm hot?
I be shaking my ass
like what? Nigga what?
I be shaking my ass
I get paid a lot
I be shaking my ass
'cause it's all I got.

(She turns her back to the audience.)

I be shaking my ass
shaking my ass.
Unh! Unh!

(She thrusts her rear end from side to side, punctuating the "Unh! Unh!")

Shaking my ass
shaking my ass.
Unh! Unh!

(She thrusts her rear end out toward the audience twice, punctuating the "Unh! Unh!")

Shaking my ass
shaking my ass.

(She slowly turns back around to face the audience.)

I be shaking, shaking, my ass.

I talk big shit
I know you want it
I be servicing the brothers
ain't discovered my clit
I make big money
bought a phat-ass home
I can have any nigga
I ain't neva alone.

And I be shaking my ass
do you think I'm hot?
I be shaking my ass
like what? Nigga what?
I be shaking my ass
I get paid a lot
I be shaking my ass
'cause it's all I got.

(She strides back across the stage and returns the microphone to the stand.)

Unh! Unh! Shaking my ass
Unh! Unh! Shaking my ass.

(The music fades. She stands center stage. Slowly, she raises her arms in a pose of glamorous triumph.)

I be shaking my ass!

(Grinning, open-mouthed) Y'all love me, right?

(Without the applause track from her entrance, the audience seems quiet and unresponsive. Her smile fades.)

(Slightly disconcerted) Y'all love me, right?

(She listens for the applause that is not there.)

(Regrouping) Oh, y'all gon' love this.

(She gets down on her knees and gyrates.)

(Grinning) You love me now? Unh! Unh! Unh! You love me now? Unh! Unh! Unh!

(Again, she is startled by the audience's lack of response) Aight.

(She gyrates some more, her smile is more tentative.)

You love me now? Unh! Unh! Unh! You love me now? Unh! Unh! Unh!
   (She looks out, assessing the quiet audience) Damn. Y'all gonna make a bitch work for it.

(She lies on her stomach, her face turned slightly to the audience, rear end thrust up into the air. This is her finale.)

(Her smile has become more of a grimace) You love me now? Unh! Unh! Unh! You love me now? Unh! Unh! Unh!

(The audience still does not respond.)

What the fuck?

(She sits up and looks out into the audience. Scanning the faces, she doesn't find the desire or approval she is seeking. She scans further and further back into the crowd, hoping to make a connection.)

(Bitterly) Y'all don't love me. Y'all don't really love me. You don't love me . . .

(She angrily repeats, "You don't love me . . ." Then the truth of it begins to dawn on her. She is indignant. How dare they not love her when she is standing onstage, half-dressed, shaking her ass for them?)

You don't love me . . . *(Coldly)* You don't know me . . .

(She repeats, "You don't know me . . ." but cannot maintain the coldness. All of her that is unknown to the public and all of the emotions associated with her life begin to surface in this moment. She has brought her one acknowledged gift—her sexual proficiency—and it has been rejected. She keeps repeating, "You don't know me . . ." Suddenly her costume seems insufficient to cover her. She draws her knees in and huddles into herself. Her face crumples. She begins to cry, just tearing up at first, but finally she begins to sob loudly, her face buried in her knees, so only her blond head is showing. She rocks back and forth, still moaning, "You don't know me . . ." through her sobs.

She cries herself out until there is only the ragged sound of her breathing, attempting to get enough air. Slowly, painfully, she lifts her head and wipes her eyes with the back of her hand. Her movements are stiff, her face unsmiling but composed, rigid. She smoothes her hair awkwardly back into place, a failing attempt to get herself together. She rises on unsteady legs, not quite looking at the audience. Once standing, she straightens her costume. She looks toward the exit, but cannot leave without a parting shot.)

(Her voice bitter but brittle) Fuck you. I don't need you. I can get any nigga I want. I can get ten niggas, you hear me? Ten! Fuck all y'all motherfuckers!

(Blackout. Lady Triple X-Rated exits. A sad, slow beat plays in the interlude. Aya reenters as herself in street clothes.)

AYA: Hip-hop, I thought you loved me! But you betrayed me. How could you do this to me? When the nineties came along, I would look at videos just horrified at what I was seeing and hearing. How could you treat women like that? How could you treat yourself like that? I was like, fuck hip-hop. I'm not even gonna listen anymore; I'm through with you! But underneath it all, I still loved you; I still wanted you to change. I still do love you. I still do want you to change *(Beat)* God, listen to me. Ugh. I don't like feeling like this. I sound like a woman in a dysfunctional relationship. I am. I'm in a dysfunctional relationship with hip-hop. I want hip-hop to change; it's not changing. OK. OK. What would I say to a woman in a dysfunctional relationship? *(Beat)* I'd say you have choices here. You have power. It doesn't have to be like this. *(Beat)* Yeah, I'm a fucking artist. Let me stop acting like I don't have a vision. Right. What's my vision? *(Beat)* Well, first of all, we need more women in the hip-hop leadership. Don't get me wrong; amidst all the madness there have been some good brothers holding it down in hip-hop. But it's time for there to be some more women in the leadership. Yeah. Kinda like affirmative action. Women could run hip-hop for a couple years. Just to get things back in balance. And then, after that we could work out some kind of shared power arrangement. Yeah, I can almost see it . . .

if women ran hip-hop

AYA:

> If women ran hip-hop
> the beats and rhymes would be just as dope
> but there would never be a bad vibe when you walked in the
>   place
> and the clubs would be beautiful and smell good
> and the music would never be too loud
> but there would be free earplugs available anyway
> and venues would have skylights and phat patios
> and shows would run all day, not just late at night

cuz if women ran hip-hop we would have nothing to be
    ashamed of
and there would be an African marketplace
with big shrines to Oya
Yoruba deity of the female warrior and entrepreneur
and women would sell and barter and prosper.

If women ran hip-hop
there would never be shootings
cuz there would be on-site conflict mediators
to help you work through all that negativity and hostility
and there would also be free condoms and dental dams
in pretty baskets throughout the place
as well as counselors to help you make the decision:
do I really want to have sex with him or her?
and there would be safe, reliable, low-cost twenty-four-hour
    transportation home
and every venue would have on-site quality child care
where kids could sleep while grown folks danced
and all shows would be all ages
'cause the economy of hip-hop wouldn't revolve around the
    sale of alcohol.

If women ran hip-hop
Same-gender-loving and transgender MCs
would be proportionally represented
and get mad love from everybody
and females would dress sexy if we wanted to celebrate our
    bodies
but it wouldn't be that important because
everyone would be paying attention to our minds, anyway.

If women ran hip-hop
men would be relieved because it's so draining
to keep up that front of toughness and power and control 24/7.

If women ran hip-hop
the only folks dancing in cages would be dogs and cats
from the local animal shelter
excited about getting adopted by pet lovers in the crowd.

If women ran hip-hop
there would be social workers available to refer gangsta rappers

to twenty-one-day detox programs where they could get clean
   and sober
from violence and misogyny.

But best of all, if women ran hip-hop
we would have the dopest female MCs ever
because all the young women afraid to bust
would unleash their brilliance on the world.

(Singing:)

'Cause it's the time for the reclaiming of hip-hop . . .

DJ *(Voice-over):* Next on rap open mic, we have a young lady who says this is her first time rapping onstage. *(Leering)* Give it up for the virgin, Aya de León.

(Aya walks into spotlight center stage.)

AYA: Virgin? I don't think so. I've rocked plenty of stages as a spoken-word artist. See I loved hip-hop back in the old school, till it started to disrespect women.

(Puts hood on and grabs mic.)

Somebody say: "I love hip-hop!"
AUDIENCE: I love hip-hop!
AYA: But it doesn't always love me. Dig it.

(Aya raps a cappella, fast and angry:)

Sisters need to be onstage
straight up ripping and freestyling
not just smiling and buck-wilding
while the brothers be profiling
yes, it's riling me to see
such sexism in hip-hop industry
you expect me to buy your CD
so I can go home and hear you insult me?
Not bloody likely.

Like take the case of Dr. Dre
he's a musical genius

but his penis gets in the way
so it's the instrumental version of his CD I love to play
I rock his dope-ass beats
but I don't even wanna know what he's got to say
and not all brothers fall in that category
some have mad integrity
and skill and creativity
and concern for the community
like Zion I and C of P
Bamuthi and Boots Riley
but when you see brothers in concert
they don't always have the OK
about who else is on the bill
in each city that they play
like ten years ago
when Public Enemy came to the Bay
gangsta rap had just started
and the opening act was NWA
I swear I'm still traumatized
by the shit they had to say
and something similar happened to me
just the other day
and it went this way.
dig it:

(Music begins.)

I'm at the Mos Def show
it's the opening act
I'm expecting conscious hip-hop but instead they came wack
dissing on my sisters like it's gangsta rap
no, I ain't having that crap
don't make me have to slap
this is a hip-hop show
not a porno flick
and you misogynistic rappers, you can suck *my* dick
you see me and my clique
you be shittin' a brick
cuz you know that we ain't having your sexist shit
I don't wanna hear about the skins you hit
and yes I'm fine, but this is mine and no you can't have it
you go grabbin' your dick
tryin' ta be legit

but your rhymes are so weak you're like a fucking half-wit
and another thing, you're smothering your creativity . . .

*(The music suddenly slows down, just like a record played on a too-slow
speed. Her voice drops in speed and pitch as well.)*

. . . droning,
"Bitch.ho.bitch.ho.freak.slut.dick.suck.pussy.pussy.pussy."
So monotonously . . .

(The music picks back up along with her voice.)

and it's gotten to me
it sounds rotten to me
you can fool these other fools but fool you can't fool me
you're scared to express your individuality
just moving with the crowd so sheepishly
you think that you're baaaaad but as sure as you're born
this is the moment that the sheep get shorn
the last MC I spanked became the sweater I was wearin'
your ass is lucky that I'm a vegetarian
you might get ganked
end up a lamb shank
or as the beat drops
I'll hack you into lamb chops
because by any means necessary you must be stopped
before you run to the cops
screaming:
(High-pitched voice) "Officer, please, there's a crazy bitch in there
    taking out MCs!"
(Disdainful) This could all be avoided if you'll just drop to your
    knees
and beg forgiveness for your weak misogynistic steeze.

(The music ends. Aya slams the microphone back into the stand. Applause.)

(As applause dies down) Thank you. *(To unseen audience members
passing by)* Thank you. Thanks so much for coming out tonight.
Oh, thank you, girl . . . Yeah, I'm glad you liked it . . . So many of
us been feeling that way for years . . . *(To unseen male character)* An
MC? Me? Oh no. I'm through with hip-hop. I'm strictly a spoken-
word artist . . . No, honey, I can't be an MC. I'm too old for all that.
I can't be an MC—I'm thirty-seven years old . . . Thank you! But

really, I am thirty-seven; I'll be thirty-eight later this year . . . Plus, I'm from Berkeley . . . No, I'm from *North* Berkeley . . . What would I look like trying to be all up in hip-hop . . . Thank you for the compliment, but . . . you're not gonna let up on this, are you? . . . OK, I'll think about it. No! I'll do you one better. I'll meditate on it. Right on.

(Aya sits on the floor, center stage, in meditation posture.)

Picture that. Me all up in hip-hop. Ha. I don't think so. But I'm a woman of my word. I said I'd meditate on it, so I will.

(She takes several deep breaths as the lights change slowly to a soft pinspot on her. She sings:)

Mos Def said hip-hop is going where we go
I'm going somewhere positive
I will take hip-hop with me.

(Aya raises her hand into the air and freezes.
The sound of a rising wind begins to swell, accompanied by chimes, bells and the same haunting subtle melody from the opening dream sequence.
Lights fade to black.)

THE END

Writer/performer/teacher/activist **Aya de León** lives in the Oakland Bay Area. She is the director of June Jordan's Poetry for the People and teaches poetry, spoken word and hip-hop at UC Berkeley. In 2004 she was named Best Discovery in Theater by the *San Francisco Chronicle*, and she received a Goldie Award in spoken word from the *San Francisco Bay Guardian*. In 2005 she was voted "Slamminest Poet" in the annual *East Bay Express* "Best of the Bay" listing.

Aya came very close to being elected in her fall 2004 show *Aya de León Is Running for President*. Her previous show, *Thieves in the Temple: The Reclaiming of Hip-Hop*, played to sold-out crowds in the Bay Area, and toured with Hip-Hop Theater All Stars.

Aya has been an artist in residence at Stanford University, and a guest artist in residence at New York Theatre Workshop. She is a Cave Canem poetry fellow, and a slam-poetry champion of West Coast Regional. In 2003 she presented her work at the Ford Foundation in New York and The Mark Taper Forum in L.A. She is the recipient of a Magic Award for community service from the Avant! Foundation and an artist fellowship in spoken word from the California Arts Council.

In 1996 Aya married herself in a ceremony on the beach with a Yoruban priest officiating and family and friends in attendance. Her article about the experience was featured in *Essence* magazine. For the past ten years Aya has been hosting annual alternative Valentine's Day celebrations in spoken word and music that focus on self-love, love of spirit, love of community, and, in recent years, love of peace and democracy. In 2004 she began a new Valentine's tradition, The Beloved Self, a mass self-marriage ceremony and workshop extravaganza. In 2004 and 2005 she married over sixty people to themselves.

She appeared on HBO's *Def Poetry Jam* in the fall of 2004, and has shared the stage with a wide range of performers, including hip-hop and spoken-word artists Mos Def, KRS-One, The Roots, Saul Williams, De La Soul, The Coup, Mystic, Sarah Jones and Danny Hoch; literary artists Sonia Sanchez, Tillie Olsen, Walter Mosley, Eve Ensler and Alice Walker; musicians Tracy Chapman, Bonnie Raitt, Alanis Morrissette, Susana Baca; and activists Danny Glover, Barbara Lee, Julia Butterfly Hill, Al Gore, Woody Harrelson, Howard Zinn, Daniel Ellsberg, Amy Goodman,

Rita Moreno and Ram Dass. She is a co-author of the 2004 book *How to Get Stupid White Men Out of Office*.

A graduate of Harvard, Aya studied theater with Whoopi Goldberg, the San Francisco Mime Troupe and the Jean Shelton School. She also studied fiction in the MFA program at Bennington College and will receive her MFA from Antioch University in Los Angeles. She is currently finishing her first novel, *The Voodoo Sorority*, and starting a second, as well as working on a collection of essays about self-love and a book project on spirituality and the hip-hop community. She has released three spoken-word CDs, and recently released the video of *Thieves in the Temple: The Reclaiming of Hip-Hop*.

For more information, visit www.ayadeleon.com

flow

by will power

author's statement

It was the fall of 1998. I remember I was walking up New York's 7th Avenue, having just come from shopping on 125th Street. It was afternoon, and I was headed uptown, back home. I was moving around a lot in those days, but at that time home was a decently spacious apartment on 147th Street in Harlem. There I was, sauntering up the street, taking in the amazingly diverse array of street activity that makes Harlem Harlem, when all of a sudden I started seeing these moving pictures in my mind. I could see these storytellers in Africa (I assume it was Africa). Their village was under siege by invaders, and these storytellers were attempting to tell everyone in their village all the community stories before the community ceased to exist. The pictures in my mind were rather graphic. People were getting hit over the head with blunt club-like objects, fires were being set off everywhere. And in the middle of the chaos were these storytellers telling stories. When they moved, they would say, "Zuu!" And when an invader was approaching, they'd beat on drums to create a rhythmic pattern of warning. It sounded kind of like "beede-kaka, beede-kaka."

Now, walking up 7th Avenue in Harlem in the fall of 1998, my brain was not used to seeing pictures such as these. I had been by that time writing and performing for almost two decades, and I was used to getting hit with ideas and melodies and words floating in my brain and whatnot. But I had never experienced something so vivid. What was this all about? Knowing a little about history, I assumed the vision was from Africa during the slave trade, though I wasn't sure. Maybe this was something ancestral, but I wasn't really sure. Walking up the street I started to chant "zuu-zuu-beede-kaka." When I got home I took out my tape recorder, pad and paper, and began to write. Since I didn't know much about Africa, I shifted the scene from an African village to an urban neighborhood, and I turned the storyteller griots into storytelling MCs. In a couple of hours, I had written a very short rhyme about rappers on the run. These rappers were trying to pass on the ancient knowledge in their raps to all those in the hood before social poisons: drugs, crime, environmental injustices, and general "playa'-hata'-ism" did everybody in. The piece ended up being about four minutes long or so. I finished it, stuck it in a drawer, and forgot about it for three years.

Over the course of those three years, however, more stories came to me, and I'd write them down. There was the one about a cockroach named Fred, and his attempt to unite all roaches worldwide for the sake of roach survival. I got an idea about a blind girl who refused to play the victim. As the stories came I'd write them down, record the rhythmic delivery pattern and whatever music I heard that would go well with them, then I'd stick them in a drawer. Eventually I realized that what I had here could make something—not a theater piece or anything that important—but at the very least a collection of stories. Maybe I could read a few at some poetry events or something. When one of my "major, really important, this-is-the-one-that's-going-to-get-me-on-Broadway!" theater projects died by the wayside, there was nothing for me to work on except these stories. By this time they were spilling out of my drawer, stories written on the backs of flyers, on napkins, in folders, stories that would finally get the attention they deserved.

I rang up Danny Hoch. I realized that I needed not only a director, but someone that could help me shape the piece. I needed someone who understood elements of theater and hip-hop, and who also had a keen dramaturgical eye. Danny said he was down, and we began to work. First thing he said to me was, "Nobody wants to hear some loose-leaf stories, man, we gotta find the story behind the story." I was like, "Say what? Naw naw, man, this ain't no real project, man, I just want to tell some stories." Danny say, "That ain't enough." From that point on I was getting my ass kicked. We decided to use the original spark, the images I had about these storytellers on the run, as the basis for the whole show. Danny encouraged me to bring to light who these storytellers were, and then vividly paint the world that they and their stories existed in. Just like that, it became a theater piece.

Danny Hoch is a mothafucka to work with, and I mean that as a compliment. Nothing gets past him. His level of dramaturgical meticulousness is astounding. A typical week would see me doing thirty, forty, sometimes fifty hours of serious writing and composing, after which Danny would read it over and be like, "Out of these twenty pages, we can keep these two paragraphs, the rest of this wack shit has got to go." Damn he was rough, but I loved every minute of it for real. We did things during the rehearsal process that probably hadn't been done before.

Discussing Rakim to illustrate a point concerning a dramatic turn of events. Putting Stella Adler and Lil' Kim in the same sentence to clarify a character's actions. Oftentimes, Danny's blunt, in-your-face-New-York energy was a bit much for my everything's-cool-dude-northern-California vibe. But our very different energies blended well, and the process of writing the piece was amazingly rewarding.

Now we needed a DJ. I had this idea to compose original beats and then press them onto vinyl. The advantage would be twofold: original composition that specifically fit the character and/or story that was being told, while adding the much-needed interpretation of a DJ to heighten the musical experience. When DJ Reborn came on board, it was like she was always supposed to be there. Her energy and talent was and is so profound, her mere presence elevated the piece. Not only did she add a cacophony of scratches, cuts, stops, rewinds, etc., but she was able to turn my often-static tracks into real live, breathing works of music. Also, when Danny, Reborn and myself got deep into the rehearsal process, there was a need for additional music (as sections were continuing to be added and deleted). Reborn would leave for a couple of hours and come back with the perfect piece of music to accompany whatever moment was in need.

Flow was created not only through the tireless work efforts of the collaborators, but also through the opportunities that were afforded me to really workshop and develop this piece. By the time we really got into *Flow*, I had been a touring artist on the road for more than six years. In that time, I had garnered a decent network of theaters, nightclubs and community centers that supported my work and were interested in my returning to develop something new. Thus *Flow* toured for more than a year as a work in progress. Throughout the 2002–2003 season, the show enjoyed workshops and performances in Indianapolis, Iowa, Holland, the United Kingdom (a five-week tour that really helped us sharpen the piece), New Orleans, San Francisco, St. Paul, and a two-week developmental session at New York Theatre Workshop. Such a long period to develop *Flow*, all the while editing the script, adding movement, and continuing to create new songs, proved invaluable to the development of the piece. In particular, I must thank my wife, Marla Teyolia, the National Performance Network and of course New York Theatre Workshop for providing the support necessary to make it all possible.

It has been a true blessing for me to be a part of this. Since the official opening in New York, we have gone all around the world with *Flow*—from Watts, California; to Bonn, Germany; to Sydney, Australia. It's been quite a ride, to say the least. I do hope you enjoy it, too.

For Marla, Omar-Sol and Sophia Renée

production history

Flow was commissioned by Legion Arts, Penumbra Theatre Company, Junebug Productions and the National Performance Network. It toured throughout the 2002–2003 Season as a work in progress. *Flow* was further developed by New York Theatre Workshop as part of the Jonathan Larson Lab.

Flow opened at Performance Space 122 in June 2003. It was produced and presented by New York Theatre Workshop and the NYC Hip-Hop Theater Festival. It was written and composed by Will Power and developed and directed by Danny Hoch. Musical direction was by DJ Reborn, with additional composition by Will Hammond, the set design was by David Ellis, costume design was by Gabriel Berry, lighting design was by Sarah Sidman and additional movement was by Robert Moses; the stage manager was Timothy Semon. The cast included Will Power and DJ Reborn.

Flow transferred to New York Theatre Workshop in September 2003. The artistic team remained the same with the following change: stage management was by Amy McCraney. The New York Theatre Workshop/Hip-Hop Theater Festival production of *Flow* went on to tour extensively. A select listing:

major festivals:
Bonn Festival (Bonn, Germany)
Bumbershoot Festival (Seattle)
The Sydney Festival (Sydney, Australia)
UCLA live (Los Angeles)
US/HBO Comedy Arts Festival (Aspen)
National Black Arts Festival (Atlanta)

regional theaters:
The Studio Theatre (Washington, D.C.)
The Children's Theatre Company (Minneapolis)
Mark Taper Forum P.L.A.Y. Program (Los Angeles)

other venues:
Battersea Arts Centre (London, England)
The Contact Theatre (Manchester, England)
Lantern Venster (Rotterdam, The Netherlands)
Vanderbilt University (Nashville)
The Flynn Center (Burlington)
Yerba Buena Center for The Arts (San Francisco)
Miami Light Project (Miami)

notes on characters

Will Power becomes each character in his play through physical, vocal and energy changes, with the assistance of sound and light cues. He does not use costumes or props to indicate character change.

notes on the dj

The DJ is an ongoing presence onstage throughout the play who "talks," using sound and music, to comment on the action or emphasize certain words and moments in the story. The DJ and the sounds she produces are integral to the play.

A DJ is onstage performing a scratch routine. She gets the audience to clap their hands as she solos over the groove. The lights fade out during a repeated scratch. The scratch stops and the lights come up. The Seventh Storyteller, Will Power, a tall, lean, light-skinned rapper/actor with cornrows stands center stage. He plays all the characters.

WILL POWER:
    Seven
    There were only seven, ya'll
    Only seven storytellers in the neighborhood
    I say
    There were only seven storytellers in the neighborhood, ya'll.

    Seven.

    (DJ brings in "Seven" theme music: an atmospheric, mid-tempo groove with a hard-edged back beat.)

    There were only seven, ya'll
    I say
    Only seven storytellers in the neighborhood, ya'll.

    Zuu
    To sing the songs
    And right the wrongs
    And carry on, on and on
    I say Zuu
    There were only seven though—I say Zuu
    Only seven storytellers in the neighborhood, yo
    Zuu
    Gotta keep it goin'
    Flowin'
    Even in the face of death

    Till the last breath.

(DJ cross-fades to a faster, up-tempo groove, scratching and cutting and pausing the beat to emphasize certain words and phrases, which she will do throughout the play.

Will Power moves outside to the block.)

Zuu
I was kickin' it out on the block
Outside the rec center, that was my favorite spot, check it
Zuu
And it was way too hot
So I stepped up the hill to get a juice from the health-food shop
I was sweaty and sticky and feelin' awight
I just got my cornrows done and they was lookin' tight
Zuu.

And I had some money from the show I did last night
I was like livin' day to day but I was doin' awight.

Yeah, I was a known rapper-slash-actor 'round the way
Makin' up rhymes, writing lines, for my plays, every day
Zuu
Never blew up
But I kept on rhymin', and I wondered, ya'll, when it's gonna be
    my time to shine 'n'.

I like bein' a rapper-slash-actor in the hood, yo
But I got no dough! And . . .

I'm getting old . . .

Zuu.

Started stressin' as I headed up to the shop
I been doin' my thang since back in the day when they was doin'
    the wop!

But it was too hot!
To start trippin' and whatnot
I'm thankful for the rhyme, 'cause you know it's all I got
Zuu.

And today it was a sunny day so it was all good
Will Power straight troopin' through the neighborhood.

Zuu.
I seen Deacon Jones rollin' in that church van,
Hey, there go Jonwon smokin' with her girlfriend
I said what up, ay now, what up and I kept movin'
Will Power through the neighborhood swervin'
Zuu.

Past the coffee shops, and taqueria spots, and brothers with the
        glocks, and empty building lots
And then I got to the health-food shop
Got a fresh-squeezed apple-ginger wolfed it down it hit the spot,
        I seen Preacha Man
He told me, "Go with God." I said, "Word."
Threw the empty juice cup away, and now I'm on my way.

Movin'!
Back outside, through the hood, ya'll
I remember over there, in the park playin' ball
And right here, near First Baptist on the cor-na
I got my first tongue-kiss from Shashaun-a.

It was a bright sunny day like usual
Every now and then it rained but nothin' we couldn't han-dle
Well like, every day or two you might, hear some shots
Somebody daddy, somebody daughter, done got popped
And yeah, we had cops, who'd harass you on the block
And families got moved out to make
Room for condos and whatnot
Zuu.

Anyway, it was a beautiful day, done got my juice fix
Now I'm headed on my way back down to the rec center, then
        damn!

The sky got gray
I mean ya couldn't even see the sun it was so cloudy.

And then the rain started to hit the ground
And you could hear this sound, kinda like:

*(DJ plays the sounds of a storm, bringing them in and out throughout
the following.)*

Beedee-ka
Beedee-ka-ka
Beedee-ka
Beedee-ka-ka-ka ka-ka
Zuu.

But I wasn't really trippin' though, yo
We had rain in the neighborhood befo', you know.

But this rain wasn't ordinary, I mean
The way it fell was quite extraordinary—NA' MEAN?

Zuu.

Like:

Beedee-ka
Beedee-ka-ka
Beedee-ka-ka-ka-ka-ka-ka-ka
Zuu.

Anyway I was getting wet and
It was about to be a frantic situation
Then I saw this man who was a walking contradiction
Zuu
Disheeky down wit' a pimp hat
Afro on the sides jheri curl in the back
Zuu
And he started comin' towards me
Was he a old black Panther or a Gangsta O.G.?
Zuu
I really didn't know
Then he said to me:

OL' CHEESY:
It's time for you to grow
Zuu.

WILL POWER:
I said, "Who the hell are you?"
He say:

OL' CHEESY:

> I'm Ol' Cheesy from the griot crew
> I am the last one so it's time to teach you
> The old stories, and then you gotta make 'em new!
> Zuu.

(DJ fades out the storm sounds.)

WILL POWER:

> My man was trippin'—was he smoked out?
> What the hell was this fool talkin' about?
> Zuu!
> But somethin' in me say follow, so I followed him
> Plus like I said befo', it was rainin'
> Zuu.

> We walked to his shack
> Behind Abdul's liquor sto' in the back
> Steppin' over bottles, and garbage and vials of crack
> And inside the shack, six storytellers sat.

(Will Power enters the shack.
>   *DJ underscores each introduction with dramatic cuts and scratches.)*

> The first one begun with cup in hand
> First a little change he'd demand
> Zuu
> Then, he take ya ta a fantasyland
> Where animals spoke, and had problems like man
> Zuu
> Like one time he told a story bout a rat and a pigeon, who found
>   love
> Though they families had different religions
> My man was crazy
> His imagination always amazed me.

> The second storyteller when she was young, she was po
> The folks said she'd be nothin' but a project ho
> But did she listen, no, as early as eight years old she say
> I'm the shit, ya'll, just don't know—OK!
> Zuu
> And then the sista grow
> She went to college, yo

Now she a storytellin' teacher, who she teach though?
Zuu—she teach young girls, in the projects, kid
So they could do like she did.

The third storyteller
Well he liked to preach
He was a preacher, tryin' a reach ya
Zuu—he was not ordained, OK but still remained a preacher at heart
When he see ya he'd start
Zuu
Wit' a word here, a quote there
From Ghandi or Leon the Pimp, he didn't care 'cause:

He say knowledge is knowledge, no matter where it came from
He be like, "Hey, let me give you some!"

New Groun'
Strong as the ground
The fourth storyteller was ground-bound
Zuu
He was a little bit a alll a ussss
But the roots they were indigenous
Zuu
His family was in the hood before the hood
When it was only sand dunes and woods
Zuu
He was the keeper of the stories of the newcomers
He knew 'em all, 'cause his family was the first-comers.

The fifth teller, that dude could move
He use body and voice to tell a story so smooth . . .

(Will Power does a dance break for four counts.)

Zuu.

The fifth teller, he say we ain't gonna win
Unless we respect the body outside and in.

(Another four-count dance break.)

The sixth storyteller was a freestyle queen
And she could rhyme on just about anything

Zuu
Like a jazz horn, breakin' apart, melodies.

But instead a notes, she freestyle-ed stories.

She was like, like supernatural times three!

Damn—she was a bad MC.

Six tellers in the place to be
They were sittin' in a circle, I turned to old Cheesy, say:

There's six tellers in the place to be
He say:

OL' CHEESY:
The seventh storyteller is you.

WILL POWER:
I said, *me*?

(The DJ comes in with "Seven" theme music.)

Zuu.

There were only seven, ya'll
Only seven storytellers in the neighborhood, ya'll.

To sing the songs
And right the wrongs
And carry on, on and on
Say Zuu
There were only seven though, I say
Only seven storytellers in the neighborhood, yo.

Gotta keep it goin',
Flowin'
Even in the face of death
Till the last breath . . .

("Seven" theme music stops. DJ leads Will Power into the next verse section with scratching.)

I said, "Look, Cheesy, you straight senile like Old Yella
I am a rapper and an actor, I ain't no storyteller."
Zuu
He said nothin', just pointed to a chair, as if to say:

OL' CHEESY:
    Sit there.

WILL POWER:
    Zuu
    So I sat
    Down
    With these other storytellers in the
    Round
    Zuu
    Most of them, I had seen around
    Jacoba, Preacher Man, my man New Groun'
    Zuu
    I seen Breeze on the stoop
    And I knew Besombee 'cause I once did some music for his group
    Zuu
    But what the hell was we doin' here?
    I wasn't the only one confused, that much was clear, 'cause I looked
        at Swea P
    You know, the freestyle queen
    She looked at me like, "I don't know a damn thang."

    Finally this Cheesy dude, he say:

    *(DJ brings in the storm sounds, cutting it in and out throughout the
    following.)*

OL' CHEESY:
    Zuu
    Once there was a time
    When griots, we did more than just rhyme
    Zuu
    We were tellin' the truth
    Passin' knowledge along,
    Helpin' the people flow on and on
    Zuu
    And things were so bright
    Nobody got snatched up 'n' sold off in the night,

Zuu

And in the day time if you wanted to get hiiiiigh

You just looked to the sky

Zuu

Then it started to rain, say, beedee-ka-ka

Then the storm came

And folk, ya'll, they started to change

They started to call each other names and 'cause each other pain

Zuu

The storm was strong, my crew was drained, one by one we were
    taken out or tamed

Except me, the last a the griot crew

So I'm passin' these stories to the seven of you

Now these tales ain't just for stayin' alive

Inside are the secrets on how to thrive

So when I'm gone, you seven go

Out in the neighborhood and pass it on! Because

Zuu

Have you noticed, outside out there

Can ya feel somethin' different in the air?

Zuu

A new storm comes

And people don't know, folks just so numb, ZUU, but it's comin'
    this way!

And it's gonna carry so many folks away, I say

Zuu

But not you seven

You seven will make it through

Zuu

Because the stories must pass through

Because the legacy will come through you, say

Zuu

The stories will get the people through

They always do

Zuu!

WILL POWER:

My man was definitely smoked out.

But we kinda understood what he was talkin' about

Zuu

Somethin' 'bout what he said came through

The seven of us knew just what we had to do—check it

Zuu.

We learned the stories from Ol' Cheesy no doubt
Stayed in the shack, never ever went out
And each storyteller got a special assignment
Depending on their flow, and the stars' alignment
Everybody got one in an envelope
But did I get one??
Nope.

When I said to Ol' Cheesy, "Where's mine?"
He just say:

OL' CHEESY:

In time.

WILL POWER:

What? That's wack! Shoot, I want an envelope.
Anyway dough, I went along
Practicing the stories and learning the songs.

But one day at the shack . . .
Ol' Cheesy was gone.

We came back the next day, Cheesy still gone.

We waited for him from the night till the early morn'.

Beedee-ka
Beedee-ka-ka-ka
Beedee-ka-ka-ka-ka
Zuu.

Did he fall down?
Did his heart attack?
Did he get shot?
Beedee-ka-ka
Maybe the po-po
Some say Five-O
Did they snatch him?

Beedee-ka-ka
Beedee-ka-ka-ka-ka-ka-ka -ka -ka
Zuu . . .

(DJ fades out the storm sounds.)

On the third night in Ol' Cheesy's shack, well, we all realized
   Cheesy wasn't comin' back.

So . . .

(DJ starts to cut to an old-school beat.)

Seven tellers, we carried on
We went out, we spread the tales in the storm.

Zuu
Like in the daytime, on a bench in the park
And in the nighttime, we told stories in the dark
Huddled in the cold, or shoutin' it in the hot
We promised Cheesy, "We-will-not!
We-won't-stop!
We-will-not!
We-won't-stop!"

(Will Power exits. DJ plays the record A Children's Story *by Slick Rick.
She begins to scratch over the groove and lead the audience in a call-and-
response. Will Power reenters.)*

Zuu
Breeeeeeezzzze!
Zuu
Breeze, his name was Breeze-zuu
His name Breeze—his name Breeze, his name
Zuu-Breeeeeeezzze!
Zuu
Breeze, his name Breeze Breeze—his name his name
His name-his name-his name
The first storyteller
(DJ underscores) Zuu
Breeze
His name was Breeze
That fool Breeze so funny bring ya down to ya knees, baby
(Underscore) Zuu
That's what the folks would say
And if his bottle was full

Breeze a go all day, he say:

(Will Power becomes Breeze, a forty-three-year-old disabled alcoholic. Breeze is the type to wear a tweed coat and alligator shoes polished to a high shine.)

BREEZE:

> *(Underscore)* Zuu
> There was a roach name Fred
> That's right, shit, a roach name Fred!
> Zuu
> Ya'll wanna hear about Fred the roach?
> I say, do you wanna hear about Fred the roach?
> Zuu
> Well I'ma tell ya 'bout 'im
> But first ya gotta
> Drop some change in the cup right here!
> Zuu shit, fifty cent is cool, ya know, huh
> A dolla' make me wanna holla!
> Yeah, I'll take a quarter
> Drop it in, drop it in, you cheap motha—
> Zuu
> Miss Washington, good afternoon
> Drop it in, ya'll, if ya wanna hear the story, soon
> Zuu
> This is the bestes most beautifulest story
> Talkin' about Fred the roach in all his glory
> Zuu
> Drop-drop it in, drop-drop-drop it in, drop it in
> And we can begin
> Zuu
> O-K
> I'm 'bout to bring Fred the roach
> Hold up
> Before I bring Fred the roach
> My cup
> Still a little light, and if the cup too light
> The story won't come right.
>
> Wha—?
> Man I know you paid
> I ain't talkin' 'bout you

I'm talkin' 'bout you, and you, and you
Zuu
Come on
Drop it in, drop-drop it in, drop it in
And we can begin
Zuu
Wanna hear that jingle jingle
Or that crinkle crinkle
When the bills fold
Zuu
Ay, yo, Lil' Petey
Take this cup, go to the sto' and get my usual
Zuu
Tell 'im it's for me
Ay, yo, Abdul—
Yeah it's for me!
Zuu
What?
Man look I tell these kids
Don't do like I do, 'n' drink like I did
Zuu
Still do
Well you sell the shit!
Shoot
Zuu
OK, you all dropped it in, drop-dropped it in, dropped it in
Now we can begin
Zuu.

There was a roach name Fred
And I don't know why his name was Fred but
Zuu.

(DJ brings in the "Roach" beat: a slowed-down, old-school funk groove that she cuts in and out throughout the story.)

This roach was smarter than other roaches
Because Fred, well, he used his head
Zuu
Or what little head he had
He got that blessed skill from his dad
Zuu.

flow

And from his moms, he learned the fact
That you should freeze in the light and walk in the black
Zuu—the other roaches thought he was hella wack
But see the other roaches, well, they had no tact
Zuu
They would scurry out for a piece of pie
They didn't understand or comprehend why
Zuu
Fred would wait.

Then that roach would investigate, ya'll, he be like this here:

And to himself debate
'Cause he knew that he didn't wanna share the same fate
Splatter!
Like his next of kin
Squash!!
Like Fred's best friend
Check in, no, check out, like his girlfriend—
Fred said, we gotta bring this genocide to an end
Zuu
He called a meeting then
Roaches from everywhere came
How they knew? Abdul, I don't know!

But they came from everywhere to Fred's house, yo
Zuu
And some came from the East O,
Some came all the way from the South Side of Chicago
Zuu.

Now when they got together Fred said look,

"We gon' be around forever so look
Use tact
You gotta freeze in the light and walk in the black
Zuu
And these chemicals worse than crack, don't eat it my fellow
    roaches
Take it back to the lab so we can adapt!"

"Naw, naw look, I don't care how good the shit taste
It's gonna leave ya on ya back
And this

Zuu
Roach-on-roach crime is wack
The toilet gang against the kitchen-counter crew—that's wack!
Look, we all roaches . . ."

"We all roaches, baby!
We gotta start usin' some different approaches!"
Zuu
So the roaches organized, all night
And by sunrise they did unite
From now on, they would work with each other
Had roach patrols, even had roach tolls
And they took the money to fund roaches going undercover!
Zuu—Now look sistas and brothas
Them roaches be watching you, studying you
Sneakin' up under yo' covers!
That's why I don't even kill roaches in my house no mo'!
'Cause you can win the battle, but ya can't win the war, now Zuu.

And that's the end a that one
Wha?
Yeah, that's the end of that one
Zuu
What you mean it ain't worth what you paid?
You only paid a quarter, you cheap motha—
I mean cheap brotha
Zuu
No Miss Washington, I was not gonna curse
Ay, Lil' Petey here to quench my thirst.

(He takes a drink.)

Zuu
Ya'll wanna hear another good story, say?
Do ya wanna hear another hella/hecka good story?
Zuu
Well then drop it in, drop-drop it, drop it in.
And we can begin again.

(DJ scratches intensely, transitioning Will Power to the next character.)

WILL POWER:
Jacoba-Jacoba-Jacoba-coba—Jacoba
Jacoba-Jacoba-Jacoba-coba-Jacoba-huuuhum

flow

Oba-Jacoba-huuh
Oba-Jacoba-huuh
Jacoba-Jacoba-Jacoba-coba-Jacoba-huuuhum
The second storyteller
Jacoba was tall and lean
And she was regal like
Nothin' you ever seen, she was a
Teacher by day storyteller all day after school, she would tutor
    kids, try ta lead 'em
In the right di-rec-tion
Especially dem bad-ass girls—she had been one—some—
Times
When she was tutoring one, or two, girls
She tell 'em just what to do
She do it kinda like this!

(DJ brings in "Jacoba" music: a light, snappy pulse of percussion instruments. Will Power becomes Jacoba, a teacher/after-school tutor in her mid-thirties.)

JACOBA:
    Zuu ta kaa!
    Ya gotta put ya best foot down
    Zuu ta kaa!
    And that's the only way you'll come around
    Zuu to kaa
    To findin' yourself, and when you're found
    Zuu ta kaa
    You'll never be a ho, slut, a clown
    Zuu-zuu
    Because you'll know just what you be
    Zuu ta kaa
    And you were never those things you see
    Zuu to kaa
    No matter what the folks say to you.
    Zuu ta kaa
    You know what is true
    Zuu ta what?
    No, why should you care though?
    Zuu ta what? No, no why should you care though?
    Zuu ta who?
    Now why you care what La Keisha say
    Zuu ta kaa

Who is she to say it anyway?
Zuu we had girls like La Keisha back in my day
Zuu—I hate them kinda . . .
Anyway
Zuu ta kaa
Let's hear the stories ya'll got today
Zuu ta kaa
Let's hear the stories ya'll got for me
Zuu-zuu
OK, Sheniqua, you first
Can ya curse? Well, if the character would curse
Say zuu zuu
But otherwise don't do it
Zuu ta kaa
OK, come on, let's do it
Zuu ta kaa, beedee-ka-ka uh-huh
Zuu ta ka, beedee-ka-ka OK
Zuu zuu, "they were" not "they was"
Zuu ta kaa, yeah, I say it but that's because
Zuu ta ka I know both dialects
Zuu ta ka you learn 'em both and you can flip
Zuu ta ka, from the office to the projects
You'll get respect, they won't be able to put you in check
Zuu ta ka
But that's a good story nonetheless
Zuu zuu
OK, Belinda girl, you next
Zuu ta ka, beedee-ka-ka, uh-huh
Zuu ta ka, beedee-ka-ka, OK
Ka, beedee-ka-ka, uh-huh
Zuu ta ka, beedee-ka-ka, OK
Zuu zuu
Not bad Belinda, not bad
But make sure, at the end, we know that it's your dad
Zuu ta what?
But I told one last week
Zuu ta— Now look, don't give me attitude
Zuu ta weeell, you want a story huh?
Zuu to weeell, ya gotta have a story? Uh-uh
Well OK
Are ya ready?
Zuu ta ka
This is a story bout a girl named Betty.

(DJ brings in "Betty" music: a light, snappy percussive pulse with a thundering kick drum underneath. She mixes in all the story's voice-overs.)

And she was about ya'll age, maybe a little younger
Once upon a time
In the neighborhood
There was a blind girl, her name was Betty
When Betty was nine, well
She said she ready
To go outside without her sista Netty
Her father said:

FATHER *(Voice-over)*:
    Hell naw!

JACOBA:
    So late that night, after they ate spaghetti
    She tiptoed over the bed a sista Netty
    She climbed out the window she was happy as confetti.

NEIGHBOR 1 *(Voice-over)*:
    Look at that blind girl on the seesaw.

NEIGHBOR 2 *(Voice-over)*:
    Mmmm-mh . . .

JACOBA:
    And she was just laughin', and goin' up and down
    Then she climbed up the slide, slid back down
    Then she hung from the rings, hit the ground
    She got in trouble with her father but her freedom she had found
    OK the years passed by, Betty is grown
    With a husband and a cat yeah a real nice home
    But even with her man
    She told him again and again
    That she could make it on her own, yo
    Didn't need no shadow
    Like one time Betty, she wanted to go out
    Walkin' by herself in the dark no doubt
    Her man said it was wack, "Betty ya can't do that."
    Betty said, "We've been through this, I can do this."
    She left the house 'bout quarter to nine
    Then these crackheads Marv and White Boy Double Shine
    They said:

MARV *(Voice-over)*:
> Man, that bitch blind, man, she all by herself.

WHITE BOY DOUBLE SHINE *(Voice-over)*:
> Let's jack that lady, man, before she can call for help.

MARV *(Voice-over)*:
> Lets do it! I can't believe it, man, a blind lady walkin' 'lone in
>> the neighborhood.

WHITE BOY DOUBLE SHINE *(Voice-over)*:
> SHHH! Be quiet man, those blind people hear hella good.

JACOBA:
> Now Betty was scared
> No doubt, that was a fact
> But she said to herself
> She said I gotta fight back
> Now the crackheads was on her
> Had a knife to her back
> She turned around with her stick
> Crack-crack.

MARV *(Voice-over)*:
> Uuuw, uuuuw, she got me in the family jewels.

JACOBA:
> Then she took out a whistle and she blewwwwwh
> The two dirty, dirty crackheads fleeewww!

WHITE BOY DOUBLE SHINE *(Voice-over)*:
> She like daredevil, man!

MARV *(Voice-over)*:
> Let's go!

JACOBA:
> OK now Betty is older, and she is just the same
> The folk in the neighborhood still think she's kinda strange
> 'Cause she run for the bus, stretch yoga in the park
> And the folk, man, they trip, when she reads, in the dark, outside—
>> all by herself
> But Betty say if she need help she'll call for help

'Cause she ain't no victim, come test me, come get some
And don't step with no sympathy just because she can't see
Blind Betty.

(The "Betty" music changes back to the "Jacoba" music.)

Zuu ta kaa
And that's the story of Blind Betty
Zuu zuu
Uh-huh the story of Blind Betty
Zuu ta kaa
Well tell another one? Nooo
Zuu ta kaa
I think it's time for ya'll to go
Zuu ta kaa
Sheniqua, say hi to ya moms
Zuu ta kaa
Belinda say hi to your Uncle Dom
Zuu ta kaa
Tell 'em I said hello
Zuu ta ka
Uh-uh it's time for ya'll to go
Zuu zuu
Because I have a date
Zuu-ta kaa
Uh what you mean make him wait?
Zuu ta kaa
Nuh-uh it's time for ya'll to go
Zuu ta kaa
When, then, come back tomorrow
Zuu zuu
I might tell one or two
Zuu ta kaa
And hear another from each of you
Zuu ta kaa
All right, see you two.

Zuu ta kaa-beedee-beedee-beedee
Zuu ta kaa, Beedee-ka-ka uh-huh
Zuu ta kaa, Beedee-ka-ka OK
Zuu ta kaa, Beedee-ka-ka uh-huh
Zuu ta kaa, Beedee-ka-ka
Zuu.

WILL POWER:

> Preacha preach on
> Preacha preach on
> Preacha preach
> Preacha preach
> Preacha preach
> Preacha preach
> Preacha preach on
> The third storytella!
>
> Zuu
> Preach
> Go head 'n' preach
> The folk in the neighborhood, he was always tryin' aaa reach
> Zuu
> Drop a line here
> Drop some knowledge there
> If ya wasn't listenin' you know he really didn't care 'cause
> Zuu
> He say, eventually
> His words would get to ya
> They would seep deep down through ya
> Zuu
> Preacher man
> He could be found at the hip-hop spots
> And where he worked at the health-food shop *(Underscore)*
> He would talk to ya, stop, no he would not
> Strange lookin' fellow, church robe and dreadlocks
> Zuu
> He was a storytellin' modern-day bohemian
> Any check-out aisle ya went
> That's where you see 'em in.

(Will Power becomes Preacha Man, a tall, dreadlocked brother. Imagine he's wearing a church robe and a Whole Foods apron.)

PREACHA MAN:

> OK now, sista, all right
> Remember always go with God, sista, all right
> Zuu
> We together we workin' together, yeah

You ringin' 'em up, I'm baggin' 'em up, yeah

Zuu

Hey brotha, all right

Say brotha, this all right but uh

Naw, naw, it's fine this is fine, but we got Imagine over there for
    a $1.69, they got—

Zuu—

Soy milk, they got

Rice milk

On a personal level I like 'em better than Silk, you know

Zuu yeah I'll hold your place right here, brotha

Ay can he make an exchange? Go 'head an' make an exchange,
    go 'head

Zuu

Hey, ma'am, how you doin' today?

Oh I'm fine. You know Iyanla say, she say, Zuu

The truth is, God believes in Me, Amen

'N' if God believes in me, then I got to be happy. Amen. You know.

Zuu

Yeah, Iyanla Vanzant

Well, she's different than Oprah

You know what I'm sayin'

Zuu

Naw, I like Oprah too, sista

Much respect to Oprah, Oxygen 'n' all that

Zuu

Uh-huh yeah!

Zuu

Yeah! I don't care about that

Hey, Rakim, say it ain't where ya from, it's where ya at—amen?

Zuu

All right, OK

He say I gotta let you be on your way

Zuu

Uh, walk with God, ma'am.

You know, FASHEEZY, walk with God!

Zuu

How I'm makin' your job hard?

Come on, brotha

Now you are my brotha

Zuu

Hey, brotha, made the exchange, OK, let me bag it for ya, you be
    on your way—all right

Zuu

Hello, ma'am, see ya drink lotsa water. That's good

Oh, it's not for you? Oh, it's for your daughter. Who dat?

Zuu

Nubian? I know Nubian, yeah

I knew her when she was Nancy You Know?

Zuu

Well my name is Dan, but everybody 'round here call me Preacha
    Man

Zuu.

No, no, ma'am, I don't

But, I'd like to have a church

With the

Beedee-ka, beedee-ka-ka—Lord knows we need a church, amen?

Zuu

Well I mean you no offense, but uh

First Baptist not my kind of church

Zuu

Well, the kinda church I could see

Is a place where the young folk, where we could just be.

(The DJ brings up "Sunday" music: a gospel-tinged, hip-hop groove.)

Yeah, I mean it could be on Sunday could be

And it doesn't even need to be in a church

It could be in the park, you know

Hey 'cause the Lord say, if two or more people come together in
    my name . . . AMEN!

(Sunday music gets louder. Preacha Man walks to the Sunday get-together
jam in the park. He gets the audience involved clapping to the music.)

Come on everybody, that's right, uh-huh there it is, yeah get
    into it.

AND STOP!

There was a party out there on the lawn

The people started to assemble in the morn'

And by the noon time

Folks started to unwind

And talk to each other, and heal from each other, I tell ya

Sista Nancy Lopez brought tamales
She came strollin' hand in hand with Jabali
'Twas an incredible spread
Something for you and you
Chicken fried side by side with baked to-fu
And roasted corn wrapped in the foil
And don't forget, here come the brotha with the oils.

OIL MAN:

I got frankincense, frank 'n' murr, jasmine and amber
A beautiful queen
Now, brotha, what you gonna get for her?

PREACHA MAN:

And "poof," just like that, he was gone
Goin' to another get-together goin' on
In these dangerous times it gets hard
But thank God
We gotta day like Sunday.

("Sunday" music goes out. DJ solos while Preacha Man works the crowd: "Everybody say 'Sunday . . .' etc.")

Well they prayed, then they partied and they sang
Even the leaves and the trees started to swang
And folks start to scream and shout—yeah
They got a chance to let it all out—yeah
Then it broke into groups of conversation
While they conversin' they releasin' frustrations
Somebody set the soundtrack, it was the Roots band
Cindy started to talk to Joe about her man
She always went to Joe 'cause he was her best friend
And since he had a lady he could understand
And on top of the table sat Ricky and Sia, they were
Talkin' 'bout an upcoming rally for Mumia
And anybody seen Shariff and Penny Wong?
Somewhere in the park they was getting it on
And Jonwan was kickin' back smokin' a fatty yeah an' Jonwan
She brought her girlfriend Patty yeah an' Jonwan
Was talkin' about the open mic last night
Where some fool said being Asian's like being white
So Jonwan stepped up to the mic like:

JONWAN:

> That's wack!
>
> How is people of color only Latino and black?

PREACHA MAN:

> Huh, then Jonwan, passed the blunt to her, ladylike . . .

JONWAN:

> Patty, these open mics are kinda sha-dy.

PREACHA MAN:

> And Jamilah strolled in late with Gra-dy
>
> You know why? They got a new born ba-by
>
> And José
>
> Was was playin' bones, at the same time, José
>
> Was talkin' to his girl on the phone, smooth like.

JOSÉ:

> Uh-huh
>
> Yeah
>
> You study long you study wrong
>
> Uh-huh, yeah yeah yeah
>
> Ay bro' come on
>
> What? No
>
> What? No
>
> Domino . . . suckas!

(The "Sunday" music comes up. The Preacha Man and the DJ engage the audience in a call-and-response:)

PREACHA MAN:

> Sunday.

AUDIENCE:

> Sunday.

PREACHA MAN:

> Sunday-day, Sunday.

AUDIENCE:

> Sunday-day, Sunday.

PREACHA MAN:

> Domingo—that's Spanish, ya'll.

flow

AUDIENCE:

    Domingo.

PREACHA MAN:

    Sunday.

AUDIENCE:

    Sunday.

PREACHA MAN:

    Well the day rolled on, it was dusk
    A cipher started, some MCs start to bust
    And all the couples they was cuddlin' close
    That's how we do it, ya'll, from coast to coast-t-ah
    And they knew the day was comin' to an end
    And the storytellers took out their pens
    And recorded the event, that seemed to be heaven sent
    For future stages and countless future pages
    Then the place was so quiet
    'Cause they calmed that innerrrr riot
    See when I
    Don' get to see ya it's hard
    But thank God
    Because we got next Sunday.

    (DJ fades out the music. Preacha Man returns to Whole Foods.)

PREACHA MAN:

    Yeah
    All right, uh good, good, say hi to Nan—NUBIAN for me
    Nice talkin' to you too, sista
    I was gonna let her through
    Just gotta drop a little somethin' on her ya know
    Uh, go with God, ma'am! Go with God
    Zuu.

    (DJ scratches.)

WILL POWER:

    Zuu.

    Whatever ya'll puttin' down
    Can't be strong enough to break the ground, say

Baby New Groun', Baby New Groun', Baby New Groun'
Zuu.
Whatever ya'll puttin' down
Can't be strong enough to break the ground.

Baby New Groun', Baby New Groun', Baby New Groun'
The fourth storytella!
Zuu
He could point to a liquor sto'
And tell ya what had been there two hundred years befo', say
Zuu
Baby New Groun', Baby New Groun', Baby New Groun' . . . because
Zuu
He knew the neighborhood his-tory
He knew 'bout every single story 'bout every etha-nica-tay
Whether they came by train recently
Or arrived on a ship way back in the day—hey
Zuu
Not only that he could talk to plants
He could run with raccoons
He would work with the ants
Side by side
So he knew their stories, too
He even could put a story in the wind as it blew-by
And catch one later, out the sky-high
He was the only one who knew
Exactly why
Ol' Cheesy come for us when he did
New Groun', been tellin' these stories since he was a kid
New Groun'
His family go way, they go way back!
They said to New Groun', tell the people the facts!
Zuu
So he told stories faithfully
With the power of the earth he casted stories out to the sea
Zuu
And for the people something we can digest
New Groun', he owned and op-erated a tour-guide business
Zuu
And everybody wanted to tour with New Groun'
'Cause in the travel books at Barnes & Nobles this shit cannot be
    found . . .
New Groun'!

(Will Power becomes New Groun', an indigenous man with strong eyes, a firm stance, headphones around his neck, etc.)

NEW GROUN':

In answer to your question, no
My family was here a long time ago
No, no, no, no
We were never immigrants
Well I guess the first immigrants, you know
Suuuu
Now any other questions about this street?
Hard to believe it was a trail before it was, 2nd Street
Suuuu
Quite a makeover I know, but still the same
Still used for trade, it now just has a different name
Suuu no, no, no, no
No, it's not a miracle that we survived
Well despite what your teacher says we're still alive
But there were times when we were killed if found
Sometimes we had to go underground, literally.

Or transform . . .
Or blend in . . .

Suuu
But let me make this clear
Despite what your teacher says, we are still here
Suuu
Now let me show you this is the rec center
It is the place to be in our neighborhood for art and for culture
There's always something going on
A dance class, a play
And on this site way back in the day, it was the same way.

Right here
The people
They came to tell stories.

Suuu
And later, every group, no matter the culture or race
They gathered in this same place.

My family's seen it all
And we always help the new

Because we do not own this land, you know, this land is for the
    new, too
Zuu
Sad though
Almost every time we help the new . . .

Suuu . . .

(DJ plays three seconds of tonal, atmospheric sounds.)

Baba-dee-da-dabeydoo-dee-da
Baba-dee-da-dabeydoo-dee-da
Baba-dee-da-dabeydoo-dee-da.

I had my headphones
Jay-Z was playing
You know Jay-Z?
Yeah the guy, big pimpin' Jigga? Yeah, right
So, I had my headphones, Jay-Z was playing
I was walkin' down the street listening to what he's saying
Something about, about "gettin' paid"
It don't mean nothin' 'cause they just brought down the World
    Trade
Then I came across a man
He was in a zone
His
Hands were all bloody he was punching a stone
He say he wanna do something wanna do it soon
I said ya probably oughtta get some healin' for those wounds
He say
Let's kill all the Arabs, man
He say
All the motherfuckin' Arabs, man
He say
Or at least get 'em out this land
He say
Every American must take a stand
I say
I don't recall making your folks pay
When the building got blown by that man McVeigh
Plus your people aren't native in this here land, bro
If somebody kicked you out, now where would you go?

Baba-dee-da-dabeydoo-dee-da
Baba-dee-da-dabeydoo-dee-da
Baba-dee-da-dabeydoo-dee-da.

(DJ plays tonal sounds again.)

I was visiting the South going from state to state
And since I was in the South "Mrs. Jackson" was the tape
You know "Mrs. Jackson"? "Mrs. Jackson"
The song by Outkast
"Sorry Mrs. Jackson, whooo, I am for real."
"Mrs. Jackson"
Yeah, that's the bomb, that's the bomb-digitty
So anyway.

From Alabama and Kentucky I had seen
I thought I would go next down to New Orleans
So I hopped on a bus, and I started to roll
Through towns where the people used to be bought and sold
Those folks worked in the heat and even the cold
Then fought Jim Crow, let the story be told, so
On the Greyhound it's so cold, hey what up? What up?
'Cause the bus driver had the air-condition way up
Then a woman with a child in her arms and one on her knee
In broken English she says to the driver, "Too cold, please."
 And the driver just ignored her, kind of shrugs it off
He said:

BUS DRIVER:
 Shoot I like the cold, it keep my jheri curl soft.

NEW GROUN':
 Now the child that's on the woman's knee is starting to cough
 And sneeze . . .
 So the woman asked the driver again, "Too cold, sir, help!"
 And the driver stopped the bus, he said:

BUS DRIVER:
 OK that's it!
 I'm tired of you Mexicans always askin' for shit
 Now this is my bussss! Tired a you people!

NEW GROUN':

I say, but sir, didn't your ancestors die so that you could be equal?
He say:

BUS DRIVER:

Why don't half a ya'll mind ya business? Hmmph.

NEW GROUN':

I say . . .

Nothing.

Baba-dee-da-dabeydoo-dee-da
Baba-dee-da-dabeydoo-dee-da
Baba-dee-da-dabeydoo-dee-da.

(DJ plays tonal sounds for several counts.)

I was sittin' in the garden bumpin' Foxy Brown
I know you know Foxy Brown? "Ill na na"? "Still na na"?
I mean, you know
But, anyway
I was sittin' in the garden bumpin' Foxy Brown
When Grandmother asked me to go to the market downtown
We use to only eat just what the garden could grow
But now the garden is polluted and the food won't grow
Then I see a little girl outside the garden gate
And she's waiting for a bus and sipping a chocolate shake
That she probably got from the new Mickey D's across the street
And she's also got a burger that she's starting to eat
And she finishes her meal, takes the container and the cup
And she throws it in the garden, "Hey, hey, whoa little girl, what
     up? What up?"
I mean
When you fling a thing away like that, no matter how small
You know you start to choke the life force that sustains us all.
The little girl said:
"I don't know why you're trippin', somebody else will pick it
     up."
Then she turned away from me and she gets on the bus.

Baba-dee-da-dabeydoo-dee-da
Baba-dee-da-dabeydoo-dee-daaaaa

flow

Beedeekaka
Beedeekaka
Beedeekaka
Suuu.

(New Groun' moves to outside the rec center.)

Any questions?

The rec center was built thirty-five years, four months, three
    weeks and two days ago
Nas
No no no no no Nas
Nas could definitely take Jay-Z
Definitely . . .

(DJ scratches dramatically, moving Will Power to the next verse section.)

WILL POWER:
    Besombeeeee
    Besombeeeee
    Besombeeeee.

The next storyteller.

Zuu
He was a dancer
Now if you ever got the chance ta
Zuu
See him, use his body, as he
Told a story, well he
Would align with the storyline, which would then blend in with
    the rhythms of his rhymes.

Zuu
And it would pulsate from the center
He taught class at the rec center
Zuu
Besombee the dancer was his name
Hard on everybody who came
Zuu.

*(We meet Besombee, a flexible dancer in a leotard and with twists in his
hair. DJ plays a slightly sped-up West African groove.)*

BESOMBEE:

    If you lookin' for fortune and fame

    So you can learn to shake yo' thang 'n' get up in the music-video
        games

    No! OK, no

    This is not the place for you, then, OK

    This is a class where I will teach you

    How to get through the

    Zuu

    Beedee-ka-ka-beedee-ka-ka-beedee-ka-ka—

    Zuu

    I'll teach you to move through

    And rhyme through

    And maneuver through

    Zuu

    So—I know you're not eatin' a Twinkie in my class

    Get rid of it, get rid of it now!

    Zuu

    Ground rules: no Twinkie eatin' in my class!

    No gum chewing, no soda drinking, none a that shit.

    Zuu

    If ya gotta chomp on something, grab a celery stick

    Or some damn tofu nuggets, or a damn carrot, I don't care!

    Zuu

    Please OK? Please, pay attention . . .

    (Besombee's physical movements outline and introduce Sister Ewalay,
    Roberto and Larry Goldberg over a hard and fast beat.)

    This was Sister Ewalay . . .

    Committed to the fight in fact

    She loved all folks that's black

    But she hated all folks that's white

    More

    So after years of anger and stress

    It all built up in her chest

    Slowly started eating away

    At her core.

    And she never did jog or work out

    Never figured how to get it out

    She kept that pain inside

flow

Of her soul.
Till one day she drivin' in her car
Cursin' white folks, wherever they are
She wrapped that jet-black car
'Round a pole.

*(Besombee does the Sister Ewalay movement. DJ plays the sound of a
car crash. Besombee mimes the crash.)*

This was Roberto . . .
Well he was a good teacher of kids
Proud of his heritage
Boricua, but one thing, ah
He liked to eat
Anything made with sofrito
Pollo
Hecka picadillo
From Mammy table to Mickey D's, hey
He loved that meat
And he would help kids through the sorrow.

Help them see the better tomorrow
But he never would see it himself
That's a fact.
'Cause he start to get a big ol' gut
Then his organs start to erupt
At age thirty-eight his colon
It collapsed.

*(DJ plays the sound of flies buzzing and someone chomping loudly on
chips. Besombee does a modern-dance representation of colon cancer.)*

This was Larry Goldberg
To the folk he was heaven-sent—a lawyer
For the environment
He represented many po' people
Who don't have a dime
But he drink coffee every morn'
Smoke cigarettes since he was born
On his inner environment he perpetrated
The same crime
He could tell ya 'bout the atmosphere
While sippin' his third or fourth beer

And he could tell ya 'bout how that soil
Would bring death
But as he tell ya that he takin' a puff
Soon his body just had enough
His lungs inhaled, then they exhaled
His last breath.

(DJ plays the sound of a heartbeat, then comes in with a hard and fast beat again. The music stops.
Besombee dances a quick montage of the three characters, then re-addresses the class.)

And that's why I don't allow Twinkies in class.

A-no, no, no, you all have the power to move
I don't care!

OK, everyone up, up, up, up, up!
Let's begin at the bar . . .

WILL POWER:
Ummmm, OK OK, ummm right, OK OK
Ummmmm, OK OK, ummm right, OK OK
Ummm, OK OK
The sixth storyteller!

(Becomes Swea P:)

SWEA P:
I am Swea P
The baby girl a Momma P
My girl, she gon' be named Double Swea P
And on and on it's gon' be a long line a Ps
'N' they all gon' be like me, a MC
Zuu
I don't write my stuff down, don't need no paper notepad
I freestyle like the jailhouse raps of my dad
Off the dome, um
The cipher's my home, um
You don't believe me? Step up, yo, come get some
Improvisation like John Coltrane
Yeah I know that stuff
Giant Steps, After the Rain but um

That stuff is past, yo, I didn't live it
It's all about knowing that old stuff, now flip it!
And give it some new funk, a new flow
So the new generation know just how it go
Yo
For the now, I'm livin' right now, I'm cool
But some fools wanna take it back to the old school.

(DJ plays a song by Run-DMC and fades it in and out periodically throughout the scene.)

MC OLD SCHOOL:

Swea P! Hey, Swea P!

SWEA P:

Hey, MC Old School, how you doin' baby?

MC OLD SCHOOL:

I'm funky fresh, Swea P
And you know I got yo' back girl, I forever got yo' back
'Cause yo' moms, she from the old school!
Me and her, we go back to the old school rrrrrahhh!

SWEA P:

Yeah I seen pictures of you and my moms back in the day
Big ol' radio, big ol' piece of linoleum
Matching Adidas sweat suits, fat shoelaces
Big ol' furry bushy, bushy Kangol
But you still got the same shit on!

MC OLD SCHOOL:

What your moms ain't rockin' the funky fresh gear no more?

SWEA P:

Hell no, man! My moms went corporate, baby
She way different than when ya'll was together.

MC OLD SCHOOL:

Well that's a shame Swea P, 'cause those were the days.

So look, are you fresh enough now, and are you do-do def
    enough now
To appreciate real hip-hop, old-school hip-hop?

SWEA P:

> Ay old school is cool, you know, but I like some of the new shit, too
> Like Outkast, Lauryn, Common, Dead Prez, my nigga Mos Def,
>   Medusa—
> You don't know Medusa? Aw, man, Medusa.

MC OLD SCHOOL:

> Naw. Naw. If they ain't from the old school, they get the gas face
> 'Cause I only like the old school before '92—hua!
>
> Swea P! I got some tickets for you, Swea P
> Being how you coulda been my daughter and all
> And it's about time you start learnin' 'bout true hip-hop . . .
> Bam! Two tickets to the Suga'hill Gang, baby bubba.

SWEA P:

> The Suga'hill Gang? Uh—are they still alive?

MC OLD SCHOOL:

> What?

SWEA P:

> Ay my bad, I thought they was hella dead for reals dough
> But you know I'll take the tickets, but I like freestylin'
> Expressin' yourself right here right now! I mean
> The old school was tight right, but
> We gotta keep this thing movin', baby. You feel me, dough? You
>   feel me, baby?

MC OLD SCHOOL:

> Not really. Ya'll be wastin' ya'll time with all that freestylin'
> Look, how you gon' perfect yo' rhymes, if you makin' 'em up as
>   you go along?
> What if you mess up or somethin'?

SWEA P:

> If you mess up you just keep goin' and flowin' with it, baby, you
>   know.

MC OLD SCHOOL:

> Naw, naw that ain't how you do it. All the great rappers of the
>   old school, Mell-e Mel—it's nasty!
> Joeski Love: Bu-Bu-Bu-Bu-Bu-Bu-Bu-Bu—

flow

Kool Moe Dee, the "Wild Wild West," aaaaahhh!
They all took time to write they rhymes. That's why they was so
    stupid fresh.

SWEA P:

But I ain't got time like that, MC Old School!
When I feel somethin', I need to let it out right here right now
I ain't tryin' to wait till when I get home, or when I get to school
    or somethin' like that.

Yo, freestylin' in the cipher, yo, the cipher is like a party
A therapy session and a jam session all in one
My nigga June on my left. My nigga Joe on my right . . .

*(DJ plays a recording of a B-boy beatboxing. Swea P goes to the cipher
where she plays June, Joe, Ma and Father.)*

Ummmmmm OK OK, ummm right, OK OK
Ummmmmm OK OK, ummm right, OK OK.

JUNE:

Uh, yeah yeah yeah, uh, yeah yeah yeah.

JOE:

It's like, it's like, it's like, it's like, it's likity like like, likity like like.

SWEA P:

Ummmmmm OK OK, ummmmmmm right, OK OK.

JUNE:

Uh yeah, yeah yeah.

JOE:

It's like, likity liky like.

SWEA P:

Ummmmmm OK OK, ummm right, OK OK.

JUNE:

Uh, yeah yeah yeah, uh-uh here I go
Yo, son, I gets
Straight ferocious, New York macadocious
Make MCs nervous
Like if they had neurosis

Blow up the spot
Give you that shit that's hot
And I got what it takes to rock the mic right
Like Bennie C
Flexin' verbals
Smokin' mad herbals
Be up in yo' ass like Richard Gere wit' a gerbil
Bustin' out niggas
Bustin' on niggas
Got my hand on the trigga
So nigga how you figure you gon'
Come test me
That ain't gon' be
At age twenty-three
Nothin' ever could stop me
Even though I sometimes feel like a tree with no roots even
    though I
Sometimes get hassled by Ma Dukes.

(The beatbox fades out. June is on a street corner with his mother.)

How you doin', Ma?

MA:

How it look like I'm doin', Junior?
Shit, I'm cool, I'm cool, Momma cool
Junior, Junior, help ya momma out with a lil' somethin' somethin'.

JUNE:

I can't do that no more, Ma.

MA:

What you done did it before! Shit, hook me up, Junior!
Ey, ey, don't don't be lookin' at me like that
Like you different, you ain't no different than me
You slang the shit, you ain't no different than me! You slang the
    shit.

JUNE:

But I don't smell though, Ma, and I pay my bills.

MA:

You still ain't no different than me, Junior. Come on! Come on
Hook me up, Junior, come on now shit, I'm ya momma

flow

I'm still ya momma, and I wouldn't ask if I didn't need it
Come on, Junior, shit.

JUNE:

All right, Ma.

(He hands her the shit.)

. . . Bye, Ma.

(The beatbox fades back in. June comes back to the cipher.)

Yeah, I'm all alone in this world but I
Won't cry, and a nigga won't die 'cause I'm strong
Even wit' all the stress wit' my fam'
Ya'll niggas need to understand that I'm a
Straight titan, never stop fightin'
I bring it on the mic, son
My words enlighten
Help you find peace
In the cipher I release
I'm a lyrical beast
My shit jus' increase
Uh yeah, yeah, yeah.

JOE:

It's like, it's like, it's like, it's like, it's like—it's like, it's like—it's like
It's like my words expand
Yo, kid, I'm in demand
I'm wiser than my years
Older than that man on American Bandstand I got the master plan
The king MC of this land
In my bank account I got grands upon grands upon grands
Yo, so many Gs
You can call me G
But really all that I am
Is just the top MC
Make all you suckas freeze
Proud to be Chinese
I'm straight steppin' on fools like the Han dynasty
Wish they all could see
How I put in work
I wish my father could see
That this is my work.

(Beatbox fades out. Joe stands in his house with his Father.)

I'm a rhymer. I'm a MC.

FATHER:

An M-what?

JOE:

An MC. I make up rhymes. And I'm good at what I do, and I get
respect for what I do
It's like, it's like, this is what I want to do.

FATHER:

You want . . . to make rhymes. Are you in a nursery? You want to
make nursery rhymes?

JOE:

Nah it's not like that it's like—

FATHER:

This is what you will do. You will stay in school
You will graduate with honors in biology; you will get a good job
And you will make your family proud. Míng Bái?

JOE:

Yes, sir, I understand . . .

(DJ fades the beatbox back in. Joe returns to the cipher.)

It's like, even if you can't see me I'm still here
I am an MC let me make it clear and like
Even if you disrespect it's all good
'Cause I am respected in the neighborhood 'cause I
Bring that hot shit
A Yosemite fire
I make yo' ass go crazy
Like if you was Mariah
Or better yet Jim Carrey
Scare yo' ass like Carrie
It's like
What would I do without the cipher, kid?
It's like, it's like, it's like, it's like, it's like, it's like . . .

SWEA P:

Ummmmm OK OK.

Ummmmm OK OK ummm right OK OK
Swea P comin' and ya scared as hell
Um
The queen MC, baby, can't you tell
Um
Ya mumblin' 'n' stumblin' ya best to quit
Because
This cipher here I'm runnin' this shit
So tell all ya friends that you are my foe.

I give love to my nigga June and my nigga Joe
Right
Freestyle all night, make it up, on the spot, till the early light
And to all you boys that did not invite
Me up into the cipher now you feel my might
And I am forever gonna come hecka tight
In the circle wit' no rehearsal we do not write.

Now I used to be just like my moms and shit, when
I had problems I would never deal with it.

Just like when my brother died
And then my uncle lied
Yo, fuck an accident we all know it was suicide.

And Moms, she ain't fine
'Cause every night she cryin'
So instead I freestyle
Put it in a rhyme.

The cipher baby boy it keep me intact you know
Sometimes I wish even Moms could rap, you know
That she could have a place to let it go
And um like me and my nigga June and my nigga Joe, um
Swea P that's the way it go and um
I'm in the cipher fa-sho.

Ummmmm OK OK, ummm right, OK OK
Ummmmm OK OK, ummmm right, right, right, right
Yeah that's the shiznick, MC Old School, you feel me though?
    You feel me though?

MC OLD SCHOOL:

Ehhh. It's awight. All that freestylin' and stuff. But it still—

SWEA P:

I know I know, it can't mess with the old school.

MC OLD SCHOOL:

(Hands her the tickets) Who-ha!

SWEA P:

Ay thanks for the tickets for real.

MC OLD SCHOOL:

Anytime, Swea P. And may the old school never die, sista. Enjoy
the concert tonight.

SWEA P:

I will, MC Old School. Peace out, baby . . . Ay, June. Ay, Joe!
Yeah come on! Ay, Greg, go get Tony. Well, yeah, that's what I'm
sayin',
Go get 'im so we can get this cipher started like
Ummmmmmmmm OK OK, ummmmmmm right.

WILL POWER:

Seven.

(DJ brings in "Seven" theme music.)

There were only seven, ya'll
I say
There were only seven storytellers in the neighborhood, ya'll
Zuu
To sing the songs and right the wrongs and carry on, on and on . . .

(DJ cross-fades from "Seven" theme music into two loud scratches.)

BREEZE:

There was a seagull name Aquanetta
And unlike other gulls, she let ya walk up and pet her
Zuu
Come on, drop-drop some cheddar
Zuu
Aaaay Lil' Petey!
Take this cup, go to the sto', gimme—

Breeeeze, he had that delicate balance

I'm talkin' 'bout stories and liquor

Zuu

Then the storm blew a truck through the neighborhood, introducing, a new malt liquor

Zuu

The truck would stop every block, giving caseloads of it away for
free!

Zuu

Guess they knew, just what to do, ya get 'em hooked first

Then you could charge that fee

Zuu

And this wasn't no, usual, run-of-the-mill, alcoholic drink, naw
buddy

Zuu.

This was some nuvo

Scientific

One sip and a nigga already on the brink!

Zuu

They called this new drink . . .

Mack Daddy Malt Liquor

Zuu

Shoot, St. Ides?

Old E?

Shoot, Mack Daddy was way way sicker

Zuu

They even got the best gangsta MCs

To spread the slogan through the hood like a disease

Mack Daddy Malt Liquor, make the girls come quicker, if ya
drink Mack Daddy Malt Liquor

We-dee-we we-we we-we we-we we! Bling, bling, bling, ching,
ching, ching

Zuu, Breeeze, he lost the storytellin' ability

He became a zombie slave to Mack Daddy

Zuu

His liver followed—fast

Breeze passed.

Zuu

There were only six, ya'll

I say only six storytellers in the neighborhood, ya'll

Zuu

To sing the songs and right the wrongs—

("Seven" theme music goes out. As Jacoba:)

JACOBA:

Zuu ta kaa

Well tell LaWanda you not havin' that!

Zuu ta ka

Now what you mean you want to know about my date?

Ta ka

Uh-huh OK not bad, pretty good

Zuu ta ka

Belinda let me hear the one about—

WILL POWER:

Jacobaaaa

Zuu

She was commended, by the school board

She was doin' great thangs, even won an award, for what?

Teacher of the Year

Because

She could make them frownin' girls smile from ear to ear

But then

Three sistas from around the way

Who used to hang with Jacoba way back in the day

Yeah they would

Zuu

Have fun, in each other they'd confide

Before these three jealous sistas turned to the dark side.

(DJ scratches. Will Power as Sistas:)

SISTA 1:

We used to have fun back in the day, didn't we? Didn't we? Oh
    yes we did. We had big fun!

Who messed it up? And who messed everything up? Jacoba.

SISTA 3:

Jacoba!

SISTA 2:

Jacoba!

SISTA 1:

    Jacobaaaaalllaallaaaa! Yeah she started talkin' about she wanna
        make something of herself, follow all her little dreams and shit
    I said look, ho, I don't wanna be white.

SISTA 3:

    Me neither.

SISTA 2:

    But wait um how does—

SISTA 1:

    Shut up! Anyway, like I said, I coulda lived with all that white shit
    'Cause I had mad love for Jacoba in my heart, you know
    But then, but when, but then when she started talkin' 'bout how
        she still loved me
    And accepted me, for who I am, and
    Wanted me to love her, and respect her, for who she was, too?
    I said fuck you, fuck Jacoba!

SISTA 3:

    Jacoba!

SISTA 2:

    Jacoba!

SISTA 1:

    (Laughing/crying) Jacobaaaaa-ha-ha-ha!

WILL POWER:

    All day long them sistas carried on
    Jacoba
    Jacoba
    Jacoba
    From dawn to dawn
    24/7 them sistas talked shit
    But they wasn't gon' do nothin', they was talkers—that was it

    (DJ brings in the sounds of the storm.)

    But then the storm hit!
    And it found a crack
    In they cavernous little act

Made the three sistas react
And they turned from sistas . . .

To witches.

All day long they'd stir that bubblin' pot of camel snot, jealousy
Poprocks—remember that shit? Rage, Cheezewhiz,
Self-hate and Cheetos talkin' about:

WITCH 1:
When shall we three witches meet again?

WITCH 2:
Oh, I know this one, I know this one
When the hurly-burly's done, when the battle's lost and—

WITCH 1:
What the hell are you talkin' about?

WITCH 3:
I think she been readin' again.

WITCH 2:
Nah, nah I ain't been readin' again!

WITCH 1:
You betta' not be readin' again! Come on, girls. Let's do this . . .

WILL POWER:
They grabbed that bubblin' pot
An' headed towards the window . . .

WITCH 1:
There's Jacoba, there she go.

WILL POWER:
The stew went out the window.

(DJ pauses the sounds of the storm.)

They meant it as a joke; they wanted her drenched from head to
    toe
The stew hit the steps

Jacoba jumped and leapt . . .
Jacoba—slipped and broke her neck.

WITCH 3:

> *(Looking out the window)* Jacoba!!

WITCH 2:

> Jacoba!!

WITCH 1:

> . . . Jacoba.

(DJ brings up "Seven" theme music.)

WILL POWER:

> Zuu.
>
> There were only five, ya'll
> I say only five storytellers in the neighborhood, ya'll.

(DJ cross-fades from "Seven" theme music to scratching.)

PREACHA MAN:

> Zuu
> Organic, non-irradiated coconut milk? Aisle three
> Zuu
> Hey, sista, you was in the park yesterday
> Zuu
> The Dalai Lama brother
> He breaks it down like KRS-ONE, Chuck D
> Zuu
> OK, brotha, I'll let her through
> Zuu.

WILL POWER:

> Preacha preach on
> In the night or in the morn'
> He couldn't, he wouldn't be stopped
> Couldn't be blocked
> On the avenue standing on a soapbox
> Zuu
> Or like I showed you before, at the health-food store
> Preacha man he preach more and more

Zuu

And pretty soon folks start to listen and uh

And some folks started to pay attention and uh

Zuu

They shared his vision, of what?

A new kind of religion, that what?

Zuu

That still had them ancient truths

But beedee-ka the storm was breaking loose and

Zuu

(DJ brings the storm sounds in and out.)

It shot a lightning bolt, straight at First Baptist

Now check this

Zuu—at First Baptist Church, they had a secret meetin'

To discuss this Preacha Man sitcha-asion:

DEACON JONES:

    Ya'll heard about this Preacha Man?

    Lawd, what we gon' do?

MISS WASHINGTON:

    He's spreading lies.

SISTA/MOTHER/FEATHER HEN/GRANDMA/JENKINS BROWN:

    He's the devil in disguise!

DEACON JONES:

    He is! This is true!

    Now, Miss Washington/Sista/Mother/Feather Hen/Grandmother/
        Jenkins Brown

    I have heard this Preacha Man preach

    In the park, and on the block

    And everywhere that this fool preach

    The young folk

    They just flock!

MISS WASHINGTON:

    Not only that Deacon Jones, but we startin' to lose our own flock.

SISTA/MOTHER/FEATHER HEN/GRANDMA/JENKINS BROWN:

    His punk ass must be stopped!

flow

DEACON JONES:

    Amen, Sista/Mother/Feather Hen/Grandmother/Jenkins Brown,
        he must be stopped
    Just like Martin Luther King, Junior say, "By any means necessary."

SISTA/MOTHER/FEATHER HEN/GRANDMA/JENKINS BROWN:

    I was there when he said it!

DEACON JONES:

    Now look we gon' have to do somethin'
    Somethin' to bring this Preacha Man down
    'Cause he takin' all the young folk
    Pretty soon First Baptist won't be around.

MISS WASHINGTON:

    Well we can't bribe 'im or nothing like that Deacon Jones, because
        I heard the boy got too much class.

SISTA/MOTHER/FEATHER HEN/GRANDMA/JENKINS BROWN:

    Well then fuck it!
    Fuck it then!
    Let's do a drive-by on his ass!

WILL POWER:

    So the next Sunday

(Storm sounds still in and out.)

    Deacon Jones
    Ms. Washington
    And Sista/Mother/Feather Hen/Grandmother/Jenkins Brown
    Tiptoed out to the church van, when nobody else was around
    They loaded up the van with potato salad, collard greens and fat
        back
    And underneath all that
    Rocket launchers, grenades, sub-atomic missiles, shark harpoons
        and hella gats
    Then they drove around . . . lookin' for Preacher Man.

    Three holy, holy backbiters, in a white drop-top church van
    Deacon Jones and Ms. Washington sat in front
    Sista/Mother/Feather Hen/Grandmother/Jenkins Brown laid low
        in the back

will power

To calm they nerves, Deacon Jones slapped one of them tight
new beats up on the 8-track.

DEACON JONES:
(Singing) "What a friend we have in Jesus"
This my jam right here, dog, this the bomb, oh yeah
(Singing) "All the day we have in Jesus"
Look, look, look, there he go there he go right there, there go
Preacha Man, RIGHT THERE
So . . . which one of us is gon', uh, actually do it?

SISTA/MOTHER/FEATHER HEN/GRANDMA/JENKINS BROWN:
Man gimme that gun
Shit you know I'll pull the trigga.

WILL POWER:
And as they did the drive-by
Sista/Mother/Feather Hen/Grandmother/Jenkins Brown yelled:

SISTA/MOTHER/FEATHER HEN/GRANDMA/JENKINS BROWN:
First Baptist, nigga!!!!!!!

(DJ brings up "Seven" theme music.)

WILL POWER:
There were only four, ya'll
I say, only four storytellers in the neighborhood, ya'll.

NEW GROUN':
Zuu
Any more questions, about the park, or the school, anybody?
Suuu
These projects are built on an ancient burial ground
Suuu
You know Nelly? . . . *(Singing)* "It's gettin' hot in here, so take off
all your . . ." You know, Nelly—

WILL POWER:
Zuu
New Groun'
Strong as the ground
The fourth storyteller was ground bound.

Zuu
New Groun', New Groun'
He was never gettin' up he was always gettin' down, say
Zuu
New Groun', and when the storm hit he just rolled with it
Because—check it:

Nothin' could take him out . . .
But!

The storm was gettin' grand
And it whupped on the earth like an abusive man.

And people started dumpin' they garbage on the land, man
They wouldn't even wait for the garbageman, and
Companies chopped the trees and spilled oil in the seas
Causin' hella animal deformities—
We started to see fifty-pound fleas, 'leven-headed bees
Turkeys eatin' turkeys on Thanksgivin', beatboxin' pigeons
Mother Earth screamed, "This is too much for me!"

And New Groun' listened. And he began to descend but to save
    the earth
He knew what would happen to him, check it
Zuu
First his body would bend, and assimilate with the dirt
Then his molecules would go to work
Pumping life, into the seas and the trees
Restoring balance to the earth.

New Groun' melted down, and became one with the ground
And vanished
Just like that
Gone
Without a sound.

(DJ cuts "Seven" theme music; scratches.)

BESOMBEE:
Look I have no time for games, is that clear?
Move, move yes, move, move yes
Get rid of that a Tootsie Roll!
And point, flex, point, flex, and up, up, up, up, up . . .

WILL POWER:

Zuu

Besombee

He was so healthy

Had a vegan diet supplemented with vitamin B

Zuu

And he exercised

And he didn't drink

He was invincible or so you'd think.

Check it, under his house

Something was rotten, a toxic dump that had long been forgotten

Zuu

And Besombee didn't know when he moved in

Now the storm gathered up a big wind

And rustled the dust releasing toxic fumes

Eventually leading Besombee to his tomb.

(DJ fades in "Seven" theme music.)

'Cause you can build up immunity and fight disease

But the air you breathe? Please—Besombee.

All we could do really was love 'im and, wait

Zuu

Then we painted a mural outside the rec center dedicated to our
   brother . . .

Besombee the dancer.

(DJ cuts "Seven" theme music; scratches.)

SWEA P:

Ummmmmm, OK OK, ummmm right, OK.

WILL POWER:

Swea P, she didn't see, the Suga'hill Gang, see

'Cause the cipher wit' her June, Joe, Greg and Ton-y

Zuu,

Stopped

When two fools on the block started wit'

"What up nigga?" "What up nigga?" "Nigga what up?"

And these two fools, recitin' them same old lines

Like a bad play bein' performed a thousand times

Just—

Zuu

Wrapped in they own drama
They vision was cloudy from beer and marijuana
So they couldn't see the cipher or its sacredness
Naw they was to busy puttin' each other's manhood to the test
One fool flexed, the other undressed
Just the same ol' story, so you know what come next.

Beedee-ka-ka-beedee-ka-ka-ka-ka-ka-ka-ka!

Ya ever been in a storm, but instead a rain, bullets fly?
The first bullet ricochet, hit Swea P in the thigh.

(He pantomimes getting shot in the thigh.)

And the second one . . .
In the eye.

(He pantomimes getting shot in the eye and the death of Swea P. "Seven" theme music in.)

There is only one, ya'll
I say, only one storyteller in the neighborhood, ya'll
Zuu
To sing the song and right the wrong and carry on . . . on and on
Zuu
But there is only one, dough.

I say, only one storyteller in the neighborhood, yo
Zuu
Only one teller
One teller
Me . . .

(DJ abruptly stops "Seven" theme music.)

And I used to be . . . Zuu
Sweaty and sticky and feelin' good.

I was a known rapper-slash-actor in the hood . . .

But there is only one, dough
I say, only one storyteller in the neighborhood, yo.

And the neighborhood is coming down *around* me
It's on!
Breeze, Jacoba, Preacha Man, New Groun', Besombee

And Swea P
They all gone!

Carried away by the storm!
And now it's coming towards ME . . .

So IIIIIIIIII . . .
Zuu . . . put on my raincoat . . .

AND I GO . . .

(DJ brings in an African beat.)

Past the burnin' blocks
And all the looted spots
Brothers shootin' glocks
Yeah I might get got
But as I'm flowin' I'm getting strong and carryin' on
Even though the storm blew through and my crew is gone
But, yo, they still here with me Cheesy and my crew
And all the Ol' Cheesies and crews before them, too
And they help me get through
And all the Fred the Roaches and Blind Bettys before them, too
And they help me get through
Hey you got it, too.

What about the stories and storytellers that's inside YOU?
What about the stories and storytellers that's inside YOU?

(DJ brings down African beat.)

From ya grandma, to ya friend, or your cousin Wood
Even if you ain't from my neighborhood check it
Zuu.

The storm, watch it, it's comin' your way
Maybe next year, next week, or maybe today.

When ya hear that beedee-ka-ka
And ya feelin' trapped-trapped
Nowhere to go-go
You got to flow, yo . . .
I said:

flow

When ya hear that beedee-ka-ka
And ya feelin' trapped-trapped
Nowhere to go.

Use the stories that you know and just flow . . .
I just flow

(DJ pumps up the music.)

I just flow . . .

WHO got next!
WHO got next!
WHO got next!
WHO got next!

I JUST FLOW . . .
You JUST FLOW . . .
You JUST FLOW . . .

Who got NEXT!
Who got NEXT!
Who got NEXT!
Who got NEXT!

I JUST FLOW . . .
YOU JUST FLOW . . .
YOU JUST FLOW . . .

WHO got next!
WHO got next!
WHO got next!
WHO got next!

I JUST FLOW . . .

(DJ brings the music down.)

YOU JUST FLOW
I JUST FLOW
I JUST FLOW
I JUST FLOW
I JUST FLOW
I JUST FLOW
I JUST FLOW
I JUST FLOW

I JUST FLOW
I JUST FLOW
I JUST FLOW
I JUST FLOW
I JUST FLOWWWWWWWW.

(DJ fades out the music. Silence.)

And so.

ZUU
I'm in motion out on the block, and I'm movin' up the hill
Towards the ruins of the health-food shop
A little ray a sun peepin' through the clouds in a spot
Then I stop, 'cause I see a little boy . . . he got
Zuu
A Birkenstock sandal on the left foot
A Nike sneaker on the right
A cowrie-shell necklace with a platinum Jesus piece
And a T-shirt on the front say, "Break yo'self."
And on the back it say, "Peace."

Zuu
And he got a microphone, and he
Zuu
Makin' up rhymes with ease, and inside his rhymes, he is actually
    tellin' stories
It sound like hip-hop, but naw
It's not, it's some new futuristic, hyper-kemetic, kinetic-internetted,
    instigated
I don't know what the fuck that shit is, yo
But it's hot!
Zuu
And since I am the last storytella of my crew, I know just what
    I have to do
I says, "Uh, ay little man . . . ay
I wanna teach you the old stories."

And then you GO, "Make 'em new . . ."

(DJ plays dramatic scratches.)

ZUU!

THE END

Will Power is an award-winning playwright, rapper, actor and educator.

He received the 2006 Lucille Lortell Award for Outstanding Musical for his play *The Seven*; Theatre Communications Group's 2006 Peter Zeisler Memorial Award, recognizing innovation; the Joyce Award; a 2005 NYFA Fellowship; a 2004 Jury Award for Best Theatre Performance at the HBO/US Comedy Arts Festival; a 2004 Drama Desk nomination for Best Solo Performance; two AUDELCO award nominations for his solo shows, including *The Gathering: A Hip-Hop Theater Journey to the Meeting Places of Black Men* and the Trailblazer Award from The National Black Theater Network for his contributions to theater.

His adaptation of Aeschylus's *Seven Against Thebes (The Seven)* was produced at New York Theatre Workshop in 2006. They co-produced *Flow*, with the NYC Hip-Hop Theater Festival and P.S. 122 in 2003.

Recent guest appearances include *Bill Moyers on Faith and Reason* (PBS), *The Colbert Report* (Comedy Central), *Last Call with Carson Daly* (NBC) and Russell Simmon's *Def Poetry Jam* (HBO). He was the lead male in the film, *Drylongso*, a hit at the 1999 Sundance Film Festival. He was featured in the documentary *All Fathers Are Sons*.

A pioneer of hip-hop theater, Power has created his own style of theatrical communication, fusing original music, rhymed language and dynamic movement. In addition to the music composed for his own theater pieces, Power has composed lyrics and music for MTV, *Moesha* (UPN) and *Kingpin* (NBC). He has been featured on four critically acclaimed albums: *Free Roots, Spirit of the Roots, Bembon*, and as lead vocalist for Omar Sosa's Sextet on *Prietos*.

Power is also a teacher, providing communities around the world with tools of self-expression. He frequently gives workshops to help youth empower themselves through theater and rhyme. He is a professor at The City College in New York.

Visit: www.willpower.tv

Kim Euell is a playwright, producer, dramaturg and educator. She is passionately committed to developing and promoting socially relevant new plays. While serving as Director of New Play Development at Hartford Stage, she founded and produced the Voices! Playreading Series, which featured new work by African American and Latino/a playwrights. She has also served on the artistic staff of Center Theatre Group's Mark Taper Forum and San Jose Repertory Theatre. She is a company member of the Penumbra Theatre Company. Ms. Euell has worked as a new-play dramaturg at the Sundance Institute's Theatre Lab, the Eugene O'Neill Playwrights Conference and the Bay Area Playwrights Festival.

Ms. Euell's play *The Diva Daughters DuPree* was named Outstanding New Show of 2004 by the Minneapolis–St. Paul *StarTribune*. The 2006 production was designated a Critics Choice by the Seattle *Post-Intelligencer*. A winner of the Theodore Ward Prize, *The Diva Daughters DuPree* was published in an anthology entitled *Best Black Plays* by Northwestern University Press. Ms. Euell's plays have also been seen at Detroit's Plowshares Theater Company, Portland's Imago Theatre, Seattle's Langston Hughes Performing Arts Center, Actor's Theatre of Louisville, Hartford Stage, San Francisco's Lorraine Hansberry Theatre, The Los Angeles Theatre Center, New Perspectives Theatre Company in New York City and the Iowa New Play Festival.

Ms. Euell has published articles and reviews in *American Theatre* magazine, *African American Review* and the *Oakland Tribune*. The University of Pennsylvania, The University of Iowa and Wesleyan University are some of the institutions where she has enjoyed teaching theater courses. She has directed playwriting labs for Center Theatre Group's Mark Taper Forum and The Robey Theatre Company, where she was the California Arts Council's Artist in Residence. She was thrilled to have the opportunity of conducting playwriting workshops at the University of

Witwatersrand in Johannesburg, South Africa, and in Nairobi, Kenya. Ms. Euell was The August Wilson Fellow at the University of Minnesota and a Dean's Fellow at The University of Iowa, where she received her MFA in 2008. She is an honors graduate of Stanford University.

DAVID CONKLIN

Robert Alexander is the author of thirty plays, including *Servant of the People* (a play about the rise and fall of Huey Newton and the Black Panther Party), *The Hourglass, I Ain't Yo' Uncle: The New Jack Revisionist Uncle Tom's Cabin* and *Secrets in the Sands*, the latter two originally written for the San Francisco Mime Troupe. As the playwright-in-residence at the Lorraine Hansberry Theatre, he wrote several world premieres, including *Air Guitar* (a rock opera) and *We Almost Made It to the Super Bowl* (a tragicomedy about racism in the NFL). His works have been produced by theaters around the country, including The Kennedy Center, Inner City Cultural Center, Los Angeles Theatre Center, The Hartford Stage Company, Jomandi Productions, St. Louis Black Repertory Company, Crossroads Theatre Company, Oakland Ensemble Theatre Company, Center Theatre Group's Mark Taper Forum, Karamu House, The Arena Players, Trinity Repertory Company, San Diego Repertory Theatre, Horizon Theatre Company, Actors Theatre of Louisville, the Bay Area Playwrights Festival, Woolly Mammoth Theatre Company and the National Pastime Theater of Chicago.

His most recent plays: *Alien Motel 29, Freak of Nature* and *A Preface to the Alien Garden* (Broadway Play Publishing, 2001) make up his *Erotic Justice Trilogy*. *Bulletproof Hearts; Gravity Pulls at the Speed of Darkness; Erotic Justice; The Neighbor's Dog Is Always Barking; Hatemachine; The Last Orbit of Billy Mars; Will He Bop, Will He Drop?; On a Street with No Name* and *Forty Acres* have come to be known as the *Erotic Justice Play Cycle*. Many of Mr. Alexander's early plays have been printed in various anthologies and *I Ain't Yo' Uncle* is available through Dramatic Publishing Company.

Mr. Alexander has edited several play anthologies, including *Plays from Woolly Mammoth* (Broadway Play Publishing, 1999), *The Fire This Time* (edited with Harry J. Elam, TCG, 2004); *Colored Contradictions: An Anthology of Contemporary African American Plays* (edited with Harry J. Elam, Penguin/ Plume, 1996).

He is the recipient of numerous writing awards and fellowships, including grants from the Rockefeller Foundation, the Gerbode Foundation and the National Endowment for the Arts. He is a former NEA/TCG resident playwright at Jomandi Productions in Atlanta, Georgia, and a former playwright-in-residence at Woolly Mammoth Theatre Company in Washington, D.C., through The Pew Charitable Trusts/TCG National Theatre Artist Residency Program.

A graduate of Oberlin College, Mr. Alexander also holds an MFA in theater (playwriting) from The University of Iowa, where he was a Patricia Roberts Harris Fellow.